TRANSNATIONAL CORPORATIONS AND HUMAN RIGHTS

The number of transnational corporations – including parent companies and subsidiaries – has exploded over the last forty years, which has led to a correlating rise of corporate violations of international human rights and environmental laws, either directly or in conjunction with government security forces, local police, state-run businesses, or other businesses. In this work, Gwynne Skinner details the harms of business-related human rights violations on local communities and describes the barriers, both functional and institutional, that victims face in seeking remedies. She concludes by offering solutions to these barriers, with a focus on measures designed to improve judicial remedies, which are the heart of international human rights law but often fail to deliver justice to victims. This work should be read by anyone concerned with the role of corporations in our increasingly globalized society.

GWYNNE L. SKINNER was Professor of Law and Director of the Immigration Clinic at Willamette University. Along with teaching, Skinner also served as a civil rights and international human rights attorney in Seattle, a civil litigator at Dorsey and Whitney LLP, and a federal and state prosecutor. Her cutting-edge human rights litigation included the representation of individuals in immigrant detention, clients before the European Court of Human Rights, and the Palestinian families and parents of Rachel Corrie in the suit against Caterpillar, Inc. An advisor for the International Corporate Accountability Roundtable (ICAR), she was the author of many leading human rights reports.

SARAH MCGRATH is currently the Director of International Engagement, Business and Human Rights at the Australian Human Rights Commission.

RACHEL CHAMBERS teaches corporate responsibility and researches corporate accountability mechanisms at the University of Connecticut and, formerly, SOAS, University of London.

Transnational Corporations and Human Rights

OVERCOMING BARRIERS TO JUDICIAL REMEDY

GWYNNE L. SKINNER

Willamette University College of Law

Assisted by

RACHEL CHAMBERS
SARAH McGRATH

CAMBRIDGE
UNIVERSITY PRESS

University Printing House, Cambridge CB2 8BS, United Kingdom

One Liberty Plaza, 20th Floor, New York, NY 10006, USA

477 Williamstown Road, Port Melbourne, VIC 3207, Australia

314–321, 3rd Floor, Plot 3, Splendor Forum, Jasola District Centre, New Delhi – 110025, India

79 Anson Road, #06–04/06, Singapore 079906

Cambridge University Press is part of the University of Cambridge.

It furthers the University's mission by disseminating knowledge in the pursuit of education, learning, and research at the highest international levels of excellence.

www.cambridge.org
Information on this title: www.cambridge.org/9781107199316
DOI: 10.1017/9781108185547

© Gwynne L. Skinner 2020

This publication is in copyright. Subject to statutory exception and to the provisions of relevant collective licensing agreements, no reproduction of any part may take place without the written permission of Cambridge University Press.

First published 2020

A catalogue record for this publication is available from the British Library.

Library of Congress Cataloging-in-Publication Data
NAMES: Skinner, Gwynne, author. | Chambers, Rachel E., contributor. | McGrath, Sarah (writer on human rights), contributor.
TITLE: Transnational corporations and human rights : overcoming barriers to judicial remedy / Gwynne L. Skinner, Willamette University College of Law ; assisted by Rachel Chambers, Sarah McGrath.
DESCRIPTION: Cambridge, United Kingdom ; New York, NY : Cambridge University Press, [2020] | Includes bibliographical references and index.
IDENTIFIERS: LCCN 2020013258 (print) | LCCN 2020013259 (ebook) | ISBN 9781107199316 (hardback) | ISBN 9781316648803 (paperback) | ISBN 9781108185547 (epub)
SUBJECTS: LCSH: Liability for human rights violations. | Tort liability of corporations.
CLASSIFICATION: LCC K935 .S55 2020 (print) | LCC K935 (ebook) | DDC 342.08/5–dc23
LC record available at https://lccn.loc.gov/2020013258
LC ebook record available at https://lccn.loc.gov/2020013259

ISBN 978-1-107-19931-6 Hardback
ISBN 978-1-316-64880-3 Paperback

Cambridge University Press has no responsibility for the persistence or accuracy of URLs for external or third-party internet websites referred to in this publication and does not guarantee that any content on such websites is, or will remain, accurate or appropriate.

For Beth, Lucy, and Ella.
And for a more just world for all.

Thank you for the contributions made by Julia Jacovides, Ari Alvarez, Jennifer M. Green, Jennifer Hammitt, Heather Cohen and James Yap.

Contents

Foreword	*page* xiii
List of Abbreviations	xv
Table of Cases	xvii
Table of Statutes	xxv
Introduction	1

PART I: RISE OF TRANSNATIONAL CORPORATIONS, IMPACT ON HUMAN RIGHTS, AND VICTIMS' RIGHTS TO REMEDY — 7

1 **Growth and Structure of TNCs** — 9
   1.1 Financial Benefits From Operating in Developing Countries — 11

2 **Victims' Rights To Remedy for Business-Related Human Rights Violations** — 14
   2.1 Vulnerable Communities Absorb Harm from TNCs' Activities — 14
   2.2 The Right to Remedy under International Law — 16
   2.3 Remediation for Extraterritorial Violations of International Law under US Law — 23
   2.4 Barriers to Judicial Remedy — 26

3 **Barriers to Judicial Remedies in Host Countries** — 28
   3.1 The Need for Legislative Reform — 32

4 **Limits on Subject Matter Jurisdiction over International Human Rights Violations** — 34
   4.1 An Overview of Subject Matter Jurisdiction across Multiple Jurisdictions — 34

	4.1.1 United States	35
	4.1.2 Canada	41
	4.1.3 Europe	42
5	**Limited Liability of Parent Corporations**	43
	5.1 An Overview of Parent Company Liability across Multiple Jurisdictions	44
	5.1.1 United States	45
	5.1.2 Canada	47
	5.1.3 Europe	48
	5.1.3.1 France	48
	5.1.3.2 United Kingdom	49
	5.1.3.3 Switzerland	50
6	**Lack of *In Personam* Jurisdiction over TNCs and their Affiliates**	52
	6.1 An Overview of *In Personam* (Adjudicatory) Jurisdiction	54
	6.1.1 The United States: Historical and Current Theories of Personal Jurisdiction	54
	6.1.2 Europe	57
	6.1.3 Canada	59

PART II LEGAL BARRIERS TO REMEDY AND HOW TO OVERCOME THEM — 63

7	**Overcoming Legal Barriers to Remedy**	65
	7.1 Proposals to Overcome Limited Liability of Parent Corporations	65
	7.1.1 Enterprise Liability	66
	7.1.2 Due Diligence Approach	71
	7.1.3 Parent Corporation Duty of Care for Its Own Assumptions of Obligations	74
	7.1.4 Expanded Tort Law Approach Toward Parental Duty of Care to Foreseeable Victims	81
	7.2 Ensuring Parent Corporation Liability through Legislation	86
	7.3 Proposals for Addressing Limits to Subject Matter Jurisdiction	89
	7.3.1 Expand Subject Matter Jurisdiction By Statute	89
	7.3.1.1 United States	90
	7.3.1.2 Canada	92
	7.3.1.3 Europe	92
	7.4 Adoption of Jurisdiction/Forum by Necessity	93
	7.5 More Expansive Personal Jurisdiction over TNCs	95
	7.5.1 Current Jurisdictional Rules do not Reflect How TNCs Are Structured and Operate	95

7.6	Legislation Needed to Expand Personal Jurisdiction	96
	7.6.1 The United States Should Require TNCs doing Business in the United States to Consent to General Personal Jurisdiction for Federal Causes of Action	96
	7.6.2 A Statutory Enactment Would Provide for an Even Playing Field for US Corporations	104
	7.6.3 Comity and Foreign Relations Are Not Substantial Impediments	105
	7.6.4 The EU and European Countries Should Similarly Expand Jurisdiction over TNCs	106

8 Overcoming Other Barriers to Remedy — 109

8.1	Unsettled Legal Standards for Corporate Liability	109
	8.1.1 Corporate Liability for CIL Violations is Unsettled	110
	8.1.2 Unsettled Legal Standard for Vicarious Liability	113
	8.1.3 Overcoming the Barrier of Unsettled Legal Standards for Corporate Liability	116
8.2	Dismissals Based on *Forum Non Conveniens*	117
	8.2.1 US Federal Law	119
	8.2.2 US State Law	120
	8.2.3 Canada	121
	8.2.4 Overcoming the Barrier of *Forum Non Conveniens*	124
	8.2.4.1 United States	124
	8.2.4.2 Canada	125
8.3	Barriers Presented by "Choice of Law" Doctrine	125
	8.3.1 United States	125
	8.3.2 Europe	127
	8.3.3 Canada	129
	8.3.4 Overcoming the Barrier of Choice of Law Statutes	130
	8.3.4.1 United States	130
	8.3.4.2 Europe	130
8.4	Barriers Presented by Statutes of Limitations	131
	8.4.1 US Federal Law	131
	8.4.2 US State Law	131
	8.4.3 Europe	132
	8.4.4 Overcoming Barriers Created by Statutes of Limitations	133
8.5	Barriers Created by Restrictive Discovery Rules	133
	8.5.1 United States	134
	8.5.2 Canada	135
	8.5.3 Europe	135
	8.5.4 Overcoming Barriers Created by Discovery Rules	136
	8.5.5 Reform Access to Evidence	137

8.6 Barriers Created by Costs of Litigation	137
8.6.1 United States	138
8.6.2 Canada	139
8.6.3 Europe	140
8.6.4 Overcoming Barriers of Costs of Litigation	142
8.6.4.1 United States	142
8.6.4.2 Canada	143
8.6.4.3 Europe	143
8.7 Barriers Created by Collective Redress and Class Action Mechanisms	144
8.7.1 United States	144
8.7.2 Canada and Europe	145
8.7.3 Overcoming Barriers Presented by Limits on Collective Actions	147
8.7.3.1 United States	147
8.7.3.2 Europe	147
8.8 Retaliatory Lawsuits	148
8.8.1 Addressing Retaliatory Lawsuits	150
8.9 Lack of Criminal Prosecutions and Restitution	150
8.9.1 United States	151
8.9.2 Europe	152
8.9.3 Overcoming Barriers Created by Criminal Prosecution	154
8.9.3.1 United States	155
8.9.3.2 Europe	155
8.9.3.3 Training and Awareness-Raising for Public Prosecutors and Judges	156
Conclusion	158
Select Bibliography	161
Index	169

Foreword

Sadly we live in a world where victims of corporate-related human rights abuses are often unable to obtain justice. While dam collapses, factory fires, oil spills, and child labor and exploitation regularly make global headlines, legal systems are commonly unable or unwilling to respond effectively. In today's global economy, multinational corporations operate across borders and legal systems with ease, allowing them to evade liability and ultimately profit from human rights harms.

Gwynne Skinner had a vision for a better world, one where victims have access to effective remedy and where corporate actors can no longer act with impunity.

In December 2017, Gwynne Skinner passed away in her home in Portland, Oregon, surrounded by her loved ones. Throughout her career, Gwynne provided a leading voice in the business and human rights arena, particularly on areas of access to remedy and legal standards of accountability. Her work litigating on the front lines of corporate accountability, producing scholarship and thought-leadership on issues related to access to remedy was ground-breaking. We were fortunate to have had the opportunity to work closely with Gwynne. She was a mentor, advisor, and dear friend to both of us and to many others in the business and human rights community.

This publication, *Transnational Corporations and Human Rights: Overcoming Barriers to Judicial Remedy*, is both a culmination and a celebration. It is a culmination of years of incredible work: research, reasoning, and writing conducted by Gwynne. It represents perhaps the most comprehensive exploration of the legal barriers which victims face in seeking remedy for business-related human rights harms, and offers the business and human rights field with strong, legal argumentation and practice solutions to these barriers. But it is also a celebration. It is a celebration of Gwynne's mind and intellect, as well as her dedication to shaping the world for the better. It is a celebration of community, including the incredible lawyers, advocates, and activists that have and continue to work every day to ensure that human rights are protected and that corporations are held accountable for harms caused by their operations.

In reading this book, it is our hope that you will be challenged, educated, and inspired. These are the hallmarks by which Gwynne engaged in her teaching practice, and we believe they are captured here as well. By engaging with this work, you will also be helping to chart a critical path forward for building meaningful accountability for human rights harms – one where corporations are not exempt from the harms' cause, including by their subsidiaries, and where legal loopholes that eviscerate opportunities for redress from communities and individuals harmed are ultimately closed.

We want to also note that this work could not have been completed without the support and dedication of Dr. Rachel Chambers. Rachel jumped into this process in 2018, and has held the pen since that time. Her commitment to Gwynne and to these issues has resulted in a text that is timely, compelling, clear, and directed at action.

The ability to obtain justice through the courts is fundamental to the realization of human rights globally. While judicial remedy can sound technical and esoteric, the principles behind it are fundamentally about justice, about what is right and what is fair. These principles imbue the legacy of Gwynne Skinner. Every day she is missed, but through these pages, she is not forgotten.

Amol Mehra
Sarah McGrath

Abbreviations

ATS	Alien Torts Statute
AUC	United Self-Defense Forces of Colombia
CERCLA	Comprehensive Environmental Response, Compensation, and Liability Act
CERD	Committee to End Racial Discrimination
CESCR	Committee on Economic, Social and Cultural Rights
CIL	Customary international law
CJPTA	Uniform Court Jurisdiction and Proceedings Transfer Act
ERISA	Employee Retirement Income Security Act
EU	European Union
FCPA	Foreign Corrupt Practices Act
FDI	Foreign direct investment
FDIUS	Foreign direct investment in the United States
FIDH	*Fédération Internationale des Ligues des Droits de l'Homme*
FRA	European Union Agency for Fundamental Rights
HRSP	United States Department of Justice Human Rights and Special Prosecutions Section
ICC	International Criminal Court
ICCPR	International Covenant on Civil and Political Rights
ICTY	The International Criminal Tribunal for the former Yugoslavia
IMT	International Military Tribunal of Nuremberg
LASPO	Legal Aid, Sentencing and Punishment of Offenders Act
MEPs	Members of the European Parliament
NCPs	OECD National Contact Points
OECD	Organisation for Economic Co-operation and Development
OTP	Office of the Prosecutor
RICO	Racketeer Influenced Corrupt Organizations Act
SLAPP	Strategic lawsuit against public participation

TNCs	Transnational corporations
TVPA	The Trafficking Victims Protection Act
UN	United Nations
UNGPs	United Nations Guiding Principles on Business and Human Rights

Table of Cases

UNITED STATES

The Rapid, 8 Cranch 155 (1814)
The Joseph, 12 U.S. 451 (1814)
McQueen v. Middletown Mfg. Co., 16 Johns. R. 5 (N.Y. Sup. Ct. 1819)
The Apollon, 9 Wheat. 362 (1824)
Foster v. Neilson, 27 U.S. 253, 314 (1829)
United States v. Percheman, 32 U.S. 51 (1832)
Jecker v. Montgomery, 59 U.S. (18 How) 110 (1855)
The Prize Cases, 67 U.S. 635 (1862)
Welton v. Missouri, 91 U.S. 275 (1875)
Pennoyer v. Neff, 95 U.S. 714 (1878)
Santa Clara County v. Southern Pacific RR, 118 U.S. 394 (1886)
Texas & Pac. Ry. Co. v. Behymer, 189 U.S. 468 (1903)
Shandrew v. Chi. St. P., M. & O. Ry. Co., 142 F. 320 (8th Cir. 1905)
International Textbook Co. v. Pigg, 217 U.S. 91 (1910)
St. Louis S.W. Co. v. Alexander, 227 U.S. 218 (1913)
McDonald v. Mabee, 243 U.S. 90 (1917)
Tauza v. Susquehanna Coal Co., 220 N.Y. 259 (1917)
Missouri, K. & T.R. Co. v. Reynolds, 255 U.S. 565 (1921)
Osage Oil & Ref. Co. v. Interstate Pipe Co., 253 P. 66 (Okla. 1926)
Staley-Wynne Oil Corp. v. Loring Oil Co., 162 So. 756 (La. 1935)
Milliken v. Meyer, 311 U.S. 457 (1940)
Klaxon Co. v. Stentor Electric Mfg. Co., 313 U.S. 487 (1941)
Wickard v. Filburn, 317 U.S. 111 (1942)
Int'l Shoe Co. v. Wash., 326 U.S. 310 (1945)
Gulf Oil Corp. v. Gilbert, 330 U.S. 501 (1947)
Eure v. Morgan Jones & Co., 79 S.E.2d 862 (Va. 1954)
Pennsylvania v. Nelson, 350 U.S. 497 (1956)
Green Mountain Coll. v. Levine, 139 A.2d 822 (Vt. 1958)
Confederation of Can. Life Ins. Co. v. Vega y Arminan, 144 So. 2d 805 (Fla. 1962)
Deveny v. Rheem Mfg. Co., 319 F.2d 124 (2d Cir. 1963)
Byham v. Nat'l Cibo House Corp., 143 S.E.2d 225 (N.C. 1965)

Zschernig v. Miller, 389 U.S. 429 (1968)
Ratliff v. Cooper Labs. Inc., 444 F.2d 745, 748 (4th Cir. 1971)
Shaffer v. Heitner 433 U.S. 186 (1977)
Springle v. Cottrell Eng'g Corp., 391 A.2d 456 (Md. Ct. Spec. App. 1978)
Mannington Mills, Inc. v. Congoleum Corp., 595 F.2d 1287 (3d Cir. 1979)
Gartner v. Snyder, 607 F.2d 582 (2d Cir. 1979)
Filartiga v. Pena-Irala, 630 F.2d 876 (2d Cir. 1980)
Piper Aircraft Co. v. Reyno, 454 U.S. 235 (1981)
Mittelstadt v. Rouzer, 328 N.W.2d 467 (Neb. 1982)
In re Mid-Atl. Toyota Antitrust Litig., 525 F. Supp. 1265 (D. Md. 1981), aff'd, 704 F.2d 125 (4th Cir. 1983)
Augsbury Corp. v. Petrokey Corp., 470 N.Y.S.2d 787 (N.Y. App. Div. 1983)
Pension Benefit Guar. Corp. v. Ouimet Corp., 711 F.2d 1085 (1st Cir. 1983)
Halberstam v. Welch, 705 F.2d 472 (D.C. Cir. 1983)
Ruckelshaus v. Sierra Club, 463 U.S. 680 (1983)
Johnson Creative Arts & Wool v. Masters, Inc. 743 F. 2d 947 (1st Cir. 1984)
Helicopteros Nacionales de Colom., S.A. v. Hall 466 U.S. 408 (1984)
Holloway v. Wright & Morrissey, Inc., 739 F.2d 695 (1st Cir. 1984)
Marek v. Chesny, 473 U.S. 1 (1984)
Securities Investor Protection Corporation v. Vigman, 764 F.2d 1309 (9th Cir. 1985)
Daetwyler Corp. v. R. Meyer, 762 F.2d 290 (3d Cir. 1985)
Fassett v. Delta Kappa Epsilon (New York), 807 F.2d 1150 (3d Cir. 1986)
Coulter v. Tennessee, 805 F.2d 146 (6th Cir. 1986)
In re Union Carbide Corp. Gas Plant Disaster at Bhopal, India in Dec., 1984, 809 F.2d 195 (2d Cir. 1987)
Grey Line Tours v. Reynolds Elec. & Eng'g Co., 238 Cal. Rptr. 419, 421–22 (Cal. Ct. App. 1987)
Read v. Sonat Offshore Drilling, Inc., 515 So. 2d 1229, 1230–31 (Miss. 1987)
Sternberg v. O'Neil, 550 A.2d 1105, 1109–16 (Del. 1988)
Burnham v. Superior Court of California, 495 U.S. 604 (1990)
Dow Chem. Co. v. Castro Alfaro, 786 S.W.2d 674 (Tex. 1990)
Simmers v. Am. Cyanamid Corp., 576 A.2d 376, 382 (Pa. Super. Ct. 1990)
Knowlton v. Allied Van Lines, Inc., 900 F.2d 1196, 1199–2000 (8th Cir. 1990)
Allied-Signal Inc. v. Purex Indus., Inc., 576 A.2d 942, 943-45 (N.J. Super. Ct. App. Div. 1990)
Wilson v. Humphreys (Cayman) Ltd., 916 F.2d 1239, 1245 (7th Cir. 1990)
Rykoff-Sexton, Inc. v. American Appraisal Associates, 469 N.W.2d 88, 89–91 (Minn. 1991)
Werner v. Prins, 861 P.2d 271,272–74 (Ariz. Ct. App. 1991)
Bane v. Netlink, Inc., 925 F.2d 637, 640 (3d Cir. 1991)
Wenche Siemer v. Learjet Acquisition Corp., 966 F.2d 179, 182–83 (5th Cir. 1992)
Allstate Ins. Co. v. Klein, 422 S.E.2d 863, 864–65 (Ga. 1992)
Wyoming v. Oklahoma, 502 U.S. 437 (1992)
Cipollone v. Liggett Grp., Inc., 505 U.S. 504, 532 (1992)
Paul v. Avril, 812 F. Supp. 207 (S.D. Fla. 1993)
Xuncax v. Gramajo, 886 F. Supp. 162 (D. Mass. 1995)
Kadic v. Karadzic, 70 F.3d 232, 241 (2d Cir. 1995)
In re Temporomandibular Joint (TMJ) Implants Prods. Liab. Litig. Eyeglasses, 113 F.3d 1484 (8th Cir. 1995)

Bridgestone/Firestone, Inc. v. Recovery Credit Servs., Inc., 98 F.3d 13, 18 (2d Cir. 1996)
Hilao v. Marcos, 103 F.3d 767 (9th Cir. 1996)
Ciba-Geigy Ltd. v. Fish Peddler, Inc., 691 So. 2d 1111, 1118 (Fla. Dist. Ct. App. 1997)
Wash. Equip. Mfg. Co., Inc. v. Concrete Placing Co., Inc., 931 P.2d 170 (Wash. Ct. App. 1997)
Doe v. Karadzic, 176 F.R.D. 458 (S.D.N.Y. 1997)
United States v. Bestfoods, 524 U.S. 51, 62 (1998)
First Am. Corp. v. Price Waterhouse LLP, 154 F.3d 16, 23 (2d Cir. 1998)
United States ex rel. Newsham v. Lockheed Missiles & Space Co., 190 F.3d 963 (9th Cir. 1999)
Wiwa v. Royal Dutch Petrol. Co., 226 F.3d 88, 95 (2d Cir. 2000)
Consol. Dev. Corp. v. Sherritt, Inc., 216 F.3d 1286, 1293 (11th Cir. 2000)
Freeman v. Second Jud. Dist. Court ex rel. Cnty. of Washoe, 1 P.3d 963 (Nev. 2000)
Aetna Cas. & Sur. Co. v. Leahey Const. Co., 219 F.3d 519 (6th Cir. 2000)
Northern Light Tech., Inc. v. Northern Lights Club, 236 F.3d 57 (1st Cir. 2001)
DP Aviation v. Smiths Indus. Aerospace and Def. Sys. Ltd., 268 F.3d 829 (9th Cir. 2001)
Aguinda v. Texaco, Inc., 303 F.3d 470 (2d Cir. 2002)
Papa v. United States, 281 F.3d 1004 (9th Cir. 2002)
Sinaltrainal v. Coca-Cola (Sinaltrainal I) 256 F. Supp. 2d 1345, 1354–55 (S.D. Fl. 2003)
Sosa v. Alvarez-Machain, 542 U.S. 692 (2004)
Presbyterian Church of Sudan v. Talisman Energy, Inc., 244 F. Supp. 2d 289 (S.D.N.Y. 2003); No. 01 Civ. 9882(DLC) (S.D.N.Y. 2004)
Bowoto v. Chevron Texaco Co., 312 F. Supp. 2d 1229, 1235–40 (N.D. Cal. 2004)
Van Tu v. Koster, 364 F.3d 1196, 1199 (10th Cir. 2004)
Mendez-Laboy v. Abbott Labs., Inc., 424 F.3d 35, 37 (1st Cir. 2005)
Estate of Unger v. Palestinian Authority, 400 F. Supp. 2d 541, 553 (2005)
In re Agent Orange Prod. Liab. Litig., 373 F. Supp. 2d 7, 58 (E.D.N.Y. 2005)
Jean v. Dorelien, 431 F.3d 776 (11th Cir. 2005)
Merriman v. Crompton Corp., 146 P.3d 162, 170–77 (Kan. 2006)
Bohreer v. Erie Ins. Exch., 165 P.3d 186, 191–94 (Ariz. Ct. App. 2007)
Roe I v. Bridgestone Corp., 492 F. Supp. 2d 988, 1024 (S.D. Ind. 2007)
Romero v. Drummond Co., 552 F.3d 1303, 1318 (11th Cir. 2008)
Scotts Co. v. Hacienda Loma Linda, 2 So. 3d 1013 (Fla. Dist. Ct. App. 2008)
S. Middlesex Opportunity Council, Inc. v. Town of Framingham, Civil Action No. 07-12018-DPW, 2008 WL 4595369 (D. Mass. Sept. 30, 2008)
In re South African Apartheid Litigation, 633 F. Supp. 2d 117 (S.D.N.Y. 2009)
Sinaltrainal v. Coca-Cola (Sinaltrainal II), 578 F.3d 1252, 1259 (11th Cir. 2009)
Sadler v. Hallsmith SYSCO Food Servs., Civil No. 08-4423 (RBK/JS), 2009 WL 1096309 (D.N.J. Apr. 21, 2009)
Aldana v. Del Monte Fresh Produce N.A., Inc., 578 F.3d 1283 (11th Cir. 2009)
In re Xe Servs. Alien Tort Litig., 665 F. Supp. 2d 569 (E.D. Va. 2009)
Chavez v. Carranza, 559 F.3d 486 (6th Cir. 2009)
Henry v. Lake Charles Am. Press, L.L.C., 566 F.3d 164 (5th Cir. 2009)
Cossaboon v. Me. Med. Ctr., 600 F.3d 25 (1st Cir. 2010)
Morrison v. Nat'l Austl. Bank Ltd., 561 U.S. 247, 265 (2010)
Spiegel v. Schulmann, 604 F.3d 72 (2d Cir. 2010)

Wissam Abdullateff Sa'eed Al-Quraishi v. Adel Nakhla, 728 F. Supp. 2d 702 (D. Md. 2010)
Chevron v. Bonifaz, No. 09-05371 CW, 2010 WL 1948681 (N.D. Cal. May 12, 2010)
Abecassis v. Wyatt, 704 F. Supp. 2d 623, 654–55 (S.D. Tex. 2010)
Godin v. Schencks, 629 F.3d 79 (1st Cir. 2010)
Goodyear Dunlop Tires Operations, S.A. v. Brown 131 S. Ct. 2846 (2011)
Doe VIII v. Exxon Mobil Corp., 654 F.3d 11, 57 (D.C. Cir. 2011)
re Chiquita Brands Int'l, Inc., Alien Tort Statute and S'holder Derivative Litig., 792 F. Supp. 2d 1301, 1355–56 (S.D. Fl. 2011)
King v. Am. Family Mut. Ins. Co., 632 F.3d 570 (9th Cir. 2011)
Holocaust Victims of Bank Theft v. Bank, 807 F. Supp. 2d 689 (N.D. Ill. 2011)
Flomo v. Firestone Nat. Rubber Co., L.L.C., 643 F.3d 1013 (7th Cir. 2011)
Baloco ex rel. Tapia v. Drummond Co., 640 F.3d 1338 (11th Cir. 2011)
Aziz v. Alcolac, Inc., 658 F.3d 388 (4th Cir. 2011)
Wal-Mart Stores, Inc. v. Dukes, 131 S. Ct. 2541 (2011)
Drummond Co. v. Collingsworth, No. 2:11-CV-3695-RDP (N.D. Ala. filed Oct. 21, 2011)
Abelesz v. Magyar Nemzeti Bank, 692 F.3d 661 (7th Cir. 2012)
3M Co. v. Boulter, 842 F. Supp. 2d 85 (D.D.C. 2012)
Kiobel v. Royal Dutch Shell 133 S. Ct. 1659 (2013)
Sarei v. Rio Tinto, PLC, 671 F.3d 736, 747 (9th Cir. 2011) 133 S. Ct. 1995 (2013)
Chevron v. Donziger, 296 F.R.D. 168 (S.D.N.Y. 2013)
Giraldo v. Drummond Co., No. 2:09-CV-1041-RDP, 2013 WL 3873960 (N.D. Ala. July 25, 2013)
Intercon Solutions, Inc. v. Basel Action Network, 969 F. Supp. 2d 1026 (N.D. Ill. 2013)
Martinez v. Aero Corporation, 764 F.3d 1062, 1067 (9th Cir. 2014)
Daimler AG v. Bauman 34 S. Ct. 746 (2014)
AstraZeneca AB v. Mylan Pharm., Inc., 72 F. Supp. 3d 549, 556 (D.Del. 2014)
Vera v. Republic of Cuba, 91 F. Supp. 3d 561, 566–67, 571 (S.D.N.Y. 2015)
Al Shimari v. CACI Premier Technology, Inc., 758 F.3d at 516
Forest Labs., Inc. v. Amneal Pharmaceuticals L.L.C., No. 14-508-LPS, 2015 WL 880599, *9 (D.Del. Feb. 26, 2015)
Lanham v. Pilot Travel Centers, No. 03:14-CV-01923-HZ, 2015 WL 5167268, *11 (D. Or. Sept. 2, 2015)
Otsuka Pharmaceutical Co., Ltd. v. Mylan Inc., 106 F. Supp. 3d 456, 468 (D.N.J. 2015)
Keeley v. Pfizer, Inc., No. 415-CV-00583 ERW, 2015 WL 3999488, *4 (E.D. Mo. July 1, 2015)
Fiduciary Network, L.L.C. v. Buehler, No. 3:15-CV-0808, 2015 WL 2165953 (N.D. Tex. May 8, 2015)
Doe I v. Nestle USA, Inc., 766 F.3d 1013, 1021–22 (9th Cir. 2014), reh'g en banc denied, 788 F.3d 946 (2015), cert. denied, 136 S. Ct. 798 (2016)
Brown v. Lockheed Martin Corp., No. 14-4083, 2016 WL 641392 (2d Cir. Feb. 18, 2016)
Acorda Therapeutics Inc. v. Mylan Pharm. Inc., No. 2015-1456, 2016 WL 1077048 (Fed. Cir. Mar. 18, 2016)
Leibovitch v. Republic of Iran, No. 08-C-1939, 2016 WL 2977273, *9 (N.D. Ill. May 19, 2016)

Mitchell v. Eli Lilly and Company, 159 F. Supp. 3d 967, 977–79 (E.D. Mo. 2016)
Display Works, L.L.C. v. Bartley, No. 16-583, 2016 WL 1644451, *7 (D.N.J. April 25, 2016)
Adhikari v. Kellogg Brown & Root, Inc., 845 F.3d 184, 195 (5th Cir. 2017), cert. denied, 138 S. Ct. 134 (2017)
Jesner v. Arab Bank, 138 S. Ct. 1386 (2018)
Yem Ban, Sophea Bun, Sem Kosal, Nol Nakry, Keo Ratha, Sok Sang and Phan Sophea v. Doe Corporations, Phatthana Seafood Co., Ltd., Rubicon Resources, L.L.C., S.S. Frozen Food Co., Ltd. and Wales and Co. Universe Ltd. No 2:16-CV-04271 (C.D. Cal, 15 June 2016)

ENGLAND AND WALES

Multinational Gas and Petrochemical Co v. Multinational Gas and Petrochemical Services Ltd [1983] Ch 258, [1983] 2 All ER 563 (C.A.)
Regina v. Bow Street Metropolitan Stipendiary Magistrate, ex parte Pinochet, [1999] 2 W.L.R. 827 (H.L.)
Kuwait Airways Corp. v. Iraq Airways Co. [2002] 2 A.C. 883 (Eng.)
Guerrero v. Monterrico Metals plc [2009] EWHC 2475
Arroyo v. BP Exploration Co. (Colo.) [2010] EWHC (QB) 1643
Chandler v. Cape plc [2012] EWCA Civ 525
Fish & Fish Ltd v. Sea Shepherd UK [2015] UKSC 10
His Royal Highness Emere Godwin Bebe Okpabi and Others v. Royal Dutch Shell Plc and Another [2018] EWCA Civ 191

CANADA

Moran v. Pyle National (Canada) Ltd. [1975] 1 SCR 393
Pettkus v. Becker [1980] 2 S.C.R. 834
Morguard Investments Ltd. v. De Savoye [1990] 3 S.C.R. 1077
Hunt v. T & N plc [1993] 4 S.C.R. 289
Recherches Internationales Québec v. Cambior, Inc., 1998 CarswellQue 4511 (Can. R.J.Q.) (WL)
Somers v. Fournier (2002) 60 O.R. (3d) 225 (C.A.)
Muscutt v. Courcells [2002] 60 OR (3d) 20 (Can. Ont.)
McIntyre Estate v. Ontario (Attorney General) (2002) 218 D.L.R. 4th 193 (Can. Ont. C.A.)
Teck Cominco Metals Ltd. v. Lloyd's Underwriters [2009] 1 S.C.R. 321 (Can.)
Bil'in (Vill. Council) v. Green Park Int'l, 2009 QCSC 4151 (Can. Que. Sup. Ct.)
Club Resorts, Ltd. v. Van Breda [2012] 1 S.C.R. 572
Ass'n Canadienne Contre L'Impunité (A.C.C.I.) v. Anvil Mining Ltd., 2011 QCSC 1966 (Can. Que.)
Choc v. Hudbay Minerals, Inc. [2013] ONSC 1414
Araya v. Nevsun Resources Ltd [2017] BCCA 401
Das v. George Weston Limited [2017] ONSC 4129 (Can. Ont. Super. Ct.)
Lee v. Transamerica Life Canada [2017] BCSC 843
Yaiguaje v. Chevron Corporation [2018] ONCA 472 (Can. Ont. App. Ct.)

THE NETHERLANDS

Cass. Civ. lère, 19 November 1985, Cognacs and Brandies, JDI 1986
Cass. Civ. lère, 23 May 2013, Prieur
Ktg. Amsterdam 27 April 2000, 18 Nederlands Internationaal Privaatrecht No. 315, at 472 (2000) (Saloum/Kuwait Airways Corp.) (Neth.)
Ktg. Amsterdam 5 January 1996, 14 Nederlands Internationaal Privaatrecht No. 145, at 222 (1996) (Abood/Kuwait Airways Corp.) (Neth.)
Akpan v. Royal Dutch Shell, No. 337050/HA ZA 09-1580 (District Court of the Hague, Jan. 30, 2013)

FRANCE

The ERIKA, Tribunal correctionnel de Paris, January 16, 2008; Cour d'appel de Paris, Pôle 4, 11e ch., March 30, 2010, RG n° 08/02278; Cour de cassation, No. 3439, September 25, 2012
Veolia & Alstom Lawsuit, Cour d'appel [C.A.] [regional court of appeal] Versailles, 3ème ch., Mar. 22, 2013, 11/05331 (Fr.)
Amesys Case (2011)

INTERNATIONAL

PICJ/ICJ

Factory at Chorzów (Ger. v. Pol.), Judgment, 1927 P.C.I.J. (ser. A) No. 8, at 21 (July 26)
Trail Smelter Arbitration (U.S. v. Can.), 3 R.I.A.A. 1905 (1949)
Case Concerning the Barcelona Traction, Light and Power Co (Belg. v. Spain), 1970 I.C.J. 3, 35–36, 42 (Feb. 5)

ICC

Prosecutor v. Perišić, Case No. IT-04-81-A (Int'l Crim. Trib. for the Former Yugoslavia Feb. 28, 2013)
Prosecutor v. Taylor, No SCSL-03-01-A, 10766, 10949-50 (Special Ct. for Sierra Leone Sept. 26, 2013)

COURT OF JUSTICE OF THE EUROPEAN UNION

Case C-412/98, Group Josi Reinsurance Co. S.A. v. Universal Gen. Ins. Co. (UGIC), 2000 E.C.R. I-05925
Marangopoulos Foundation for Human Rights (MFHR) v. Greece, Eur. Comm. Soc. Rights, Complaint No. 30/2005
Case C-281/02, Owusu v. Jackson, 2005 E.C.R. I-1383

INTER-AMERICAN

Velásquez-Rodríguez *v.* Honduras, Inter-Am.Ct.H.R. (ser. C) No. 4

AFRICAN COMMITTEE ON HUMAN AND PEOPLES' RIGHTS

SERAC & CESR *v.* Nigeria, Afr. Committee on Hum. and Peoples' Rts., Comm. No. 155/96, ACHPR/COMM/A004/1, ¶ 46 (2002)

Table of Statutes

UNITED STATES

Alien Tort Statute, 28 U.S.C. § 1350 (1789)
Foreign Sovereign Immunities Act, 28 U.S.C. § 1605(a)
Torture Victim Protection Act of 1991, Pub.L. No. 102-256, 106 Stat. 73, 28 U.S.C. § 1350 (1992)
Sudan Accountability and Divestment Act of December 31, 2007 ("SADA"), Pub. L. No. 110-174, 21 Stat. 2516 (2007)
Anti-Terrorism Act, 18 U.S.C. §§ 2332–33 (1996)
The Employee Retirement Income Security Act (ERISA), 29 U.S.C. §§ 1101–1461 (2012)
Trafficking Victims Protection Act, 22 U.S.C. § 78 (2012)
Sherman Antitrust Act, 15 U.S.C. §§ 1–7 (2012)
Taft-Hartley Act, 29 U.S.C. §§ 141–531 (2012) (labor)
Copyright Act of 1976, 17 U.S.C. §§ 101–810 (2012)

TEXAS

Tex. Civ. Prac. & Rem. Code Ann. § 71.051 (West 2009)

CANADA

Court Jurisdiction and Proceedings Transfer Act, S.B.C., c. 28
Civil Code of Québec, S.Q. 1991 c. 1
An Act Respecting the Class Action, R.S.Q., c. R-2.1 (Can. Que.)

EUROPEAN UNION

Regulation 1215/2012 of the European Parliament and of the Council of 12 December 2012 on Jurisdiction and the Recognition and Enforcement of Judgments in Civil and Commercial Matters, 2012 O.J. (L 351)
Council Regulation 864/2007 2007 O.J. (L 199) 40 (EC)

SWITZERLAND

Swiss Law on Private International Law, *Loi federate sur le droit international privé* [LDIP] Dec. 18, 1987, RS 291 (Switz.)

U.K.

Legal Aid, Sentencing and Punishment of Offenders Act, 2012, c. 10 (Eng.)

Introduction

The number of transnational corporations (TNCs) – including parent companies and subsidiaries – has exploded over the last forty years. In 1970, there were approximately 7,000 TNCs in the world; today, there are more than 100,000 with over 900,000 foreign affiliates.[1] TNCs are now so complex and amorphous in their structure – even compared to ten years ago – that it is difficult for even the most sophisticated legal systems to adequately hold TNCs accountable for the harms they create in countries where they operate, even as the TNCs make enormous profits at the expense of often vulnerable communities. The truth is, certain legal doctrines, often devised nearly a century ago or longer, are too outdated to sufficiently assure that TNCs are held accountable for harms they create in today's world, where TNCs operate globally, and often have structures that transcend a single country or jurisdiction.

While some TNCs benefit host countries (those that "host" transnational businesses, including their subsidiaries) through direct investment, creation of infrastructure, increased employment, and decreased poverty, many others act in violation of international human rights or environmental laws, either directly or in conjunction with government security forces, local police, state-run businesses, or other businesses. Such behavior often wreaks havoc on local, vulnerable communities, and they are often left to absorb all the costs in terms of harm, human rights violations, and environmental degradation. Where such behavior occurs in

---

[1] Damiano de Felice, *Business and Human Rights Indicators to Measure the Corporate Responsibility to Respect: Challenges and Opportunities*, 37 HUM. RTS. Q. 511, 517 (2015). I adopt the definition of a TNC set forth by the United Nations Conference on Trade and Development: "Transnational corporations (TNCs) are incorporated or unincorporated enterprises comprising parent enterprises and their foreign affiliates. A parent enterprise is defined as an enterprise that controls assets of other entities in countries other than its home country, usually by owning a certain equity capital stake." *Transnational Corporations (TNC)*, UN CONF. ON TRADE AND DEV., https://unctad.org/en/PublicationChapters/wir2014chMethodNote_en.pdf (last visited January 1, 2020).

countries with weak and fragile governments and judiciaries ("high-risk" or "fragile" countries), the victims of these violations are typically unable to obtain any compensation for the injuries which these corporations impose upon them. When they seek remedies against these corporations in the host country, these victims often find a lack of causes of action, a corrupt, ineffective, or non-independent judiciary, a lack of lawyers to take their cases, burdensome rules that make bringing a case difficult (such as "loser pays" rules), and threats of violence and other forms of intimidation.

Where the responsible party is a subsidiary that a parent corporation created or purchased in order to do business in the country, victims usually cannot obtain a judicial remedy from the parent in the parent corporation's home country ("home country") either, even though these parent corporations gain tremendous financial and tax benefits from the operation of the subsidiaries. Such victims often cannot seek a remedy from the parent corporation for a variety of reasons: lack of a cause of action for human rights violations, such that the court does not have subject matter jurisdiction over the claim; limited liability of shareholders (and thus, limited liability of parent corporations for acts of their subsidiaries); increasingly narrow personal jurisdiction over TNCs, even in countries where the enterprise engages in substantial business, and for a host of other legal and doctrinal reasons. Given their inability to seek a judicial remedy, these victims are left absorbing all the risks and costs to their life, health, and livelihood while TNCs enjoy immense profits.

This book, *Transnational Corporations and Human Rights: Overcoming Barriers to Judicial Remedy* identifies the barriers which victims face in seeking a remedy for business-related human rights violations, and offers solutions to those barriers. Part I describes the various legal and practical obstacles that prevent the victims of business-related human rights violations from seeking a judicial remedy for their harm, both in their own countries and in the countries where the TNCs are domiciled or operate. The first set of obstacles the book describes are those found in the countries where the victims live and the harm occurs – those countries that "host" transnational businesses ("host countries"). These obstacles include ineffective laws and weak or corrupt judicial systems, as well as a multitude of other practical barriers that make obtaining a remedy in host countries nearly impossible. The second set of obstacles include certain, nearly universal legal doctrines that make it difficult to bring lawsuits against parent companies, even in the country where they are domiciled, incorporated, headquartered, or where they conduct significant business. These locations (or forums) are typically in the West, such as in the United States, Europe, and Canada. The obstacles include limits on the type of cases a court can hear (called subject matter jurisdiction), and in the United States, judicial limits on claims when the harm occurs in other countries (extraterritorial jurisdiction); inability to bring claims against parent companies due to the doctrine of limited liability of shareholders; and limits of a court's jurisdiction over a particular corporate defendant not domiciled in the country where the court sits, and thus, inability to hear and adjudicate a case (called *in personam* jurisdiction, or personal jurisdiction).

If the victim is lucky enough to be able to get into court in a country where a court can and will assert jurisdiction over the case, there are additional legal doctrines that make transnational cases very difficult. They include *forum non conveniens* (where a court dismisses a case because it believes another jurisdiction is a more convenient jurisdiction to hear the case), differences in which country's laws should apply to the claim (called "choice of law" or "conflict of laws"), and doctrines relating to foreign policy concerns (such as the political question doctrine, comity, and the foreign affairs doctrine), short time frames in which to bring the case (statutes of limitation), lack of clarity regarding standards for corporate and vicarious responsibility, rules that make the cost of bringing such cases prohibitive (such as loser pays rules, the prohibiting or taxation of pro bono representation, and lack of contingency fees), and practical barriers relating to evidence-gathering, discovery, and witness testimony. Such barriers not only exist for civil litigation but also for the criminal prosecution of TNCs, meaning, for victims, a lack of any kind of restitution associated with criminal convictions.[2]

Part II offers possible solutions in addressing many of these barriers, the majority of which are suggestions for legislative bodies (such as United States Congress, the European Union, and parliaments in other home countries) to change or revise the laws relating to these barriers. The book contains recommendations that the author considers necessary to overcome some of the most substantial barriers that were found to exist in the countries reviewed. Before moving to the specific recommendations, it should be noted that although many of the recommendations made below are directed to the unique nature of the jurisdictions reviewed, lessons common to all jurisdictions may be drawn from them. These include revisions to the protections of limited liability of parent companies for the illegal conduct of their subsidiaries; ensuring that forum states can hear claims arising from illegal extraterritorial conduct; ensuring that the prosecution of such claims are economically feasible; and ensuring appropriate criminal prosecution of a business's extraterritorial criminal violations in a manner that also allows for victim compensation.

With regard to addressing barriers in home countries, these solutions include changes to judicial and bar association rules that could incentivize bringing such claims, ensuring that causes of action exist, and drilling down on the liability of the parent corporation for acts of their subsidiaries or affiliates they control through a variety of possible legal doctrines; expanding both subject matter jurisdiction so that courts can hear human rights claims, including claims for conduct that occurs in the host country, and personal jurisdiction over TNCs and their affiliates; clarifying or changing rules relating to statutes of limitations; and making changes to better

---

[2] In certain countries, civil claims can be attached to criminal prosecutions, giving the criminal process additional significance for victims. Barriers to accessing remedy unique to prosecutions include a lack of capacity of prosecutors and lack of laws that apply to corporations as a legal person; *see The Corporate Crimes Principles: Advancing Investigations and Prosecutions in Human Rights Cases*, INDEPENDENT COMMISSION OF EXPERTS 20 (Oct. 2016).

support victims' ability to bring legal cases, such as changes to litigation's financial and discovery rules.

Some might ask, why the focus on a judicial remedy? In today's global economy, powerful corporations operate across borders (and legal frameworks) with ease. The costs of such operations are often absorbed by the vulnerable or by those at the local and community level. An ongoing challenge is how to hold TNCs legally accountable for impacts and ensure meaningful and effective reparations to victims. While access to remedy is at the heart of international human rights law, judicial systems often fail to deliver justice and remedy to victims of business-related human rights abuse. Without effectively tackling the barriers to judicial remedy, we will never see the true realization of human rights.

Judicial remedy is the backbone of access to remedy. Moreover, other types of remedies have not been successful. Non-judicial grievance mechanisms, provided at both the state and company level, have failed to deliver effective remedy alone. These include company-level or project-level remedial schemes and government mechanisms such as the OECD's National Contact Points (NCPs).[3]

I also want to address what others might perceive as a limitation of this book – that it focuses primarily on the legal doctrines of the United States, and to a lesser extent, Europe and Canada. The focus on these countries is because most of the TNCs that operate globally, especially in developing countries, are incorporated or domiciled in the United States, Europe, or Canada.[4] It is true that some large TNCs also exist in Asian countries, such as China or Japan, but the numbers pale in comparison to the other three regions. Moreover, those legal systems typically do not allow victims to bring tort claims for human rights violations that take place in the host countries. The more detailed focus on the United States exists for a very simple reason: of the three regions, it has a statute that has been used for over 30 years – the Alien Tort Statute[5] – that allows courts to hear cases for violations of customary international law (CIL) (although, as will be seen, use of this statute has been severely restricted following two Supreme Court decisions). CIL is the source of law for international human rights claims, such as torture, rape, extrajudicial killing, genocide, prolonged arbitrary detention, slavery and trafficking, forced displacement, racial discrimination, and

---

[3] *Remedy Remains Rare*, OECD WATCH (2015) https://www.oecdwatch.org/publications-en/Publication_4201; *Pillar III on the Ground: An Independent Assessment of the Porgera Remedy Framework*, ENODO RIGHTS (2016), http://www.enodorights.com/assets/pdf/pillar-III-on-the-ground-assessment.pdf.

[4] See *The World's Top 100 Non-Financial MNEs, Ranked by Foreign Assets, 2017*, UN CONFERENCE ON TRADE AND DEV., U.N. doc. UNCTAD/WIR/2017, Annex 19, https://unctad.org/Sections/dite_dir/docs/WIR2018/WIR18_tab19.xlsx (last visited July 5, 2018) [hereinafter *World Investment Report*] (showing that countries where the majority of transnational businesses are headquartered include the United States, Canada, Switzerland, and many countries of the European Union such as Germany, France, Spain, and the Netherlands).

[5] 28 U.S.C. § 1350 (stating that federal district courts have jurisdiction over tort claims brought by aliens for violations of the law of nations).

other similar claims.[6] The United States also has specific statutes that grant causes of action for anti-terrorism activities, human trafficking and torture (although torture claims under the current statute can only be brought against natural persons, not corporations).

This is not to say that such claims might not be brought in other countries as well, such as various African or Asian countries, but those countries do not have the same number of TNCs operating abroad as do the United States, Canada, and Europe. Finally, such is not where my expertise lies. Thus, the scope of this book is limited to the United States, Canada, and Europe. As victims are increasingly able to bring human rights claims against corporations in their own countries, or other countries of the world, this book will become obsolete. I hope that is the case.

---

[6] The Restatement of the Law (Third) The Foreign Relations of the United States lists violations of CIL norms as including genocide, slavery or slave trade, the murder or causing the disappearance of individuals, torture or other cruel, inhumane, or degrading treatment or punishment, prolonged arbitrary detention, systematic racial discrimination, or a consistent pattern of gross violations of internationally recognized human rights.

PART I

Rise of Transnational Corporations, Impact on Human Rights, And Victims' Rights to Remedy

A transnational mining company allegedly paid the salaries of soldiers who massacred over seventy civilians – including women and children – following a protest in Democratic Republic of Congo (DRC). Twenty-eight were summarily executed and buried in mass graves, and the company was accused of using its trucks to transport the bodies. The soldiers, said to be in the company's employ, terrorized the local community, raping and sexually assaulting the daughter of the police chief, who was left paralyzed after giving birth and died.[1] Who should pay for these crimes?

Unfortunately, this is not a one-off example. In April 2004, Peruvian communities organized a peaceful march to a mine site to express their objections to a business's operations. Police responded by firing tear gas, and the resulting violence left one protester dead and numerous protesters and police officers injured. This violence led to further deterioration in business–community relations. As a result, the regional government of Piura in northwestern Peru organized talks between various stakeholders relevant to the mining project, including the surrounding communities. However, these talks broke down in July 2005 due to allegations of state bias in favor of the company, Monterrico. In response, the local communities organized a second march that culminated in several thousand protesters gathering at the mine site in August 2005. Again, the protest descended into violence after the police attempted to disperse the protesters with guns and tear gas. Many demonstrators were injured, including one protester who was killed after being shot in the neck. Following the protest, at least twenty-eight people – including two women and a teenager – were held for over seventy-two hours on the business's property. They allege that during their captivity, they were beaten, bound, forced to eat rotten food,

---

[1] UN Organization Mission in the Democratic Republic of Congo (MONUC), *Report on the Conclusions of the Special Investigation into Allegations of Summary Executions and Other Violations of Human Rights Committed by the FARDC in Kilwa (Province of Katanga) on 15 October 2004* ¶ 36 (2005).

and threatened with violence, rape, and death. Two women were sexually assaulted.[2] In situations such as this, where is the redress? How do victims of business-related human rights violations obtain effective remedy?

Or another situation – failure to adequately maintain a multinational oil company's pipelines, used to transport oil produced in Nigeria – has led to widespread and destructive pollution. Oil spills in Niger Delta villages—including Goi in 2004, Oruma in 2005, and Ikot Ada Udo between 1996 and 2006 – have reportedly resulted in the loss of hectares of commercially viable trees, fish ponds, and nurseries.[3] In addition, these spills have contaminated drinking water sources and damaged other property essential to villagers' livelihoods. Ongoing leaks in Goi have made any clean-up essentially futile, and, following a spill in September 2007, the village has been deserted. According to local people in Oruma, the clean-up in their community only consisted of setting oil-sodden soil on fire. Not only were nearby trees of economic value seriously damaged by these fires, but the oil-damaged fish ponds were largely left untouched, causing local residents to abandon fisheries.[4]

How did we get here? Why do TNCs have the power to operate above the law and immune from accountability, preventing rightful plaintiffs from accessing remedy? To answer that question, we must first investigate the growth and structure of the transnational corporation, which has markedly increased in both number and complexity. This matters, because the vast economic power of the TNCs and the complex legal and corporate structures that they embody are a major force frustrating attempts at redress for serious human rights violations.

---

[2] *Torture at the Río Blanco Mine—A State-Corporate Crime?* Chapter 3: *Communities March on the Mine (Source 9: Documentary Excerpt "The Devil Operation")*, INT'L ST. CRIME INITIATIVE, http://www.statecrime.org/testimonyproject/peru# (last visited June 22, 2018).

[3] Akpan v. Royal Dutch Shell, No. 337050/HA ZA 09-1580 (District Court of the Hague, Jan. 30, 2013).

[4] *Timeline: The Course of the Lawsuit*, MILIEUDEFENSIE, https://en.milieudefensie.nl/shell-in-nigeria/timeline-the-course-of-the-lawsuit (last visited July 3, 2018); *see also Shell lawsuit (re oil pollution in Nigeria)*, BUSINESS & HUMAN RIGHTS RESOURCE CENTRE, https://www.business-humanrights.org/en/shell-lawsuit-re-oil-pollution-in-nigeria? (last visited July 3, 2018).

1

Growth and Structure of TNCs

A description of the varied types of complex business structures employed by large, transnational businesses is outside the scope of this book. However, a few key facts about corporate growth and structure are important to note, given the current jurisdictional paradigm's focus on the "home" (or in Europe, domicile) of a corporation – a paradigm that is based on outdated notions of how TNCs are structured. First, the sheer growth in number of TNCs has changed the operation of business and the resultant potential for human rights violations at the global scale. The number of TNCs – including parent companies and subsidiaries – has grown exponentially over the last fifty years. Moreover, as companies grow in size and expand overseas, the number of subsidiaries tends to increase and companies' structures become even more complex.[1] Over the last several decades, as TNCs have grown and created other corporations, they have rapidly changed form, with the emergence of complex multi-tiered corporate structures which include numerous affiliated entities that collectively conduct the business of the enterprise.[2] As a result, it is difficult to determine ownership of TNCs' various affiliated companies or to compile complete financial data on TNCs due to their complex structure, the existence of holding companies, and the fact that a subsidiary can be owned by multiple parent corporations.[3] Lack of transparency surrounding ownership and existence of various TNC affiliates only exacerbates the problem.

---

[1] *Governance of Subsidiaries: A Survey of Global Companies*, DELOITTE (Sept. 2013), http://www2.deloitte.com/content/dam/Deloitte/in/Documents/risk/Corporate%20Governance/in-gc-governance-of-subsidiaries-a-survey-of-global-companies-noexp.pdf (last visited June 6, 2019).
[2] *See* Phillip Blumberg, *Limited Liability and Corporate Groups*, 11 J. CORP. L. 573, 604 (1986).
[3] *World Investment Report 2016: Chapter IV*, UN CONF. ON TRADE & DEV., http://unctad.org/en/PublicationsLibrary/wir2016_en.pdf (last visited July 10, 2018).

This is a far cry from the original view of the "corporation" in the comparatively provincial world that gave rise to the legal corporate structure. Even the complex multinational corporate group that most policy-makers have had in mind when considering regulations and legal doctrines – perhaps consisting of a parent corporation, sub-holding companies, and subsidiary corporations (often hundreds of subsidiaries), each organized under various countries' laws – no longer completely captures the changing structures and complexities of TNCs. This hierarchal, pyramid approach, typically used by Anglo-American and British companies, although itself complex, is now dated and becoming quickly obsolete. Yet, as one well-known scholar of corporate structure notes, this is the typical model that judges and policymakers had (and continue to have) in mind when thinking about regulation and legal doctrines pertaining to TNCs.[4]

With mergers, things are even more complex – often there is not one main "parent" company. For example, with mergers involving European companies, often there is "the creation of a twin holding company located in each home state, based on joint shareholding by the founding parent companies, and the transfer of operating activities to subsidiaries that may be jointly or separately owned and controlled by the holding companies" (as an example, this was how Royal Dutch Shell was structured until 2005).[5] Finally, transnational financial institutions pose special complexities in their structure. Many international banks either open a branch or satellite abroad, or transform their subsidiaries into satellites, in order to avoid the stricter regulations that apply to financial transactions.[6] Branches can typically transfer capital and liquid assets across national borders with little regulation, and thus little transparency.[7]

One can visualize the immense complexity of corporate structures, including "parents", subsidiaries, affiliates, and "related entities" of numerous TNCs. The United Nations Conference on Trade and Development cannot even compile complete and accurate financial data on TNCs because they are so complex, their number of categorizations of holding companies, and the fact that a subsidiary can be owned by multiple parent corporations.[8]

---

[4] PETER T. MUCHLINSKI, MULTINATIONAL ENTERPRISES & THE LAW 56 (2nd ed. 2007). The Anglo-American "pyramid group" type of structure consists of a parent company which owns and controls a network of wholly or majority-owned subsidiaries, which may themselves be intermediate holding companies for sub-groups of closely held subsidiaries. The resulting structure is that of a "pyramid" with the parent company at its apex. As noted above, when the "pyramid" crosses borders, this represents the "classic" conception of the MNE which underlies much of the thinking on MNE regulation. Id.
[5] Id. at 59.
[6] Tobias H. Trigger, Organizational Choices of Banks and the Effective Supervision of Transnational Financial Institutions, 48 TEX. INT'L L. J. 177 (2012).
[7] Id. at 182.
[8] World Investment Report 2016: Chapter IV, UN CONF. ON TRADE & DEV., http://unctad.org/en/PublicationsLibrary/wir2016_en.pdf (last visited July 10, 2018).

1.1 FINANCIAL BENEFITS FROM OPERATING IN DEVELOPING COUNTRIES

TNCs gain enormous financial benefits by operating globally, especially when operating within countries that have few regulatory mechanisms to ensure that corporations and their subsidiaries are complying with human rights and environmental norms and laws. It is difficult to compile complete financial data on TNCs due to their complex structures and a lack of transparency. However, as of 2010, the value of global foreign direct investment (FDI) exceeded $21,288.5 billion, the number of TNCs was estimated at over 100,000, and the number of TNC foreign affiliates at over 890,000, a number that likely underestimates the number and investment of TNCs due to the fact that many do not list all of their subsidiaries.[9]

Meanwhile, the benefits received by parent corporations for actions of subsidiaries are immense. They include, inter alia, lower production and labor costs, shareholder income and payouts, and preferential tax treatment.[10] Many transnational businesses have a foreign subsidiary operating abroad in order to manufacture goods in host countries where labor, manufacturing, and regulatory costs may be lower.[11] In addition, like individual shareholders, parent corporations receive foreign subsidiaries' income in the form of shareholder dividends.[12] The TNC therefore reaps the benefit of both international labor and regulatory standards, and the business-friendly legal and financial structure of the home country (where labor costs may well be higher and where the TNC, if operating locally, would likely face a more stringent regulatory regime).

---

[9] *id.*; Małgorzata Jaworek & Marcin Kuzel, *Transnational Corporations in the World Economy: Formation, Development and Present Position*, 4 COPERNICAN J. OF FIN. & ACCT. 55–70, 57 (2015) http://dx.doi.org/10.12775/CJFA.2015.004 (last visited June 6, 2019).

[10] *See* Gwynne Skinner, *Rethinking Limited Liability of Parent Corporations for Foreign Subsidiaries' Violations of International Human Rights Law*, 72 WASH. & LEE L. REV. 1769, 1777 n19 (2015); citing Daniel Chow, *Counterfeiting as an Externality Imposed by Multinational Companies on Developing Countries*, 51 VA. J. INT'L L. 785, 816–17 (2011) (describing advantages of low labor costs and lenient regulatory regimes); Christopher H. Hanna, *Corporate Tax Reform: Listening to Corporate America*, 35 J. CORP. L. 283, 298–99 (2009) (describing significant tax advantages of foreign subsidiaries, such as the tax advantages of deferral of income earned by a foreign subsidiary); Christopher H. Hanna, *The Real Value of Tax Deferral*, 61 FLA. L. REV. 203, 231–33 (2009) (describing additional tax-related benefits of foreign subsidiaries, such as advantageous accounting rules); J. Clifton Fleming, Jr., *Worse Than Exemption*, 59 EMORY L. J. 79, 84–85 (2009) (describing how foreign subsidiaries provide US resident corporations with "overly generous tax benefits" and providing examples); J. Clifton Fleming, Jr. & Robert J. Peroni, *Reinvigorating Tax Expenditure Analysis and Its International Dimension*, 27 VA. TAX REV. 437, 538 (2008) (describing how foreign subsidiaries provide advantages over domestic competitors in the United States).

[11] *See* Chow, *supra* note 10 at 816–17.

[12] *See, e.g.*, Julie Roin, *The Grand Illusion: A Neutral System for the Taxation of International Transactions*, 75 VA. L. REV. 919, 938 (1989) ("[T]he foreign earnings of a foreign subsidiary, even one owned entirely by U.S. shareholders, are subject only to foreign income tax.").

In the United States, parent corporations often use foreign subsidiaries to take advantage of the US tax code and reduce taxes they pay on the subsidiary's income primarily through two methods: deferral of subsidiaries' income, and a mechanism called "transfer pricing manipulation." With deferral of income,[13] for example, the parent corporation operates a subsidiary in a foreign country and keeps the profits abroad. Under the tax code, the subsidiary's income is not liable to taxation until it is returned to the United States, although there are certain exceptions.[14] Corporations can also treat what is supposed to be a temporary tax deferral as permanent if the parent asserts that the deferral is indefinite – in other words, that the parent does not plan on returning the profits to the United States in the near future.[15] Transfer pricing enables corporate parents to shift income from high-tax to low-tax countries by allowing their various entities to sell or transfer goods or services among each other.[16] Through transfer pricing, a parent corporation can concentrate on selling goods or services in a lower tax jurisdiction, for example.[17] Similarly, a parent can shift costs to itself or to an entity in a high-tax country so that deductions for costs will be maximized.[18]

The World Investment Report discusses FDI to indicate growth and health of the world economy.[19] According to the 2014 report, FDI outflows from developing countries also reached a record level. TNCs from developing economies are increasingly acquiring foreign affiliates from developed countries located in their regions. The report further highlights that: "Developing and transition economies together invested $553 billion, or 39 per cent of global FDI outflows, compared with only 12 per cent at the beginning of the 2000s."[20]

Where are these TNCs located? We'll begin with the United States. TNCs with headquarters abroad do business and invest in the United States more than in any

---

[13] *See generally* REUVEN S. AVI-YONAH, U.S. INTERNATIONAL TAXATION: CASES AND MATERIALS 192 (2002) (identifying the tax preference granted to US businesses operating abroad through the deferral of US tax until repatriation as having great import; and noting that the privilege of deferral is deepened in accordance with the level of tax in the low tax foreign jurisdiction).

[14] *See* Hanna, *Corporate Tax Reform, supra* note 10 at 231–32 (describing this strategy).

[15] This is accomplished through the Accounting Principles Board (APB) 23 provision. *See* Hanna, *supra* note 10 (noting that APB 23 essentially lowers the US parent's tax rate).

[16] *See* Cym H. Lowell, *Significance of Transfer Pricing for Multinational Enterprises, in* U.S. INT'L TAX: AGREEMENTS, CHECKLISTS AND COMMENTARY ¶ 2.05, (2015) (describing transfer pricing as "a quintessential three-way contest pitting tax administration against tax administration, in bilateral treaty-country matters, with the taxpayer often occupying the position of stakeholder in the middle.").

[17] *See* MICHAEL J. GRAETZ, FOUNDATIONS OF INTERNATIONAL INCOME TAX 400 (2003) (explaining transfer pricing).

[18] *See* Markus Henn, *Tax Havens and the Taxation of Transnational Corporations,* FRIEDRICH EBERT STIFTUNG (June 2013), http://library.fes.de/pdf-files/iez/global/10082.pdf (last visited June 6, 2019) (providing examples of tax evasion practices).

[19] *See generally,* UN CONFERENCE ON TRADE AND DEVELOPMENT, *World Investment Report 2014 Overview: Investing in the SDGs: An Action Plan,* U.N. Doc. UNCTAD/WIR/2014 (2014).

[20] *Id.* at ix.

country in the world.[21] FDI in the United States, known as FDIUS,[22] totaled $3.7 trillion through 2016 on a historical-cost basis.[23] As the Organization for International Investment notes, "Each year foreign firms make new investments in the United States ... They build new factories, grow their well-established U.S. operations, fund research and development, and employ millions of Americans in well-paying jobs."[24] Transnational companies from the United Kingdom do the most business in the United States, followed by Japan, the Netherlands, Canada, Luxembourg, Germany, Switzerland, and France.[25] These countries make up 80 percent of the FDI in the United States. On a regional basis, European countries are the largest investors in the United States.[26]

What do the TNCs do? Manufacturing is the largest industry for foreign businesses (spending over $1 trillion through 2014), followed by the finance and insurance industry ($355 billion); wholesale trade ($346 billion); banking ($219 billion); the information industry ($177 billion); and mining ($155 billion).[27] Foreign companies exported between $2.25 billion in goods and services into the United States during July 2016 alone,[28] as US citizens are the largest consumers in the world.

---

[21] *Foreign Direct Investment in the United States 2017*, ORGANIZATION FOR INTERNATIONAL INVESTMENT 2, https://ofii.org/sites/default/files/FDIUS%202017.pdf (last visited July 3, 2018). This is true on a cumulative basis, and has been true every year but for 2014, when flows into China and Hong Kong exceeded the United States. *Id.* at 1.

[22] Although FDI is defined differently by different organizations, the United States defines FDIUS as the ownership or control, directly or indirectly, by one foreign entity of a 10 percent or more ownership share of an incorporated or unincorporated US business enterprise. *Id.* at 1.

[23] *Id.* at 2.

[24] *Id.*

[25] *Id.* at 3.

[26] *Id.* at 5.

[27] *Id.* at 6.

[28] *See U.S. International Trade in Goods and Services*, BUREAU OF ECONOMIC ANALYSIS (U.S. DEPARTMENT OF COMMERCE) (Apr. 2018), http://www.bea.gov/newsreleases/international/trade/tradnewsrelease.htm (last visited June 6, 2019).

2

Victims' Rights To Remedy for Business-Related Human Rights Violations

2.1 VULNERABLE COMMUNITIES ABSORB HARM FROM TNCS' ACTIVITIES

While TNCs stand to benefit greatly from their work in less developed or developing countries, it is frequently the local, most vulnerable populations and communities – often nonconsenting to the development – who absorb most of the costs associated with this economic activity in the form of lower labor and regulatory costs, environmental damages, and civil and human rights violations.[1] Although many TNCs are responding to human rights violations by acting responsibly, engaging in due diligence,[2] and otherwise establishing mechanisms to assist in the prevention of

---

[1] See, e.g., Kiarie Mwaura, *Internalization of Costs to Corporate Groups: Part-Whole Relationships, Human Rights Norms and the Futility of the Corporate Veil*, 11 J. INT'L BUS. & L. 85, 85–86 (2012) (explaining how victims of human rights abuses often absorb the costs of those abuses); Meredith Dearborn, *Enterprise Liability: Reviewing and Revitalizing Liability for Corporate Groups*, 97 CAL. L. REV. 195, 205–07 (2009) (noting the large benefits corporations gain from host countries' subsidiaries' risky conduct while only bearing some of the costs); Elizabeth Barrett Ristroph, *How Can the United States Correct Multi-National Corporations' Environmental Abuses Committed in the Name of Trade?* 15 IND. INT'L & COMP. L. REV. 51, 53–54 (2004) (noting corporations externalize the costs of doing business while enjoying the benefits); Robert B. Thompson, *Unpacking Limited Liability: Direct and Vicarious Liability of Corporate Participants for Torts of the Enterprise*, 47 VAND. L. REV. 1, 29–39 (1994) (discussing corporations' externalization of costs to reap benefits from their subsidiaries' potentially abusive conduct in host country); David W. Leebron, *Limited Liability, Tort Victims, and Creditors*, 91 COLUM. L. REV. 1565, 1584–87, 1613–23, 1637–40 (1991) (same); Mark J. Roe, *Corporate Strategic Reaction to Mass Tort*, 72 VA. L. REV. 1, 39–56 (1986) (examining the practice of externalizing the risks of a subsidiary operating in a host country to allow the parent corporation to avoid liability as a result of actions taken by subsidiary).

[2] The OECD Guidelines define due diligence as follows: Due diligence is understood as the process through which enterprises can identify, prevent, mitigate and account for how they address their actual and potential adverse impacts as an integral part of business decision-making and risk management systems. *OECD Due Diligence Guidance for Responsible Supply Chains of Minerals from Conflict-Affected and High-Risk Areas: Third Edition* 66 OECD

human rights violations, when violations do occur, victims often do not have any remedy available to them.

Over the past decades, Western-based TNCs have been expanding into developing countries, which have campaigned to attract transnational business. Understandably hungry for foreign investments and the growth that comes with it, the government limits the amount of "red tape" and regulations in order to attract the foreign investment. Although such direct investment in developing countries often leads to economic growth, and improvements in infrastructure and standards of living, such is not typically without costs to human rights, health, and the environment of often vulnerable populations. Frequently, there are lax regulations or few laws that protect such populations, and when laws do exist, they are often not enforced by the host government. In many countries, government-owned enterprises partner with private business to engage in the economic activity of the TNC. We see this particularly in the extraction industries.

Some of the most severe human rights abuses occur when the host government, with the knowledge or aid of the TNC, employs state security forces to forcibly remove a population, crack down on a labor movement, violently squash a peaceful protest, or retaliate against those who speak out against business activity, often violently. Given the enormous benefits to business and the costs communities bear, policy-makers should question the fairness of allowing such TNCs to escape civil lawsuits these victims might bring.

International organizations such as the United Nations and the Organisation for Economic Co-operation and Development (OECD) recognize that both countries and TNCs owe an obligation to ensure victims have access to a remedy – and in particular a judicial remedy – for violations of human rights occasioned by the profit-making enterprise of the TNC. Nonetheless, there are many barriers to remedy that must be overcome to provide real, meaningful access to justice for victims. These barriers, and the legal structures to overcome them, are the focus of this book.

Before looking at the barriers to remedy for victims harmed by the conduct of multinational corporations, it is first important to address and understand why such victims are entitled to remedy in the first place. After all, the notion of "tort law" and its extraterritorial application is not universal and there may be arguments, based in notions of sovereignty and territory, that victims are only afforded whatever remedy is available in the legal system where they reside, such that any lack of accountability for corporate behavior should be taken up with the governments of the victims' countries.

(2016), http://www.oecd.org/daf/inv/mne/OECD-Due-Diligence-Guidance-Minerals-Edition3.pdf (last accessed June 25, 2018). See also OECD, *Due Diligence Guidance for Responsible Business Conduct* (2018), http://mneguidelines.oecd.org/OECD-Due-Diligence-Guidance-for-Responsible-Business-Conduct.pdf (last accessed June 25, 2018).

Therefore, it is important to elucidate the legal underpinnings of the notion of victims' rights to remedy. The first, and oldest, is found in international law notions of comity and the responsibility of the sovereign for the actions of his subjects. This international law basis for remedy has been further developed through various treaties, agreements, and jurisprudence. As such, there is now a general principle of international law that every violation of international law should be accompanied by the provision of remedy.[3]

The notion that all victims of human rights violations should have access to remedy is at the heart of human rights law. This notion has been developed and articulated in numerous human rights treaties and their accompanying bodies. Recently, the UN Committee on Economic, Cultural and Social Rights stated in a General Comment on state obligations under the International Covenant on Economic, Social and Cultural Rights in the context of business activities that "States parties have the duty to take necessary steps to address these challenges in order to prevent a denial of justice and ensure the right to effective remedy and reparation."[4] Recognizing the right to remedy under international human rights law, there is a current movement toward a United Nations Treaty on Business and Human Rights. Discussions thus far include how such a treaty might affect the right of victims of business-related abuses to a judicial remedy. The basis for remediation for human rights violations committed by TNCs is therefore strong and well supported at the international level.

Similarly, and as discussed below, the history of the United States and its enactment of the Alien Torts Statute (ATS) demonstrates that the United States has continually supported and developed a law of remedy for violations of international law by US citizens, including corporate citizens. Yet despite the strong evidence that CIL requires nations to provide a remedy to victims who are noncitizens for injuries arising from that nation's violation of international law, victims still face numerous barriers to accessing, let alone achieving, a remedy for human rights related abuses.

2.2 THE RIGHT TO REMEDY UNDER INTERNATIONAL LAW

Although the notion that international law requires countries to provide victims with civil remedies for the harms that arise from international human rights violations has ancient roots,[5] it has been a pillar of international law only during the relatively

---

[3] *See, e.g.*, Factory at Chorzów (Ger. v. Pol.), Judgment, 1927 P.C.I.J. (ser. A) No. 8, at 21 (July 26).
[4] Comm. on Econ., Soc. and Cultural Rights, General comment No. 24 (2017) on State obligations under the International Covenant on Economic, Social and Cultural Rights in the context of business activities, ¶ 44, U.N. Doc E/C.12/GC/24 (2017).
[5] *See* M. Cherif Bassiouni, *International Recognition of Victims' Rights*, 6 HUM. RTS. L. REV. 203, 206–08 (2006) (discussing the historical evolution of victims' rights).

modern times of the last three centuries. One of the most influential international law commentators to recognize a right to remedy was Emmerich de Vattel, a famous international scholar during the 1700s.[6] Vattel wrote in his influential international law treatise in 1758 that "[a] sovereign who refuses to repair the evil done by one of his subjects, or to punish the criminal, or, finally, to deliver him up, makes himself in a way an accessory to the deed, and becomes responsible for it," and further noted that a sovereign needed to ensure a remedy for an "evil done by one of his subjects."[7] Similarly, William Blackstone, a respected English legal scholar and international law authority during the 1700s, noted that a sovereign should ensure that injured "strangers" receive restitution from those individuals who harmed them through violations of international law.[8]

This obligation to ensure a remedy was reaffirmed in the mid-twentieth century through various U.N. resolutions and treaties.[9] Not only does the Universal Declaration of Human Rights state that "[e]veryone has the right to an effective remedy by the competent national tribunals for acts violating the fundamental rights granted him by the constitution or by law,"[10] various treaties ratified by the US, Canada, and Europe all contain a provision guaranteeing a remedy to a noncitizen whose rights under international law have been violated, such as the International Covenant on Civil and Political Rights (ICCPR)[11] and the Convention Against Torture.[12] Several treaties also specifically note that countries are required to ensure that victims have

[6] Anthony D'Amato, *The Alien Tort Statute and the Founding of the Constitution*, 82 AM. J. INTL. L. 62, 64 (1988).
[7] EMMERICH DE VATTEL, THE LAW OF NATIONS 137 (Carnegie Institute of Washington ed., Charles G. Fenwick trans. 1916) (1758).
[8] WILLIAM BLACKSTONE, COMMENTARIES ON THE LAWS OF ENGLAND, IN FOUR BOOKS, 69–70 (1803) (noting that with violations of safe conduct, "the injured stranger should have restitution out of [the violator's] effects" and that "the Lord Chancellor... may cause full restitution and amends to be made to the party injured").
[9] *See, e.g.*, Universal Declaration of Human Rights, art. 8, G.A. Res. 217 (III), at 73, U.N. Doc. A/810 (1948); International Covenant on Civil and Political Rights, art. 2(3)(a), *opened for signature* Dec. 19, 1966, 999 U.N.T.S. 171; Convention Against Torture and Other Cruel, Inhuman or Degrading Treatment or Punishment, art. 14, *opened for signature* Dec. 10, 1984, 1465 U.N.T.S. 85.
[10] Universal Declaration of Human Rights, G.A. Res. 217A (III), art. 8, U.N. GAOR, 3d Sess., U.N. Doc. A/810, at 73 (Dec. 10, 1948).
[11] "Each State party to the present Covenant undertakes: (a) To ensure that any person whose rights or freedoms as herein recognized are violated shall have an effective remedy, notwithstanding that the violation has been committed by persons acting in an official capacity." International Covenant on Civil and Political Rights, *opened for signature* Dec. 16, 1966, art. 2(3)(a), 999 U.N.T.S. 171, 174 (entered into force Mar. 23, 1976).
[12] "Each State Party shall ensure in its legal system that the victim of an act of torture obtains redress and has an enforceable right to fair and adequate compensation, including the means for as full rehabilitation as possible. In the event of the death of the victim as a result of an act of torture, his dependents shall be entitled to compensation." Convention Against Torture and Other Cruel, Inhuman or Degrading Treatment or Punishment, *opened for signature* Dec. 10, 1984, art. 22, S. Treaty Doc. No. 100-20, at 27, 1465 U.N.T.S. 85, 120 (entered into force June 26, 1987).

access to judicial remedies when their human rights are violated.[13] For example, human rights treaties' expert bodies, such as the Human Rights Committee of the ICCPR, as well as regional human rights courts and bodies have repeatedly found that countries have the duty to protect human rights by regulating nonstate actors.[14] Several of these bodies, such as the Committee to End Racial Discrimination (CERD) and the Committee on Economic, Social and Cultural Rights (CESCR),

---

[13] International Convention on the Elimination of All Forms of Racial Discrimination, *opened for signature* Mar. 7, 1966, art. 6, S. Exec. Doc. C, 95-2, at 5, 660 U.N.T.S. 195, 222 (entered into force Jan. 4, 1969); Convention on the Rights of the Child, *opened for signature* Nov. 20, 1989, art. 19, 1577 U.N.T.S. 3, 50 (entered into force Sept. 2, 1990); American Convention on Human Rights, *opened for signature* Nov. 22, 1969, arts. 25, 63(1), O.A.S.T.S. No. 36, 1144 U.N.T.S. 123, 151, 159 (entered into force July 18, 1978); African Charter on Human and Peoples' Rights, *adopted* June 27, 1981, art. 7(1)(a), 21 I.L.M. 58, 60; Council of the League of Arab States, Arab Charter on Human Rights, Sept. 15, 1994, arts. 12, 23, *reprinted in* 18 HUM. RTS. L. J. 151, 152 (1997); European Convention for the Protection of Human Rights and Fundamental Freedoms, *opened for signature* Nov. 4, 1950, art. 13, Europ. T.S. No. 5, 213 U.N.T.S. 221, 232 (entered into force Mar. 1, 1985).

[14] Human Rights Comm., *General Comment No. 31: Nature of the General Legal Obligation Imposed on States Parties to the Covenant*, ¶ 8, U.N. Doc. CCPR/C/21/Rev.1/Add.13 (May 26, 2004) (the obligations of States Parties to ensure Covenant rights require state protection "against acts committed by private persons or entities that would impair the enjoyment of Covenant rights in so far as they are amenable to application between private persons or entities"); Comm. on Econ., Soc. and Cultural Rights, General Comment No. 12: The right to adequate food, Art. 11, ¶ 15, U.N. Doc. E/C.12/1999/5 (May 12, 1995) ("[T]he obligation to protect requires measures by the State to ensure that enterprises or individuals do not deprive individuals of their access to adequate food."); *see* Young, James & Webster *v.* United Kingdom, 44 Eur. Ct. H.R. (ser. A) ¶ 49 (1981) (observing that a state is responsible for a violation of the Convention for the Protection of Human Rights and Fundamental Freedoms that is the "result of non-observance of that obligation in the enactment of domestic legislation"); *see also* X & Y *v.* Netherlands, 91 Eur. Ct. H.R. (ser. A) ¶ 27 (1985) ("Effective deterrence ... can be achieved only by criminal-law provisions."). Under the European Social Charter, *see* Marangopoulos Foundation for Human Rights (MFHR) *v.* Greece, Eur. Comm. Soc. Rights, Complaint No. 30/2005, ¶ 14 (decision on admissibility Oct. 10, 2005) ("The state is responsible for enforcing the rights embodied in the Charter within its jurisdiction. The Committee is therefore competent to consider the complainant's allegations of violations, even if the State has ... simply failed to put an end to the alleged violations in its capacity as regulator."). Under the American Convention on Human Rights, *see* Velásquez-Rodríguez *v.* Honduras, Inter-Am.Ct.H.R. (ser. C) No. 4, ¶ 172 (1988) ("An illegal act which violates human rights and which is initially not directly imputable to a State ... can lead to international responsibility of the State ... because of the lack of due diligence to prevent the violation or to respond to it as required by the Convention."). Under the African Charter of Human and Peoples' Rights, *see* Commission Nationale des Droits de l'Homme et des Libertés *v.* Chad, Afr. Comm. on Hum. & Peoples' Rts., Comm. No. 74/92, ¶ 20 (1995) ("[I]f a state neglects to ensure the rights in the African Charter, this can constitute a violation, even if the State or its agents are not the immediate cause of the violation."); *see also* SERAC & CESR *v.* Nigeria, Afr. Committee on Hum. and Peoples' Rts., Comm. No. 155/96, ACHPR/COMM/A004/1, ¶ 46, (2002) ("The State is obliged to protect right-holders against other subjects by legislation and provision of effective remedies ... Protection generally entails the creation and maintenance of an atmosphere or framework by an effective interplay of laws and regulations so that individuals will be able to freely realize their rights and freedoms.").

have taken the position that this duty extends to the private actors' extraterritorial conduct.[15] This obligation has also been recognized by recent scholars[16] and at least one international arbitration body.[17]

Moreover, it has become increasingly recognized that CIL requires that nations provide a remedy to victims who are noncitizens for injuries arising from that nation's violation of international law, as evidenced by the US's Restatement of the Law,[18] and the work, current and historical, of the United Nations.[19]

---

[15] Comm. on Econ., Soc. and Cultural Rights, General Comment No. 14: The Right to the Highest Attainable Standard of Health, Art. 12, ¶ 39, U.N. Doc. E/C.12/2000/4 (Aug. 11, 2000) ("States parties have to respect the enjoyment of the right to health in other countries, and to prevent third parties from violating the right in other countries."); see also Comm. on Econ., Soc. and Cultural Rights, General Comment No. 15: The Right to Water, arts. 11–12, ¶ 23, 31, U.N. Doc. E/C.12/2002/11 (Nov. 26, 2002) ("The obligation to *protect* requires States parties to prevent third parties from interfering in any way with the right to water... International cooperation requires States parties to refrain from actions that interfere, directly or indirectly, with the enjoyment of the right to water in other countries."); Comm. on Econ., Soc. and Cultural Rights, Statement on the Obligations of States Parties Regarding the Corporate Sector and Economic, Social and Cultural Rights, ¶ 5, U.N. Doc. E/C.12/2011/1 (May 20, 2011) ("States Parties should also take steps to prevent human rights contraventions abroad by corporations which have their main seat under their jurisdiction, without infringing the sovereignty or diminishing the obligations of the host States under the Covenant."); Comm. on the Elimination of Racial Discrimination, Consideration of Reports Submitted by States Parties Under Art. 9 of the Convention, ¶ 17, U.N. Doc. CERD/C/CAN/CO/18 (May 25, 2007) ("[T]he Committee encourages the State Party to take appropriate legislative or administrative measures to prevent acts of transnational corporations registered in Canada which negatively impact on the enjoyment of rights of indigenous peoples in territories outside Canada.").

[16] OLIVIER DE SCHUTTER, INTERNATIONAL HUMAN RIGHTS LAW: CASES, MATERIALS AND COMMENTARY 163 (2010) ("[A]n emerging scholarship insist[s] that the extraterritorial obligations imposed under the ICESCR entail ... that States ... should control the activities of private actors ... which they recognize as having their 'nationality'"); IAN BROWNLIE, SYSTEM OF THE LAW OF NATIONS: STATE RESPONSIBILITY 165 (1983); see also NICOLA JÄGERS, CORPORATE HUMAN RIGHTS OBLIGATIONS: IN SEARCH OF ACCOUNTABILITY 172 (2002) ("[A] State has the obligation not knowingly to allow its territory to be used for acts contrary to the rights of other States — that home State responsibility can arise where the home State has not exercised due diligence in controlling parent companies that are effectively under its control.").

[17] See Trail Smelter Arbitration (U.S. v. Can.), 3 R.I.A.A. 1905 (1949).

[18] The Restatement (Third) of Foreign Relations Law of the United States art. 14, § 711 (1987) reads:

> State Responsibility for Injury To Nationals of Other States
> A state is responsible under international law for injury to a national of another state caused by an official act or omission that violates
>
> (a) a human right that, under § 701, a state is obligated to respect for all persons subject to its authority;
> (b) a personal right that, under international law, a state is obligated to respect for individuals of foreign nationality; or
> (c) a right to property or another economic interest that, under international law, a state is obligated to respect for persons, natural or juridical, of foreign nationality, as provided in § 712.

[19] In 2005, the United Nations issued the Basic Principles and Guidelines on the Right to a Remedy and Reparation. See Basic Principles and Guidelines on the Right to a Remedy and

The United Nations' Human Rights Council endorsed the Guiding Principles for Business and Human Rights (UNGPs) in 2011.[20] The UNGPs are divided into three "pillars": (1) the state duty to protect human rights; (2) the corporate responsibility to respect human rights; and (3) ensuring access to remedy for victims of human rights abuses.[21] It is important to note that the UNGPs, which outline obligations of both states and businesses, apply "to *all business enterprises*, both transnational and others, *regardless of* their size, sector, *location, ownership and structure*."[22]

Of particular interest for this treatise are the Principles outlining the obligations to ensure access to remedy for victims of human rights abuses in the third section (also called the Third Pillar or Pillar Three). The concept embraced by these Principles is that states should ensure remedies, including judicial remedies, for their business's human rights violations.[23] Although Principle 25, the first Principle in Pillar Three, applies only to states where abuses occur in their territory or jurisdiction in requiring such to have effective remedies, Principle 26, which discusses remedies, provides that states should take appropriate steps to ensure the effectiveness of domestic judicial mechanisms when addressing business-related human rights abuses, including considering ways to reduce legal, practical, and other relevant barriers that could lead to a denial of access to remedy.[24] The Commentary to Principle 26 then notes that "legal barriers that can prevent legitimate cases involving business-related human rights abuse from being addressed can arise," inter alia, (1) by the way in which legal responsibility is attributed among members of a corporate group in a way that facilitates the "avoidance of appropriate accountability; and [(2)] where claimants face a denial of justice in a host State and *cannot access home State courts* regardless of the merits of the claim."[25]

Thus, when read in totality, the UNGPs suggest that when victims of harm caused by a subsidiary corporation, owned by a foreign parent, cannot obtain a remedy in their own country, the country where the parent corporation is located should

---

Reparation. G.A. Res. 60/147, U.N. Doc. A/RES/60/147 (Dec. 16, 2005). The UN noted the right to "equal and effective access to justice." *See id.* at Annex, part II, ¶ 3(c), part VII, ¶ 11(c). It also noted the right to an effective judicial remedy for victims of violations of human rights. *Id.* at Preamble, part VII, ¶ 12. It further noted the right to "[a]dequate, effective and prompt reparation" and "compensation, rehabilitation, [and] satisfaction" required by international law. *Id.*, part IX, ¶¶ 15–22.

[20] *Id.*; Human Rights Council Res. 17/4, U.N. Doc. A/HRC/17/L.17/Rev.1 (June 16, 2011) (discussing human rights, transnational corporations and other business enterprises).

[21] *See* John Ruggie, *Guiding Principles on Business and Human Rights: Implementing the United Nations "Protect, Respect, and Remedy" Framework*, U.N. Doc A/HRC/17/L.17/31 (June 16, 2011) (outlining United Nations principles on business and human rights).

[22] *See id.* at princ. 17–35 (emphasis added) (offering United Nations principles on business and human rights).

[23] *See id.* (outlining the Third Pillar of the UNGPs).

[24] *See id.* at princ. 26 (discussing the appropriate steps which states should take to ensure the effectiveness of domestic judicial mechanisms when addressing business-related human rights abuses).

[25] *Id.* at princ. 26, Commentary.

ensure that the victims receive a remedy for the harm.[26] Although such a remedy can include a non-judicial grievance procedure that meets certain criteria, the UNGPs are clear that a remedy must ultimately include resort to a judicial remedy.[27] Indeed, the UNGPs provide that countries should ensure that effective judicial mechanisms exist and should remove barriers to accessing remedies for such violations.[28] The importance of a judicial remedy is further heightened in the commentary, which specifically notes that countries should not erect barriers to prevent legitimate cases from being brought before their courts where judicial access is essential to accessing a remedy.[29] This language is not limited to countries that host such businesses.[30] In fact, the UNGPs' commentary notes that countries are to address barriers "[w]here claimants face a denial of justice in a host State and cannot access home State courts regardless of the merits of the claim."[31] Thus, the commentary suggests that even though countries may not be legally obligated to control their businesses' conduct within another sovereign's jurisdiction (although they certainly can), they are to ensure that there are no barriers preventing victims from seeking remedies against transnational businesses, especially where victims cannot access legal remedies in their host countries.[32]

Similarly, the OECD issued its updated Guidelines on Multinational Enterprises in 2011 ("the OECD Guidelines"), which apply to OECD countries including the United States, Canada, and most of Europe.[33] Like the UNGPs, the OECD Guidelines state that they should "extend to enterprise groups" and subsidiaries, including those that cross national borders. With regard to remedy, the OECD Guidelines are supported by the NCPs, which were partly established to provide mediation and conciliation for "resolving practical issues that may arise." The expectation is that the

---

[26] See id. at 1–31 (outlining guiding principles on business and human rights).
[27] See id. at princ. 29, Commentary ("They should not be used to undermine the role of legitimate trade unions in addressing labour-related disputes, nor to preclude access to judicial or other non-judicial grievance mechanisms.").
[28] Id. at princ. 26.
[29] Id. at Commentary.
[30] Id.
[31] Id.
[32] The OECD Guidelines on Multinational Enterprises also set forth obligations of both states and businesses with regard to the protection of human rights. The Guidelines are part of the OECD Declaration on International Investment and Multinational Enterprises. The Guidelines state that they provide voluntary principles and standards for responsible business conduct consistent with applicable laws and internationally recognized standards. The Guidelines further state: "[h]owever, the countries adhering to the Guidelines make a binding commitment to implement them in accordance with the Decision of the OECD Council on the OECD Guidelines for Multinational Enterprises." OECD Guidelines for Multinational Enterprises, OECD (2011), http://www.oecd.org/daf/inv/mne/48004323.pdf (last visited February 1, 2020).
[33] List of OECD Member Countries – Ratification of the Convention on the OECD, OECD, http://www.oecd.org/about/membersandpartners/list-oecd-member-countries.htm (last visited June 22, 2018).

NCPs will help provide victims with a remedy in situations where a remedy may be unavailable in the host country. However, the chapter on human rights notes that TNCs should "[p]rovide for or co-operate through legitimate processes in the remediation of adverse human rights impacts where they identify that they have caused or contributed to these impacts."[34] Like the UNGPs' discussion regarding company-level grievance mechanisms, the OECD Guidelines commentary on the human rights chapter notes that a company's own grievance mechanisms should not preclude victims' access to judicial mechanisms.[35] Thus, it is clear that current international bodies support the availability of a remedy for victims of international human rights violations by TNCs despite a lack of judicial recourse or availability of remedy in the host country. Furthermore, it is evident that while alternative dispute resolution mechanisms or administrative processes may be an adequate adjunct to a judicial remedy, these processes cannot and should not replace a functioning judicial system to provide redress to victims in the country where the transnational corporation is domiciled.

Finally, at the UN level, there is a current movement to move beyond non-binding principles toward a binding Treaty on Business and Human Rights. Such a treaty, if enacted, would become obligatory for those countries that ratify it. Even if the United States, European countries, and Canada do not ratify such a treaty, it is possible that countries where subsidiaries operate will. This might lead to the argument that parent companies of such subsidiaries are bound by the treaty, due to their subsidiaries' business operations within treaty-bound countries.[36] Moreover, the obligations contained in the treaty may at some point "ripen" into CIL, which would bind all countries regardless of their ratification status.[37] Discussions thus far include how such a treaty might affect the rights of victims of business-related abuses to a judicial remedy, and given the international embrace of diminishing barriers to effective legal remedy, may also include a mechanism to enforce such rights.[38]

---

[34] *OECD Guidelines, supra* note 32, Section IV (Human Rights) 6.
[35] *Id.*, Commentary to Section IV, ¶ 46.
[36] *See* Gwynne Skinner, *Rethinking Limited Liability of Parent Corporations for Foreign Subsidiaries' Violations of International Human Rights Law*, 72 WASH. & LEE L. REV. 1769, 1816 n162 (2015).
[37] *See Kadic v. Karadzic*, 70 F.3d 232, 241 (2d Cir. 1995) (citing H.R. Rep. No. 367, at 4 (1991), *reprinted in* 1992 U.S.C.C.A.N. 84, 846) (explaining that the ATS "should remain intact to permit suits based on other norms that already exist or may ripen in the future into rules of customary international law").
[38] *Ten Key Proposals for the Treaty: A Legal Resource for Advocates and Diplomats Engaging with the UN Intergovernmental Working Group on Transnational Corporations and Other Business Enterprises* 89–95 INTERNATIONAL NETWORK FOR ECONOMIC, SOCIAL AND CULTURAL RIGHTS (ESCR-NET) & INTERNATIONAL FEDERATION FOR HUMAN RIGHTS (FIDH) (2016), https://www.escr-net.org/sites/default/files/attachments/tenkeyproposals_final.pdf (last accessed June 25, 2018).

2.3 REMEDIATION FOR EXTRATERRITORIAL VIOLATIONS OF INTERNATIONAL LAW UNDER US LAW

CIL is not the sole foundation for a notion of victims' right to a judicial remedy for violations of international human rights law. It is well documented that the United States, very early in its history, wanted to ensure that noncitizens had the ability to seek a civil remedy when one of its citizens violated a noncitizen's international rights, including for extraterritorial violations.[39] Providing civil remedies for violations of international law (then often referred to as "law of nations") was important in order to demonstrate that the young country took the law of nations seriously[40] and to prevent foreign conflicts.[41]

The founders ensured the availability of such remedies by enacting the ATS[42] in 1789, which allowed "aliens" (i.e. noncitizens) to sue for violations of the law of

---

[39] See, e.g., David M. Golove and Daniel Hulsebosch, *A Civilized Nation: The Early American Constitution, the Law of Nations, and the Pursuit of International Recognition*, 85 N.Y.U. L. REV. 932 (2010); Ralph G. Steinhardt, *The Alien Tort Claims Act; Theoretical and Historical Foundations of the Alien Tort Claims Act and its Discontents: A Reality Check*, 16 ST. THOMAS L. REV. 585 (2004); William Dodge, *The Constitutionality of the Alien Tort Statute: Some Observations on Text and Context*, 42 VA. J. INT'L L. 687, 705–08 (2002); Curtis Bradley, *Attorney General Bradford's Opinion and the Alien Tort Statute*, 106 AM. J. OF INT'L LAW 509, 587 (2012); Julian G. Ku, *Customary International Law in State Courts*, 42 VA. J. INT'L L. 265 (Fall 2001); WILLIAM R. CASTO, THE SUPREME COURT IN THE EARLY REPUBLIC: THE CHIEF JUSTICESHIPS OF JOHN JAY AND OLIVER ELLSWORTH 9 (Herbert A. Johnson ed. 1995); Anne-Marie Burley [Slaughter], *The Alien Tort Statute and the Judiciary Act of 1789: A Badge of Honor*, 83 AM. J. INT'L L. 461 (1989); D'Amato, *supra* note 6 at 63; William Casto, *The Federal Courts' Protective Jurisdiction Over Torts Committed in Violation of the Law of Nations*, 18 CONN. L. REV. 467, 490 (1986); Kenneth C. Randall, *Federal Jurisdiction Over International Law Claims: Inquiries into the Alien Tort Statute*, 18 N.Y.U. J. INT'L & POL. 1, 11–12 (1985).

[40] See, e.g., William S. Dodge, *The Historical Origins of the Alien Tort Statute: A Response to the "Originalists,"* 19 HASTINGS INT'L & COMP. L. REV. 221, 224 (1996) (finding that the ATS "was designed to ensure that those who violated the law of nations could be held liable not just criminally but civilly as well"). *See also* Sosa v. Alvarez-Machain, 542 U.S. 692, 715 (2004) (describing that the founders found it critical to ensure that the federal courts have jurisdiction over aliens' claims for torts in violation of the law of nations because they were the type of violations that potentially "threatened serious consequences in international affairs"); Casto, *supra* note 39, *The Federal Court*, at 481 (noting that scholar William Blackstone, the Continental Congress, and the courts all indicated that "a judicial remedy was necessary in order to assuage the anger of foreign sovereigns"); and *id.* at 491 (explaining the reasoning behind granting a civil remedy).

[41] See Casto, *supra* note 39, *The Federal Court*, at 490 (citing 21 J. CONT. CONG. 1137 (1781)). *See also* Randall, *supra* note 39, at 20–21; *see also* John M. Rogers, *The Alien Tort Statute and How Individuals "Violate" International Law*, 21 VAND. J. TRANSNAT'L L. 47, 47 (1988) (arguing that the First Congress intended to limit the ATS to tortious acts "which, if unaddressed, would result in international legal responsibility on the part of the United States"); Slaughter, *supra* note 39, at 464 (noting that the ATS "was a straightforward response to what the framers understood to be their duty under the law of nations").

[42] The First Congress enacted the ATS in 1789 as part of the First Judiciary Act. The ATS reads, "The district courts shall have jurisdiction over tort claims for violations of the law of nations

nations in federal courts.[43] Although the traditional thinking has been that Congress enacted the ATS in response to an incident where a foreign citizen was the perpetrator – the Marbois affair[44] – there is also strong evidence that Congress had US citizens equally in mind as likely defendants in these claims. For example, in 1781, the Continental Congress passed a resolution calling upon states to enact legislation providing for the vindication of rights under the law of nations because it felt "hamstrung" by its inability to "cause infractions of treaties, or of the law of nations to be punished."[45] The 1781 Resolution specifically stated that noncitizens would have the ability to receive compensation for violations of their rights protected by international law when perpetrated "by a citizen."[46] Similarly, President George Washington stated in an address to Congress that "aggressions by our citizens on the territory of other nations" was a violation of the law of nations.[47] Each of these suggests that the founders likely had violations by their own citizens as well as foreign citizens in mind when contemplating possible civil remedies such as the ATS.

Indeed, in addition to the Marbois affair, other events likely contributing to the enactment of the ATS were violations perpetrated by US citizens.[48] These included well-publicized incidents of criminal and tortious offenses against ambassadors and other foreign dignitaries in the United States;[49] the arrest of the Dutch Ambassador's

---

and treaties." 28 U.S.C. § 1350 (2000). The ATS was enacted as Section 9 of the Judiciary Act of 1789. See Judiciary Act of 1789, ch. 20, § 9, 1 Stat. 73 (1789).

[43] The First Judiciary Act provided federal courts with diversity jurisdiction over claims where an alien was a party when the amount in controversy was over $500. Id. § 11, 1 Stat. at 78–79. The $500 requirement for claims involving aliens was the result of a compromise involving the difficulty of British debt collections under the Treaty of Paris. By providing for federal jurisdiction over cases involving aliens only where the amount in controversy exceeded $500, a large majority of such litigation would be forced to proceed in state courts, which were much more sympathetic to US citizens. Id. Thus, without the ATS, there would have been no federal court jurisdiction generally involving aliens for claims under $500. By enacting the ATS, Congress ensured federal court jurisdiction for claims brought by aliens even if the amount in controversy was less than $500, as long as the suit was a tort claim for violation of the law of nations.

[44] The Marbois affair involved an assault on a French diplomat by French adventurer De Longchamps on the streets of Philadelphia in 1784. The international community was "outraged" and demanded that the Continental Congress take action, but Congress lacked the authority to do anything under the Articles of Confederation. See, e.g., Dodge, supra note 39, at 694; Randall, supra note 39, at 24; CASTO, THE SUPREME COURT IN THE EARLY REPUBLIC supra note 39, at 7–8.

[45] Sosa v. Alvarez-Machain, 542 U.S. 692, 716 (2004) (citing JAMES MADISON, JOURNAL OF THE CONSTITUTIONAL CONVENTION 60 (E. Scott ed. 1893); 21 JOURNALS OF THE CONTINENTAL CONGRESS 1136–37 (G. Hunt ed. 1912)).

[46] See Dodge, supra note 39, at 692–93.

[47] George Washington, Fourth Annual Address, in 1 A COMPILATION OF THE MESSAGES AND PAPERS OF THE PRESIDENT 125, 128 (James D. Richardson ed. 1911).

[48] See Randall, supra note 39 at 20–21 (stating their injuries to aliens may occur at the hands of the state).

[49] See Randall, supra note 39 at 24 (citing 1 WILLIAM WINSLOW CROSSKEY, POLITICS AND THE CONSTITUTION IN THE HISTORY OF THE UNITED STATES 457–65 (1953)); Edwin Dickinson, The

coachman by a New York State court officer in 1787;[50] American citizens mounting private military expeditions against Spanish territories in Florida;[51] American citizens' attacks against noncitizens who, under US treaties, were entitled to the free exercise of religion and to safe passage through the country;[52] and US privateers causing damage in prize cases to the other party (or the ships' inhabitants) in violation of the several treaties the United States had entered into before passage of the ATS.[53]

In fact, the first Attorney General opinion regarding the ATS concerned acts of an American who led a French fleet in attacking and plundering a British slave colony in Sierra Leone.[54] Attorney General William Bradford issued an opinion in 1795 making it clear that although the United States did not have criminal jurisdiction over the matter – which he acknowledged was a violation of the law of nations – the ATS provided federal jurisdiction for a civil remedy against Americans who had taken part in the acts.[55] In explaining that the law of nations would provide the rules of decision for domestic remedies of such violations, Justice William Paterson, one of the primary drafters of the First Judiciary Act, used an example of a US citizen enlisting in the British Army to fight the French in violation of the United States' position of neutrality (and thus also in violation of the law of nations).[56] These examples demonstrate both that the ATS was clearly intended to apply to foreign and US citizens for violations of international law, and that the founders felt the importance of providing a remedy for extraterritorial violations.[57]

After the founding period, throughout the 1800s, and into the 1900s, the US Supreme Court issued several decisions demonstrating the importance, in its view,

---

Law of Nations as Part of the National Law of the United States–Part I, 101 U. PA. L. REV. 26, 30–32 (1952).

[50] Ku, *supra* note 3 at 281–82 (citing 1 JULIUS GOEBEL, JR., HISTORY OF THE SUPREME COURT OF THE UNITED STATES: ANTECEDENTS AND BEGINNINGS TO 1801 at 310–11 (Paul A. Freund ed. 1971); *see also* Casto, *supra* note 39, *The Federal Court*, at 494.

[51] CASTO, *supra* note 39, THE SUPREME COURT IN THE EARLY REPUBLIC at 43–44.

[52] Id.

[53] *See* Bradley, *supra* note 39, at 616–17. However, it may well be these cases were not a reason for the ATS, given the admiralty grant of jurisdiction. *Id.* at 617. However, to the degree the ATS was viewed as also providing a cause of action, then they may well have been. For a list of the treaties, *see id.* at 616 n130. For a list of the treaties, *see id.* at 616 n130.

[54] 1 Op. Atty. Gen. 57, 58 (1795); *see also* Casto, *supra* note 39, *The Federal Court*, at 502–03.

[55] *Id.* at 58–59 (1795) ("But there can be no doubt that the company or individuals who have been injured by these acts of hostility have a remedy by a *civil* suit in the courts of the United States; jurisdiction being expressly given to these courts in all cases where an alien sues for a tort only, in violation of the laws of nations, or a treaty of the United States"). *See also* Bradley, *supra* note 39 at 510, 521 (noting that original documents associated with the opinion demonstrate that Attorney General Bradford contemplated that the ATS would apply extraterritorially with regard to US citizens).

[56] *See* Casto, *supra* note 39, *The Federal Court*, at 480 (internal citations omitted).

[57] *See id.* at 483–84 (noting that the founders had not only violations within the United States on their minds, they also likely had transgressions by US citizens abroad in their sights as well); *see also* Bradley, *supra* note 39 at 521.

of the "strictest fidelity" of the United States to its duties under international law, cognizant that not doing so would negatively impact the United States' foreign relations.[58] Most were prize cases, piracy cases, or cases involving the rights of belligerents and the obligations of neutrals.[59] Of these, many involved United States citizens as principal perpetrators or aiders and abettors,[60] and in one case, a US customs official who unlawfully seized a French ship in Spanish waters.[61] The United States has continued to affirm this international obligation to provide remedies, including ratifying treaties that require victims receive such remedies, as discussed in section 2.2, and remains party to international bodies, such as the OECD, who champion such remedies.[62]

2.4 BARRIERS TO JUDICIAL REMEDY

Even with the UNGPs and other remedy-related documents and arguments, and the increasing emphasis at the United Nations on the right to effective remedy,[63] victims still face numerous barriers to accessing, let alone achieving, a remedy for human rights-related abuses, including those where TNCs are involved, whether directly or vicariously. In addition to practical barriers that exist, which will be discussed in Part II, many older, traditional legal doctrines commonly recognized around the world prohibit victims obtaining a remedy for harm against the TNCs involved. These doctrines are particularly problematic when victims cannot otherwise obtain a remedy against the TNC's subsidiary or affiliate in their own countries where the harm occurred, which is often the case, as described in more detail in Chapter 3.

One of the most problematic of these doctrines is that of limited liability of shareholders, which can shield a parent corporation from liability for its subsidiary's human rights violations. Another doctrine, "subject matter jurisdiction," limits the type of case the courts can hear. Other than the United States (and Canada since perhaps 2016), the countries where most TNCs operating in developing countries

---

[58] See CHARLES WARREN, THE SUPREME COURT IN UNITED STATES HISTORY 1789–1835, at 565–86 (revised ed. 1937).

[59] See id. at 573–75.

[60] See, e.g., Jecker v. Montgomery, 59 U.S. (18 How) 110, 112 (1855); The Prize Cases, 67 U.S. 635, 637–38 (1862); The Rapid, 8 Cranch 155, 159 (1814); The Joseph, 12 U.S. 451, 454 (1814). See also WARREN, supra note 58 at 570–71, 573–79.

[61] WARREN, supra note 58 at 581–82 (citing The Apollon, 9 Wheat. 362 (1824)).

[62] Those the United States has ratified include: Universal Declaration of Human Rights, art. 8, G.A. Res. 217 (III), at 73, U.N. Doc. A/810 (1948); International Covenant on Civil and Political Rights, art. 2(3)(a), opened for signature Dec. 19, 1966, 999 U.N.T.S. 171; Convention Against Torture and Other Cruel, Inhuman or Degrading Treatment or Punishment, art. 14, opened for signature Dec. 10, 1984, 1465 U.N.T.S. 85.

[63] UN Working Group on the Issue of Human Rights and Transnational Corporations and other Business Enterprises, Report, U.N. Doc. A/72/162 (2017) §§ 38–42.

are domiciled do not have a cause of action available for human rights claims.[64] In the United States, which has a history of allowing claims for violations of CIL (the source of law for most human rights claims), there are now restrictions on extraterritorial violations given the Supreme Court decision in 2013, Kiobel v. Royal Dutch Shell[65] and the Court's decision prohibiting ATS claims against foreign corporations in 2018 in Jesner v. Arab Bank.[66]

A third doctrine that creates barriers for victims is that of a court's *in personam* jurisdiction, or personal jurisdiction, over a defendant TNC. Personal jurisdiction over TNCs, even those that have significant operations in the United States, has significantly narrowed in the United States in recent years due to two significant US Supreme Court decisions, Goodyear Dunlop Tires Operations, S.A. v. Brown,[67] and Daimler AG v. Bauman.[68] Personal jurisdiction over TNCs operating in Europe is also fairly restrictive. These limits on personal jurisdiction have sometimes allowed TNCs to operate without any court able to hear human rights claims against them, not unlike how countries at one time lacked ability to assert jurisdiction over pirates operating on the high seas.

These doctrines often work together to prevent victims from seeking, let alone obtaining, a remedy against a parent corporation. In addition, these doctrines were developed unilaterally and at a time when immense global economic activity by TNCs did not exist. Today, these rules are simply outdated and no longer adequate to address the issues an increasingly global population faces when it comes to properly attributing costs for transnational economic activity – costs that are often absorbed by the least powerful and most vulnerable communities. Thus, it is time to re-examine these rules and advocate for changes in laws to reflect today's complex, global economy and its transnational corporate players, including rules regarding jurisdiction and limited liability of shareholders – rules which almost always result in protections of TNCs at the expense of vulnerable populations, and which act as barriers to the remedy of serious human rights violations by these same corporations.

---

[64] Plaintiffs have brought claims in tort law containing allegations that, in addition to be tortious wrongs, are also human rights violations. See, for example, Guerrero v. Monterrico Metals plc [2009] EWHC 2475.
[65] 133 S. Ct. 1659 (2013).
[66] 138 S. Ct. 1386 (2018).
[67] 131 S. Ct. 2846 (2011).
[68] 134 S. Ct. 746 (2014).

3

Barriers to Judicial Remedies in Host Countries

Before discussing the barriers to bringing claims against TNCs in countries where they are incorporated or domiciled ("home countries"), or where they engage in significant business, it is first important to understand why victims cannot, and thus do not, bring claims against TNC affiliates in their own countries where the harm occurs – the host country. In an ideal world, all countries would have regulatory systems sufficient to prevent harm to individuals and communities, and judicial or judicial-like mechanisms to provide for a remedy in the event that businesses engage in tortious actions, whether directly or vicariously. Many wonder why the victims simply do not bring a claim in their own country and question whether bringing a case outside their country is appropriate. Even the US Supreme Court has suggested that victims of human rights abuses should simply bring the case in their home country.[1] However, it is not so simple. Indeed, if the victims could bring a claim in their own country and obtain a remedy, it would be much easier for them given the difficulty in bringing a case abroad against a parent company, and they would typically prefer to do so.[2] Yet, the sad reality is that this is often not possible in many host countries where TNCs operate. First, many of these host countries do not have sufficient regulations to prevent harm; in fact, as a result of globalization, many have done away with regulations in order to attract transnational business.[3] Second, when

---

[1] *Kiobel v. Royal Dutch Petro. Co.*, 569 U.S. 108, 129 (2013) (citing *Sosa v. Alvarez-Machain*, 542 U.S. 692, 733 n21 (2004)).

[2] *See* Gwynne Skinner, *Beyond Kiobel: Providing Access to Judicial Remedies for Corporate Accountability for Violations of International Human Rights Norms by Transnational Corporations in a New (Post-Kiobel) World*, 46 COLUM. HUM. RTS. L. REV. 158, 172 (2014) (recognizing that "victims... would much rather bring cases in the host countries as long as the judiciary was fair, stable, and effective, and the victims felt safe bringing such claims").

[3] *See* Christen Broecker, Note, *"Better the Devil You Know": Home State Approaches to Transnational Corporate Accountability*, 41 N.Y.U. J. INT'L L. & POL. 159, 184–85 (2008); Brittany T. Cragg, Comment, *Home is Where the Halt Is: Mandating Corporate Social Responsibility Through Home State Regulation and Social Disclosure*, 24 EMORY INT'L

human rights violations do occur, countries should ensure that causes of action exist, that their judiciaries are fair, corruption-free, and functional, and that companies, including foreign-owned subsidiaries, have sufficient funds to pay any award of compensation (or are otherwise insured for negligent torts). However, when human rights violations occur in countries with weak and fragile governments and judiciaries, the victims are often unable to obtain any compensation for their injuries in their home country.

One of the biggest problems is that in many countries where human rights violations occur, including by TNCs either directly or indirectly, there is often a weak and ineffective judicial system, or worse, a high level of corruption in the judicial system.[4] In particular, many countries hosting subsidiaries that engage in extraction or other industries, which have a high potential for human rights abuses, often have ineffectual and corrupt judicial systems.[5] Sometimes there is simply no legal mechanism available to seek redress or no cause of action available – in other words, no statutory or common law basis to bring a claim.[6] For example, in the case against Bhopal for the gas leak disaster in India, the plaintiffs and the Government of India argued that the case should be heard in a US court due to the fact that Indian law does not have the substantive nor the procedural law to deal with the magnitude and complexity of the case.[7]

L. Rev. 735, 751–55 (2010); Jodie A. Kirshner, *Why is the U.S. Abdicating the Policing of Multinational Corporations to Europe?: Extraterritoriality, Sovereignty, and the Alien Tort Statute*, 30 Berkeley J. Int'l L. 259, 266–67 (2012); Lesley K. McAllister, *On Environmental Enforcement and Compliance: A Reply to Professor Crawford's Review of Making Law Matter: Environmental Protection and Legal Institutions in Brazil*, 40 Geo. Wash. Int'l L. Rev. 649, 679–80 (2009); Benjamin Mason Meier, *International Protection of Persons Undergoing Medical Experimentation: Protecting the Right of Informed Consent*, 20 Berkeley J. Int'l L. 513, 532–33 (2002); Skinner, *supra* note 2 at 169–73, quoting Samantha Evans, *The Globalization of Drug Testing: Enforcing Informed Consent Through the Alien Tort Claims Act*, 19 Temp. Int'l & Comp. L. J. 477, 479 (2005).

[4] See Gwynne Skinner, *Rethinking Limited Liability of Parent Corporations for Foreign Subsidiaries' Violations of International Human Rights Law*, 72 Wash. & Lee L. Rev. 1769, 1800 n110 (discussing the failings of host countries in holding transnational corporations accountable for their wrongs) and n108 and accompanying text (2015); (citing sources describing the challenges faced by host countries, which are often developing countries).

[5] See, e.g., Catherine Boggs, *Project Management: A Smorgasbord of International Operating Risks*, Introduction Rocky Mountain Mineral Law Inst., Paper No. 13 (2008), Kirshner, *supra* note 3 at 266–67. The fact that many host countries involved in the extraction industry have corrupt or ineffective judicial systems, and that human rights are often violated with impunity, is also confirmed by the US Department of State. *See Country Reports on Human Rights Practices for 2013*, U.S. Dep't of State, Bureau of Democracy, Hum. Rts, and Lab., https://www.state.gov/j/drl/rls/hrrpt/2013humanrightsreport/index.htm#wrapper (last visited June 22, 2018) (evaluating human rights practices in various countries. See in particular the reports for the DRC, Guatemala, Indonesia, and Nigeria as examples).

[6] See Skinner, *supra* note 4 at 227 (explaining how "[c]hoice of law" principles can "create unforeseen barriers to recovery").

[7] Memorandum of law in opposition to Union Carbide Corporation's motion to dismiss these actions on the grounds of forum non conveniens, In Re Union Carbide Gas Plant Disaster at

Even where a claim might exist and there exists some potential for the country's judiciary system to hear it, it is often very difficult, if not impossible, to find a lawyer in the host country willing to take the case. There are several reasons for this. First, lawyers themselves may fear retaliation from the government or others in the community. This might include threats to their own lives or safety, or their families. The lawyers might find themselves blacklisted, or subject to retaliatory lawsuits or criminal charges. Over the course of 2015 to 2017, the Business and Human Rights Resource Center documented over 140 cases of legal retaliation against human rights defenders working on corporate accountability issues.[8] It is not only lawyers and human rights defenders that may be subject to reprisals or legal retaliation. Victims themselves may have legitimate fears of retaliation by the business or the members of the community if they bring a claim.[9] In addition, it might be that victims bring a suit against the subsidiary in the host state and receive a verdict, but are then unable to collect due to lack of funds, bankruptcy, or the inability to enforce judgments.[10] For example, the widely cited case against Chevron (which acquired Texaco) in Ecuador highlights the challenges of seeking enforcement of judicial decisions.[11] The plaintiffs, who are seeking compensation for severe environmental contamination and damage, have yet to see any justice despite the Ecuador Supreme Court ruling against Chevron in 2013 ordering damages in the amount of $9.51 billion.[12]

Second, the lawyers may not have the resources to pursue the case due to facing an uphill battle in getting the case adjudicated in their clients' favor, given the legal and evidentiary barriers. Moreover, there is a lack of contingency fees available (where a lawyer gets a percentage of the recovery) in most countries. In addition, plaintiffs, often the most vulnerable community members, have few resources

---

Bhopal, India in December 1984, MDL Docket No.626, 85 Civ 2696 (JFK) US Southern District Court of New York. *See* also, PETER T. MUCHLINSKI, MULTINATIONAL ENTERPRISES & THE LAW 117 (2nd ed. 2007).

[8] *See Business, Civic Freedoms & Human Rights Defenders Portal*, BUSINESS & HUMAN RIGHTS RESOURCE CENTRE (search under Attack type for "Law & lawsuits"), https://www.business-humanrights.org/bizhrds (last visited July 3, 2018).

[9] *See* Skinner, *supra* note 4, at 172, 231-34 (discussing how the potential for "unwarranted counterclaims or retaliatory claims" can dissuade victims from litigating human rights issues).

[10] *See* Gwynne Skinner, *Expanding General Personal Jurisdiction Over Transnational Corporations for Federal Causes of Action*, 121 PENN ST. L. REV. 617, 660 (2017); *see also* Skinner, *supra* note 4 at 227 (2014) (explaining how "[c]hoice of law" principles can "create unforeseen barriers to recovery").

[11] Sarah Joseph, *Protracted Lawfare: The Tale of Chevron Texaco in the Amazon* 3(1) JOURNAL OF HUMAN RIGHTS AND THE ENVIRONMENT (2012) 70-91.

[12] *See* Lauren Carasik, *Chevron Uses Deep Pockets to Win Ecuador Legal Battle*, ALJAZEERA AMERICA (May 16, 2014). For an overview of efforts to seek enforcement of the judgment *see also* Fenner L. Stewart, *Foreign Judgments, Judicial Trailblazing and the Cost of Cross-Border Complexity: Thoughts on Chevron Corp v Yaiguaje*, 34 J. OF ENERGY & NAT. RESOURCES L. (2016) and Anil Yilmaz-Vastardis & Rachel Chambers, *Overcoming the Corporate Veil Challenge: Could Investment Law Inspire the Proposed Business and Human Rights Treaty?* INTERNATIONAL AND COMPARATIVE LAW QUARTERLY, 389-423 (2018).

available to retain a lawyer and pay lawyers' fees. In some jurisdictions, victims and sometimes even their lawyers at times have to pay costs and fees to the defendants if they lose – called loser pays systems.[13] Yet, few countries provide legal aid for plaintiffs for this type of work. Even where a lawyer might be willing to take the case for free – pro bono – she might not be able to. In much of the developing world, there is not only sometimes a lack of a culture of pro bono representation, but some countries either prohibit pro bono representation or tax pro bono representation. While some nonprofit organizations exist to provide free legal representation in these sorts of cases, they also lack resources and as such, have to be extremely strategic with which cases they decide to pursue.

Where a victim is lucky enough to find a lawyer, have a cause of action, and is before a court that is willing to hear the case, there are other barriers. For example, due to the complexity of corporate structures, victims and their lawyers are sometimes simply unable to identify which subsidiary is operating in their area and cannot get the parent to supply the information, and thus, are unable to determine which entity to bring a claim against.[14] What can be even more confusing is that the subsidiary may be using the logo of the parent company, leading to confusion about what entity is operating in the area and is thus responsible for the violations. This was reported to have occurred in Nigeria with Shell in Kiobel v. Royal Dutch Shell,[15] where parent corporation Shell's logo appeared on the side of the trucks owned by the Nigerian subsidiary directly responsible for the abuses.

Additionally, victims may not have the ability to gather the evidence they need to bring a lawsuit against a TNC in their home country. Knowing that you or your family have been harmed is one thing; being able to find the evidence you need to allege that a TNC is responsible in some way can be daunting, if not impossible. TNCs are typically not very transparent about their internal operations, and they do not willingly provide information that might lead to a lawsuit against them. Their complex legal structures, opaque operations, and economic power make it difficult for even the most sophisticated individuals to gain information about inside decision-making and what they know might have taken place. Populations with low literacy levels, and those with little economic power, may find it nearly impossible to access the necessary information. Even if a victim has enough information to file a suit in court, countries' often restrictive discovery rules and biases toward the TNCs bringing investment make evidence difficult to obtain. These evidentiary hurdles make it difficult to bring cases in host countries, let alone prevail. Moreover,

---

[13] *See* Skinner, *supra* note 2 at 172 (noting how the loser pays system common in host countries can serve as a barrier to representation).
[14] *See id.* at 244 ("For example, parent companies over which the courts have jurisdiction may deny any involvement in subsidiaries' actions, yet often will not produce information regarding the subsidiaries, including information regarding their relationships to the subsidiaries.").
[15] Kiobel v. Dutch Royal Shell, 133 S. Ct. 1659 (2013).

witnesses may be too afraid to come forward, either because their identity will become known or because of an overall lack of rule of law.[16]

Weak rule of law, political instability, and corruption also play an important role in limiting the ability to seek remedy in the host state. In such contexts, it can be almost impossible to hold powerful actors accountable, particularly those that bring investment and infrastructure to a country. Corruption in the justice sector primarily takes two forms. The first is the direct bribery of judges by private parties through the exchange of cash, land, or goods and services. The second is through political interference, such as through pressure from executive or the legislative authorities.[17] According to the International Commission of Jurists, there are a number of factors that enable and contribute to corruption within the judicial system. These include low salaries, heavy caseloads, insecurity of tenure, and no or ineffective accountability systems.[18] Ideally, victims should be able to access remediation in the country where the harm was suffered. As such, strengthening the rule of law and tackling corruption in host states should be a priority for policy-makers globally. However, until host state judiciaries operate free from corruption and interference, additional avenues for providing remediation need to be provided.

All of these factors converge to create a situation where victims are likely to have little recourse in their own countries. It is no wonder that they often have little choice but to bring a claim against a TNC parent corporation in a country where they have more hope of finding a remedy.

3.1 THE NEED FOR LEGISLATIVE REFORM

For the reasons discussed in the Introduction, if victims of business-related human rights violations are not able to seek a remedy in their own countries, they ought to be able to seek a remedy from a TNC that is the parent company of the subsidiary or affiliate causing the harm. This is because the TNC parent corporation receives enormous economic benefit from the operations of the subsidiary or affiliate in the host country, yet the victims bear all the costs. This is simply not fair, and not sustainable from an ethical, moral, or economic point of view. Such claims against the parent TNC will typically be in the country where the parent TNC is domiciled or headquartered.[19] However, if victims are not able to seek a remedy in the country

---

[16] Skinner, *supra* note 2 at 205 (citing Joel Samuels, *When is an Alternative Forum Available? Rethinking the Forum Non Conveniens Analysis*, 85 IND. L. J. 1059, 1095–96 (2010)).

[17] INTERNATIONAL COMMISSION OF JURISTS, "Judicial Accountability: A Practitioners' Guide" (June 2016) at 108.

[18] *Id.* at 109–10.

[19] A state-owned enterprise may also be benefiting from the economic activity. However, foreign sovereign immunity may prevent a victim from suing a state or a state-run enterprise, although there are exceptions. Foreign Sovereign Immunities Act, 28 U.S.C. § 1605(a). In such situations, businesses may have a legitimate argument that they should not bear all the costs.

of domicile – and they may well not be able to for a variety of reasons – then they ought to be able to seek and obtain a remedy in any country where the TNC does significant business, given that the TNC is benefiting from doing business there as well as in the host country. However, as the following chapters will demonstrate, numerous barriers exist when bringing such claims.

4

Limits on Subject Matter Jurisdiction over International Human Rights Violations

The limitations of subject matter jurisdiction present significant barriers to victims seeking a remedy for business-related human rights violations. Even if courts can assert personal jurisdiction over a corporate defendant, the government of any particular country may not give its courts permission to hear and adjudicate the *types of claims* that arise from human rights or severe environmental torts. In order to bring a lawsuit, a person has to be able to have a legal claim. Sometimes these claims, which are called causes of action, come from the parliament, legislature, or other legislative body, which decides what sort of claim its citizenry can bring before court. In some systems, typically the common law system, courts can also recognize a claim based on the common law.

4.1 AN OVERVIEW OF SUBJECT MATTER JURISDICTION ACROSS MULTIPLE JURISDICTIONS

In the United States, a court's ability to hear a particular type of claim, or case, is called "subject matter" jurisdiction. European courts typically refer simply to jurisdiction, not making a distinction between subject matter jurisdiction and personal jurisdiction, and setting forth circumstances where European courts will have jurisdiction over a type of claim against a certain defendant.[1] As discussed in more detail below, Canada and most of Europe allow certain claims to be brought against TNCs domiciled in their countries,[2] even where the harm took place

---

[1] However, technically speaking, one can review the European Regulations and give examples of jurisdictional rules related to types of claims – subject matter – and rules relating to who can be defendants – personal jurisdiction. As discussed in Chapter 6, personal jurisdictional rules in Europe are not constitutional as they are in the United States, but merely a matter of regulation.

[2] *See* Gwynne Skinner, *Expanding General Personal Jurisdiction Over Transnational Corporations For Federal Causes of Action*, 121 PENN ST. L. REV. 617, 624 n24 (2017); *see also*

extraterritorially, such as in a host country, but they have historically not allowed claims brought by victims alleging violations of international human rights law in the host country. Only recently have Canadian courts began exploring common law claims for violations of CIL. Few other countries allow claims for extraterritorial violations of CIL.

4.1.1 United States

For decades, the United States was a rare exception, allowing federal courts to assert jurisdiction over tort claims for violations of CIL against under the federal ATS. This included claims against TNCs over which its courts could assert personal jurisdiction (which was fairly liberal until 2011; see Chapter 6), even where the harm to victims that grounded such claims occurred abroad. Before discussing the ATS in more detail, it is important to understand how state and federal courts operate with regard to tort claims.

In the United States, state courts have quite expansive jurisdiction, or ability to hear claims, including common law claims. Federal courts, however, are courts of limited jurisdiction. This means that claims can only be typically brought in federal court if Congress has granted courts the ability to hear such claims; in other words, granted them subject matter jurisdiction. This means that Congress typically has to enact a statute to give a person the right to bring a claim in federal court.

In the United States, most tort claims, or claims for personal injuries, are brought as state common law claims. Typically, they are brought in state court. However, where the individual and the defendant are citizens of different states or one is a citizen of the United States and one is a citizen of a foreign country, then claims can either be brought in or removed to federal court under diversity jurisdiction,

---

Resolution on the Commission Green Paper on Promoting a European Framework for Corporate Social Responsibility, Eur. Parl. Doc. (COM 366) 2 (2001) (noting that "the 1968 Brussels Convention ... enables jurisdiction within the courts of EU Member States for cases against companies registered or domiciled in the EU in respect of damage sustained in third countries," urging "the Commission to compile a study of the application of the extraterritoriality principle by courts in the Member States of the Union," and urging "the Member States to incorporate this extraterritoriality principle in legislation"); *see generally* Council Regulation 1215/2012 (recast), 2012 O.J. (L 351) (EU) at pmbl. 14; *id.* at ch. II, § 1, art. 6. For corporations not domiciled in an EU country, each country in Europe has its own jurisdictional laws that govern such entities, and personal jurisdiction over such non-EU corporations ranges and can be quite broad. As Skinner notes, in Canada, jurisdiction is broader than it now exists in the United States post-*Daimler*. *See* Club Resorts, Ltd. v. Van Breda [2012] 1 S.C.R. 572 (Can.) (explaining that jurisdiction over out-of-province or out-of-country defendants is based on whether the foreign corporation has a "real and substantial connection" to Canada (and the province asserting jurisdiction)); *see also* Caroline Davidson, *Tort Au Canadien: A Proposal For Canadian Tort Legislation on Gross Violations of International Human Rights and Humanitarian Law*, 38 VAND. J. TRANSNAT'L L. 1403, 1437–38 (2005). *Id.*

meaning diversity of citizenship, as long as the claim is over a certain amount of dollars, currently $75,000.[3]

Most state courts recognize only typical tort claims that might arise in the human rights context, such as assault, battery, and unlawful death. Most states have not yet recognized claims that violate CIL, including what is referred to as international human rights law, such as extra judicial killing, torture, prolonged arbitrary detention, and the like. However, some states have, and scholars predict that international human rights claims will increasingly be filed in state courts, under the theory that state common law incorporates CIL.[4] In these state cases, there are no limits on defendants that the courts otherwise can assert personal jurisdiction over,[5] and under transitory tort theories, claims may be brought for extraterritorial violations. However, for a variety of reasons, claims for extraterritorial human rights claims in state court present numerous obstacles.[6]

Although tort claims are typically the province of states, Congress has occasionally enacted statutes that allow individuals to bring federal human rights-related tort claims. There are a few of these in the area of international human rights law in addition to the ATS. One example is the Torture Victim Protection Act,[7] which allows individuals to bring claims "under color of foreign law" against foreign officials for torture (but not US officials). Another example is the Trafficking Victims Protection Act,[8] which allows individuals to bring claims for those involved, or who benefit from, human trafficking. The Anti-Terrorism Act[9] also provides a civil claim for US citizens who have been harmed, or whose family has been killed, by terrorist acts.

In the area of tort claims for violations of international human rights, the United States is perhaps most famous for the ATS. As discussed above, the ATS grants federal courts jurisdiction to hear claims brought by noncitizens for torts in violation of the law of nations, also referred to as CIL, or treaties. Although the Supreme Court has said that individuals can only bring claims for violation of treaties where

---

[3] 28 U.S.C. § 1332.
[4] *Symposium Issue: Human Rights Litigation in State Courts and Under State Law*, 3 U.C. IRVINE L. REV., (2013).
[5] When regular common law torts – often referred to as "garden-variety torts" are filed against the federal government, or a federal official that the Justice Department finds was acting within the scope of her authority, the claim proceeds under the Federal Tort Claim Act, the act where the United States, the sovereign, has waived its rights of immunity as a sovereign, to be sued in federal court.
[6] See Gwynne Skinner, *Beyond Kiobel: Providing Access to Judicial Remedies for Corporate Accountability for Violations of International Human Rights Norms by Transnational Corporations in a New (Post-Kiobel) World*, 46 COLUM. HUM. RTS. L. REV. 158, 201–202 (2014).
[7] Torture Victim Protection Act of 1991, Pub.L. No. 102-256, 106 Stat. 73 (codified at 28 U.S.C. § 1350 (1992)).
[8] 22 U.S.C. § 78.
[9] 18 U.S.C. §§ 2332-33 (1996).

Limits on Subject Matter Jurisdiction

Congress has provided a cause of action for such a claim,[10] it has allowed courts to recognize claims for violations of CIL as a matter of their common law powers.[11] This is discussed in more detail below.

The statute itself places no limits as to who can be a defendant in such claims or where the tort giving rise to the claim takes place (thus allowing claims for extraterritorial conduct).

The ATS was rarely used for near 200 years, until the 1980 ground-breaking case of Filártiga v. Peña-Irala.[12] In that case, the Second Circuit court of appeals rejected the federal district judge's decision that courts did not have jurisdiction over the case because the tort giving rise to the claim occurred abroad and involved a foreign official.[13] The Second Circuit court noted that under the ATS, US courts indeed have jurisdiction over human rights claims, even though such claims occur abroad and involve foreign officials. The court noted that the statute itself made no limitations, and that in the wake of the Second World War, violations of international human rights, regardless of where they took place, were seen as violations against all of humankind.

After *Filartiga*, victims of human rights violations began bringing cases in federal court, with courts adjudicating such cases, as long as they had personal jurisdiction over the defendants. Historically, this was achieved either by the individual defendant residing in the United States, being served while in the United States (called tag jurisdiction); or, for a TNC, where the corporation was incorporated in the United States,[14] where it did continuous and systematic business in the United States,[15] or where such had a subsidiary or agent in the United States.[16] New limitations on personal jurisdiction are discussed in Chapter 6 below.

---

[10] See Skinner, *supra* note 6 at 191 n132 (citing Foster v. Neilson, 27 U.S. 253, 314 (1829), overturned in part on other grounds by United States v. Percheman, 32 U.S. 51 (1832) (noting that "when either of the parties engages to perform a particular act, the treaty addresses itself to the political, not the judicial department; and the legislature must execute the contract before it can become a rule for the Court"); Mannington Mills, Inc. v. Congoleum Corp., 595 F.2d 1287, 1298 (3d Cir. 1979); see also Restatement (Third) of the Foreign Relations Law of the United States § 111(2) (1987) ("Cases arising under international law or international agreements of the United States are within the Judicial Power of the United States and ... are within the jurisdiction of the federal courts."). This is not the case with violations of certain claims under customary international law.)

[11] See Sosa v. Alvarez-Machain, 542 U.S. 692, 724–25 ("[N]o development in the two centuries from the enactment of [the Alien Tort Statute] to the birth of the modern line of cases beginning with *Filartiga v. Pena-Irala*, 630 F.2d 876 (2d Cir. 1980), has categorically precluded federal courts from recognizing a claim under the law of nations as an element of common law.").

[12] 630 F.2d 876 (2d Cir. 1980).

[13] 630 F.2d 885 (2d Cir. 1980).

[14] Goodyear Dunlop Tires Operations, S.A. v. Brown, 564 U.S. 915, 918–19 (2011); Daimler AG v. Bauman, 134 S. Ct. 746, 751, 761 (2014).

[15] Int'l Shoe Co. v. Wash., 326 U.S. 310, 317 (1945).

[16] Skinner, *supra* note 2 at 617, 638 n99 (citing Wiwa v. Royal Dutch Petrol. Co., 226 F.3d 88, 95 (2d Cir. 2000) (holding that a New York subsidiary investor relations office was an "agent" of

The initial cases were often against individuals, typically those who had committed human rights violations in their capacity as foreign officials. But soon, victims began bringing cases against corporations, either for their direct involvement in human rights violations or for complicity in human rights violations, such as for aiding and abetting. More often than not, these cases arose in a context where the corporations were working in conjunction with state security agents.[17]

In 2004 the US Supreme Court heard a case involving the ATS for the first time. In Sosa v. Alvarez-Machain, the question was whether the ATS was a jurisdictional statute only, and courts could only hear a claim under the statute if Congress enacted a cause of action, or whether it also provided a cause of action.[18] The Supreme Court found that the ATS was a jurisdictional statute, but that when Congress enacted it in 1789, Congress had anticipated that the federal courts would use their common law powers to recognize such claims and provide a remedy. Thus, the Court found that federal courts could continue to use their common law powers to recognize such claims for violations of CIL, as long as the claims were as similarly defined as the claims Congress probably had in mind in 1789 – piracy, attacks on diplomats, and attacks on safe passage.[19] Importantly, in its holding, the Supreme Court cited, with approval, cases such as *Filartiga* and other cases that had involved extraterritorial claims.[20]

Thus, beginning in 1980, US courts continued to hear hundreds of human rights claims brought under the ATS.[21] Although victims were often not successful

the parent companies for purposes of jurisdiction because all of the subsidiary's time was devoted to the companies' business, the companies fully funded the subsidiary's expenses, and the subsidiary sought the companies' approval on important decisions). This decision was important, as the case ultimately settled. See Jad Mouawad, *Shell to Pay $15.5 Million to Settle Nigerian Case*, N.Y. TIMES (June 9, 2009), https://www.nytimes.com/2009/06/09/business/global/09shell.html (last visited January 1, 2020); *see also* Presbyterian Church of Sudan v. Talisman Energy, Inc., 244 F. Supp. 2d 289, 330 (S.D.N.Y. 2003); Presbyterian Church of Sudan v. Talisman Energy, Inc., No. 01 Civ. 9882(DLC), 2004 WL 1920978, at *2–3 (S.D.N.Y. Aug. 27, 2004) (finding that the court could assert general personal jurisdiction over Talisman given its subsidiary's presence in New York because the subsidiary was a "mere department" of the parent corporation); Bauman v. DaimlerChrysler Corp., 644 F.3d 909, 920–23 (9th Cir. 2011), rev'd, 134 S. Ct. 746 (2014) (holding that a wholly owned US subsidiary, Mercedes-Benz USA, LLC ["MBUSA"], which served as the US general distributor of automobiles of the German parent manufacturer DaimlerChrysler Aktiengesellschaft (DCAG), was DCAG's agent for general jurisdictional purposes). At other times, courts have found either actual consent through the naming of a registered agent, or implied consent through the corporations' engaging in business in the state, although both theories have increasingly been rejected.)

[17] Sosa v. Alvarez-Machain, 542 U.S. 692, 714.
[18] *Id.* at 712.
[19] *Id.* at 724–25. The Court cautioned lower federal courts, however, to evaluate the claims brought in each case with a prudential eye toward whether the recognition of such a claim in a particular case might cause foreign policy complications. *Id.* at 727–28.
[20] *Id.* at 725.
[21] Between 1980 and 2011, approximately 312 ATS cases were brought against businesses or organizations. *See* Skinner, *supra* note 2 at 617, 635 (2017), citing the dataset attached to Cortelyou C. Kenney's article, *Measuring Transnational Human Rights*, 84 FORDHAM

in achieving a remedy under the ATS, sometimes they were,[22] and in any event, it allowed them both their day in court as well as the ability to create a historical record about human rights abuses. Human rights advocates throughout the world praised the United States and Congress in particular for allowing these claims in US courts.[23]

In 2013, the Supreme Court issued Kiobel v. Royal Dutch Shell, in which it significantly limited cases brought under the ATS by finding that principles underlying the presumption against extraterritoriality applied to the ATS. Under the presumption against extraterritoriality, statutes enacted by Congress are presumed only to apply to acts within the United States, and not abroad, unless Congress states otherwise.[24] The Court found that even though the presumption typically has applied only to statutes that are substantive in nature and create a cause of action, "principles underlying the presumption" would apply it to claims brought under the ATS, even though the Supreme Court has said that the ATS is a jurisdictional statute only.[25] Moreover, the Supreme Court also held that Congress had not made clear that it intended claims brought under the ATS to apply to extraterritorial conduct,[26] although many scholars disagreed with this assessment.[27]

The Court held that the presumption can be overcome by showing a claim "touches and concerns" the United States, but the fact that the defendant is a US corporation alone is not enough to overcome the presumption.[28]

Although *Kiobel* was not the death knell to ATS human rights cases in the way that some imagined, it has certainly limited such claims. Numerous ATS cases were thrown out by federal district courts.[29] Some courts allowed ATS claims to proceed,

---

L. REV. 1053 (2015). The table of cases she compiled and relies upon can be found at http://fordhamlawreview.org/assets/Documents/Kenney_December_Dataset.xlsx (last visited June 26, 2018). This number of 312 cases is not to be confused with the 325 non-frivolous cases she explains were resolved between 1980 and 2015, that she references in her article, *id.* at 1067.

[22] See Kenney, *supra* note 21 at 1091–92 (citing Xuncax v. Gramajo, 886 F. Supp. 162 (D. Mass. 1995) (awarding plaintiffs $45.5 million); Paul v. Avril, 812 F. Supp. 207 (S.D. Fla. 1993) (awarding plaintiffs $41 million)).

[23] The *Filartiga* case was cited as precedent in the English case Regina v. Bow Street Metropolitan Stipendiary Magistrate, ex parte Pinochet [1999] 2 W.L.R. 827 (H.L.).

[24] Morrison v. Nat'l Austl. Bank Ltd., 561 U.S. 247, 265 (2010).

[25] Sosa v. Alvarez-Machain, 542 U.S. 692, 712, 724 (2004).

[26] Kiobel v. Royal Dutch Petro. Co., 569 U.S. 108, 117–18 (2013).

[27] *See, e.g.*, Beth Stephens, *Extraterritoriality and Human Rights After Kiobel*, 28 MD. J. INT'L L. 256 (2013).

[28] This chapter will also note that US Congress has provided subject matter jurisdiction over extraterritorial claims of torture and extrajudicial killing through the Torture Victim Protection Act (TVPA) (28 U.S.C. § 1350, note 2), but the US Supreme Court has held that only natural persons can be defendants in TVPA claims.

[29] William Dodge, *Business and Human Rights Litigation in U.S. Courts Before and after Kiobel*, in BUSINESS AND HUMAN RIGHTS: FROM PRINCIPLES TO PRACTICE 250 (Dorothée Baumann-Pauly & Justine Nolan eds. 2014); Jennifer M. Green, *The Rule of Law at a Crossroad: Enforcing Corporate Responsibility in International Investment Through the Alien Tort Statute*, 35 U. PENN. J. INT'L L. 1085 (2014).

finding that such claims touched and concern the United States, for example where decisions were made in the United States.[30]

The recent case of Jesner v. Arab Bank,[31] in a much-criticized ruling and a strong dissent, held in a 5–4 decision that foreign corporations could not be sued under the ATS. This decision reversed almost twenty years of specific US court rulings that had allowed such cases.[32] The rationale by the majority was that the court could not create "new" causes of action because of separation of powers concerns,[33] and because cases against foreign corporations would raise foreign policy questions.[34] Four justices[35] dissented, and their opinion explained the important reasons to allow ATS suits against US and foreign corporations. It forcefully argued that "Immunizing corporations that violate human rights from liability under the ATS undermines the system of accountability of law-of-nations violations,"[36] and that the decision created a system of unequal access to remedies based on the plaintiffs' citizenship.[37] Challenging the central foreign policy argument of the majority, the dissent noted that the majority argued strenuously about the need for deference to the US executive and legislative branches but ignored the positions actually taken in this case across administrations led by each of the two major political parties.[38] The dissent also noted that the majority

---

[30] Dodge, *supra* note 29. (citing Al-Shimari v. CACI Premier Technology, Inc., 758 F.3d at 516.) See also Doe I v. Nestle USA, Inc., 766 F.3d 1013, 1021–22 (9th Cir. 2014), reh'g en banc denied, 788 F.3d 946 (2015), cert. denied, 136 S. Ct. 798 (2016); Doe VIII v. Exxon Mobil Corp., 654 F.3d 11, 57 (D.C. Cir. 2011), vacated on other grounds, 527 Fed.Appx. 7 (D.C. Cir. 2013), Adhikari v. Kellogg Brown & Root, Inc., 845 F.3d 184, 195 (5th Cir. 2017), cert. denied, 138 S. Ct. 134 (2017).

[31] 138 S. Ct. 1386 (2018).

[32] *See, e.g.,* Wiwa v. Royal Dutch Shell, *supra* note 16.

[33] "Foreign corporate defendants create unique problems. And courts are not well suited to make the required policy judgment that are implicated by corporate liability in cases like this one." Jesner, *supra* note 31, Slip Op at 26–27.

[34] *Id.* at 19, 27; see also Alito concurrence at 1 and Gorsuch concurrence.

[35] *Id.* Justice Sotomayor (joined by Justices Ginsburg, Breyer, and Kagan).

[36] *Id.* Dissent at 34.

[37] *Id.* Dissent at 28. (Under US law, US citizens can sue for damages caused by acts of terrorism under the Anti-Terrorism Act, enacted to provide same remedy already available to foreign citizens under the ATS.)

[38] *Id.* The US Solicitor General and State Department Legal Adviser filed briefs that "twice urged the court to the exact opposite conclusion of the majority" and confirmed during oral argument that the position of the US government was that there was "no 'sound reason to categorically exclude corporate liability.'" Slip Op dissent at 24. Members of Congress weighed in with a friend of the court brief in favor of corporate liability (https://www.scotusblog.com/wp-content/uploads/2017/07/16-499-tsac-senators-sheldon-and-lindsey.pdf, last visited January 1, 2020). Beyond this particular case, in the US, courts have found that where there is a universally condemned human rights violation, there is no interference with US foreign policy. One example is in a case against the Unocal Corporation for violations including slave labor and torture; there the government stated that since torture was against US policy, allegations against a private company would not interfere with US interests.

decision violates the principle that a nation should not allow human rights violators to enter its territory with impunity.[39]

The decision contradicts the international principle on the right to remedy. All victims of human rights violations have a right to an effective remedy for harms they have suffered. This right lies at the very core of international human rights law. It stems from a general principle of international law that a breach of rights gives rise to a commensurate obligation to provide a remedy: it has been recognized under all core international and regional human rights treaties and as a rule of CIL. In its unjustified creation of immunity for foreign corporations, the *Jesner* decision undercuts this right.

In some subsequent cases, defendants have attempted to apply *Jesner* dicta to US corporations, but courts have rejected these attempts and have allowed cases against US corporations to proceed.[40]

4.1.2 *Canada*

Canada, home to many mining operations that have seen their share of allegations of human rights violations, has begun to see more cases involving human rights violations. These claims have been brought under general tort law. Although Canada has not limited such tort claims to only those that occur in Canada, its courts have made liberal use of the doctrine called *forum non conveniens*, finding that another jurisdiction is more appropriate to hear the case and therefore dismissing it. More positively, certain Canadian courts can hear these cases based on "jurisdiction by necessity," which is in some ways the opposite of *forum non conveniens*. It allows the court to hear the case if no other forum exists.

There is a recent case from Canada in which the claimants have pleaded breaches of CIL by the corporate defendants. In this litigation, Araya v. Nevsun Resources Ltd,[41] three Eritrean refugees claim, on behalf of themselves and more than 1,000 Eritrean workers, that Nevsun is liable in negligence and for breaches of CIL including forced labor, torture, slavery, and crimes against humanity. The claims relate to Nevsun's alleged complicity in the use of forced labor at the Bisha mine in Eritrea by Nevsun's local sub-contractors. An attempt by Nevsun to have the claims under CIL struck out was unsuccessful, the court finding it is at least arguable that CIL forms part of Canada's common law.[42]

---

[39] Id. Dissent (Slip Op at 18): "our Nation has an interest ... in preventing our Nation from serving as a safe harbor for today's pirates."
[40] Al-Shimari, *supra* note 30, 320 F. Supp. 3d 781 (2018).
[41] Araya v. Nevsun Resources Ltd [2017] BCCA 401.
[42] Id. paras 177–97. The defendant company has petitioned the Supreme/Superior Court for permission to appeal this decision: *Nevsun appeals to Canada Supreme Court in Eritreans' forced labor lawsuit*, REUTERS (Jan. 26, 2018).

4.1.3 *Europe*

No country in Western Europe allows a cause of action for human rights violation against a private, nonstate actor. Switzerland is a possible exception, but such a case has never been attempted. European law does allow claims to be brought against corporations in the country of their domicile for extraterritorial torts. The United Kingdom has seen several common law cases involving violations of human rights, but they have been brought as garden-variety torts rather than directly pleaded as human rights violations. There are several reasons why human rights violations are not well-suited to be brought as regular, garden-variety torts however, besides the fact that there are those that argue that human rights violations should be classed as human rights violations, not simple torts.[43] Certain economic, social, and cultural rights are not amenable to civil suit as a tort law claim, for instance the right to education.

---

[43] *See* STÉFANIE KHOURY & DAVID WHYTE, CORPORATE HUMAN RIGHTS VIOLATIONS: GLOBAL PROSPECTS FOR LEGAL ACTION 78 (2016): "[t]he procedural substance of [tort] cases is defined as the resolution of a dispute rather than a serious infraction of legal or normative standards that requires punishment or admonishment by a ... supra state institution."

5

Limited Liability of Parent Corporations

There are multiple obstacles to accessing judicial remedies for transnational harms, all of which combine to make access to justice for victims of human rights violations by TNCs exceptionally difficult and frequently impossible. The twin principles of separate legal personality and limited liability, together with limitations on extraterritorial jurisdiction and the evidentiary burdens of bringing a claim, are major barriers that victims encounter. While each issue plays an important role in denying victims a chance of obtaining access to remedy, the complex corporate structures that characterize the organization of modern business are at the heart of these obstacles. In the absence of legislation clarifying standards for parent company liability, victims face an enormous challenge to demonstrate how a parent company of a multinational enterprise, domiciled in the home state, bears responsibility for the harm carried out by its subsidiary in the host state.

The doctrine of limited liability often results in situations where victims of subsidiaries' human rights abuses are unable to access remedy, even where these subsidiaries are wholly owned by the parent corporation. The doctrine applies no matter how egregious the harm, and no matter how much financial benefit the parent receives from the operations of the subsidiary. Where a subsidiary committing abuse is incorporated or headquartered in the host country, which it typically is, a victim's only option is likely to be suing the subsidiary in the host state. For the reasons discussed in Chapter 3, this simply may not be a realistic option. Even where victims are awarded a remedy from a subsidiary corporation within a host country, there may be enforcement issues, such as failure or inability to pay the judgment ordered. Here too, victims will be left without a remedy.

While some positive legal developments have taken place, in general, governments are reluctant to address the challenges posed by the doctrine of limited liability. A major limiting factor is the extent to which the legal doctrine is entrenched throughout most legal systems. The doctrine of limited liability of shareholders is so ingrained in the law of the United States and nearly all other countries, that the

International Court of Justice has gone so far as to characterize limited liability of shareholders as CIL.[1] Moreover, because there is generally an exception to the doctrine in which plaintiffs can "pierce the corporate veil" by showing that the parent corporation essentially controlled the subsidiary,[2] there is arguably a way to overcome this barrier. However, this practice creates perverse incentives whereby parent companies are essentially incentivized to keep subsidiaries at arm's length. They are deterred from working with the subsidiary to ensure compliance with the law and from conducting due diligence with respect to potential human rights violations. This is yet another reason why the doctrine has undermined attempts to prevent human rights abuses: any action on the part of a parent corporation to improve the human rights profile of its subsidiaries is potentially *more* likely to result in an allegation of control or a finding of duty, and therefore in liability, at least when compared to distance from the subsidiaries' affairs.

5.1 AN OVERVIEW OF PARENT COMPANY LIABILITY ACROSS MULTIPLE JURISDICTIONS

The doctrine of limited liability of shareholders originated in English law potentially predating the 1600s, but was not firmly entrenched in both England and the United States until the early nineteenth century.[3] Governments adopted limited liability of shareholders to protect individuals' assets beyond the investment into the corporation, thereby eliminating any risk that they could be required to provide

---

[1] See Gwynne Skinner, *Beyond Kiobel: Providing Access to Judicial Remedies for Corporate Accountability for Violations of International Human Rights Norms by Transnational Corporations in a New (Post-Kiobel) World*, 46 COLUM. HUM. RTS. L. REV. 158, 215 n237 (2014); *see also* Case Concerning the Barcelona Traction, Light and Power Co (Belg. v. Spain), 1970 I.C.J. 3, 35–36, 42 (Feb. 5) (noting the limited liability of a parent company is municipal law applicable as international law).

[2] For United States cases on veil-piercing, see Gwynne Skinner, *Rethinking Limited Liability of Parent Corporations for Foreign Subsidiaries' Violations of International Human Rights Law*, 72 WASH. & LEE L. REV. 1769, 1774 n6 (2015); *see also* United States v. Bestfoods, 524 U.S. 51, 62 (1998) (noting the "equally fundamental principle of corporate law, applicable to the parent-subsidiary relationship as well as generally, that the corporate veil may be pierced ... when, inter alia, the corporate form would otherwise be misused to accomplish certain wrongful purposes ... on the shareholder's behalf"); Bridgestone/Firestone, Inc. v. Recovery Credit Servs., Inc., 98 F.3d 13, 18 (2d Cir. 1996). In making this determination (to pierce the corporate veil), courts look to a variety of factors, including the intermingling of corporate and personal funds, undercapitalization of the corporation, failure to observe corporate formalities ... failure to pay dividends ... and the inactivity of other officers and directors (citations omitted); *see also* Gartner v. Snyder, 607 F.2d 582, 586 (2d Cir. 1979) (explaining that alter-ego liability exists when the corporation is used "to achieve fraud, or when the corporation has been so dominated by an individual or another corporation (usually a parent corporation), and its separate identity so disregarded, that it primarily transacted the dominator's business rather than its own").

[3] Fredrick G. Kempin, Jr., *Limited Liability in Historical Perspective*, 4 AM. BUS. LAW ASSN. BULLETIN 11, 14–15 (1960).

compensation if the corporation became liable for damages. In this way, states believed they could encourage investment, spurring economic activity and growth.

5.1.1 United States

In the United States, there have been numerous cases of courts dismissing claims against parent companies in human rights litigation due to the doctrine of limited liability. In Doe v. Unocal Corp[4] the court held that the parent oil corporation was not liable since it was not an alter ego of its subsidiary for purposes of jurisdiction in a class action suit brought by Burmese citizens. The parent company was not held liable because: (1) there was not such unity of interest between the corporate personalities of the parent and subsidiary that the two did not function as separate personalities, and (2) there was no failure to disregard the separate nature of the corporate entities that would result in fraud or injustice. In the case of Sinaltrainal v. Coca-Cola (Sinaltrainal I),[5] a district court in Florida found Coca-Cola not to be liable for the murder of an employee by a paramilitary group for his efforts to unionize the Coca-Cola USA bottling plant run by a subsidiary, because the plaintiff failed to make sufficient allegations that the bottling facility was acting as an agent of Coca-Cola USA.

While these are only a couple of many dismissals, they do not even account for the likely hundreds of times that potential plaintiffs and their lawyers have simply chosen not to bring suit as a result of the doctrine. Lawyers who engage in human rights litigation have indicated that the doctrine of limited liability has persuaded them not to take on certain cases, leaving these victims without judicial remedy.

In the United States, the doctrine was initially limited to actions for a corporation's breach of contract, but was eventually expanded to include tort actions. However, many scholars have criticized this later expansion of the doctrine as being outside its original purpose.[6]

---

[4] 248 F.3d 915, 926 (9th Cir. 2001), aff'd Doe v. Unocal Corp., 27 F. Supp. 2d 1174 (C.D. Cal. 1998).

[5] 256 F. Supp. 2d 1345, 1354–55 (S.D. Fl., 2003). See also Sinaltrainal v. Coca-Cola (Sinaltrainal II), 578 F.3d 1252, 1259 (11th Cir. 2009) (noting that in Sinaltrainal I, the district court dismissed the case against Coca-Cola USA due to the plaintiff's failure to sufficiently allege facts to pierce the corporate veil (alter ego)).

[6] See Skinner, supra note 2 at 1792–93 n77–83, citing David W. Leebron, Limited Liability, Tort Victims, and Creditors, 91 COLUM. L. REV. 1565, 1566–67 (1991) (seeking to establish the "valid justifications for limited liability and the implications of those justifications for limiting the tort liability of investors"; "[T]he doctrine of limited liability has its origins in quite a different time and circumstance, when the protection of contractual creditors, not tort victims, was the overwhelming countervailing concern."); Robert B. Thompson, Unpacking Limited Liability: Direct and Vicarious Liability of Corporate Participants for Torts of the Enterprise, 47 VAND. L. REV. 1, 2, 4 (1994) ("Indeed, some believe that corporate law undercuts tort law and represents a nineteenth-century relic that should be swept away in the face of current tort learning"; acknowledging that owners of closely held businesses or corporations regularly

Initially, at least in the United States, corporations were not allowed to own other corporations. It was not until New Jersey permitted corporate ownership of other corporations in 1888 that corporations began to create subsidiaries.[7] Courts began to apply the doctrine of limited liability to corporate shareholders shortly thereafter. Neither policymakers nor the judiciary paused to consider the purpose behind the doctrine before expanding its application. In fact, according to one well-known legal scholar, Phillip Blumberg, "[l]imited liability for corporate groups, one of the most important legal rules in modern economic society, appears to have emerged as an historical accident."[8] Professor Blumberg further noted that courts began to apply the doctrine of limited liability without recognizing the different relationship between a parent and subsidiary, which together comprise one economic entity or enterprise, versus an individual investor and a corporation.[9]

Indeed, many scholars and some jurists believe that the doctrine should not apply to corporate parents because there are not the same policy reasons for doing so. Thus far, these critiques have been largely ignored. While some courts have explored theories such as enterprise liability for the purpose of holding a parent corporation liable for the acts of its subsidiaries, such decisions have been limited.[10] Instead, most jurisdictions require a plaintiff to "pierce the corporate veil" in order to hold a parent corporation liable for the acts of its subsidiary. This is notoriously difficult to do, and in the United States, the factors for doing so vary from state to state. However, all states require that the parent "control" the subsidiary and have structures and operations in common with it, such as similar boards of directors, common policies, or even bank accounts. Essentially, the subsidiary must be almost an alter ego of the parent; in other words, it must really be one and the same entity. In addition, many states require that a plaintiff establish that the subsidiary was created for the purpose of committing fraud or

---

escape liability for torts); Virginia Harper Ho, *Of Enterprise Principles and Corporate Groups: Does Corporate Law Reach Human Rights?* 52 COLUM. J. TRANSNAT'L L. 113, 136 (2013) (reasoning that limited liability can encourage unreasonable risk-taking that leads to tortious harm of third parties who are unable to protect themselves from injury by corporate negligence, unlike creditors who are able to contract); Daniel R. Kahan, *Note, Shareholder Liability for Corporate Torts: A Historical Perspective*, 97 GEO. L. J. 1085, 1089–91 (2009) (showing how limited liability for shareholders protects the shareholders' assets, but still allows those harmed by the corporation's actions to seek a remedy from the corporation's own assets).

[7] Phillip Blumberg, *Limited Liability and Corporate Groups*, 11 J. CORP. L. 573 (1986) at 605, 607; Meredith Dearborn, *Enterprise Liability: Reviewing and Revitalizing Liability for Corporate Groups*, 97 CAL. L. REV. 195, 203 (2009); Jodie A. Kirshner, *Why is the U.S. Abdicating the Policing of Multinational Corporations to Europe?: Extraterritoriality, Sovereignty, and the Alien Tort Statute*, 30 BERKELEY J. INT'L L. 259, 263 (2012); Phillip Blumberg, *Asserting Human Rights Against Multinational Corporations Under United States Law: Conceptual and Procedural Problems*, 50 AM. J. COMP. L. 493 (2002).

[8] Blumberg, *Limited Liability and Corporate Groups*, supra note 7 at 605.

[9] *Id.* at 607–08.

[10] PETER T. MUCHLINSKI, MULTINATIONAL ENTERPRISES & THE LAW (2nd ed. 2007).

for engaging in wrongful activity. Courts applying the test have had differing outcomes, but this author knows of no transnational human rights case where the corporate veil has been pierced.[11]

5.1.2 *Canada*

In Canada, holding parent corporations liable for the human rights abuses of their subsidiaries can be even more difficult than in the United States. In fact, limited liability is one of the main barriers to victims seeking accountability in Canada for human rights abuses committed abroad.[12] Most litigation in Canada against parent companies is based on direct involvement in the acts at issue or, as a back-up line of argument, on "piercing the corporate veil." In order to do the latter, the plaintiff must show that the parent had *complete* control or domination over the subsidiary *and* that the incorporation was done for the improper purpose of hiding the fraud. Alternatively, the plaintiffs can prove that the subsidiary acted as the *authorized* agent for the parent.[13] Given that avoiding liability is not considered an improper purpose, piercing the corporate veil is nearly impossible.

Limited liability and piercing the corporate veil were discussed in Choc, et al *v.* Hudbay Minerals, Inc.,[14] a case alleging that the security personnel at Hudbay Minerals' former mining project in Guatemala engaged in numerous human rights abuses, including the killing of an outspoken critic, the shooting of another, and rape. The plaintiffs seek to pierce the corporate veil as an alternative to the main argument alleging Hudbay's direct involvement in some of the wrongful conduct by its subsidiary (direct parent company liability). The Court rejected Hudbay's argument that the claims should be dismissed on the grounds of limited liability, finding that the plaintiffs properly alleged that the subsidiary was acting as an authorized agent of Hudbay, and concluding that if the plaintiffs could establish this at trial, they would be able to pierce the corporate veil. In addition the Court noted that the parent company could be directly liable for its own actions. The case remains in active litigation following years of discovery battles.[15] In any event, piercing the corporate veil has yet to be tested in cases where there is no clear allegation of authorized agency and/or direct involvement.

---

[11] There have been occasions where a court has found that a subsidiary is the alter ego of a parent corporation for purposes of establishing personal jurisdiction, discussed below in Chapter 6, although that is now very difficult due to the recent Supreme Court decisions regarding personal jurisdiction, as will be discussed.

[12] *See* Yaiguaje *v.* Chevron Corporation [2018] ONCA 472 (Can. Ont. App. Ct.); *see also* Das *v.* George Weston Limited [2017] ONSC 4129 (Can. Ont. Super. Ct.).

[13] *See* Choc *v.* Hudbay Minerals, Inc., 2013 ONSC 1414 (July 22, 2013), at 9.

[14] *Id.*

[15] For an overview of the timeline of the case from the perspective of the plaintiffs, see http://www.chocversushudbay.com/ (last visited February 24, 2020).

5.1.3 Europe

Throughout Europe, different countries take varying approaches to the doctrine of limited liability, but one consistency is that the parent must control the subsidiary to the extent that the entities are one and the same, although control on its own may not be enough. Whether the corporate veil can be pierced and whether a parent company can be held liable for the conduct of subsidiaries that it controls or ought to control will of course depend on the law applicable to the case. However, the principle of limited liability remains dominant, and under most legal systems, it will only exceptionally be possible to pierce the corporate veil. This approach makes it difficult for victims of actions by a subsidiary to seek reparations from parent companies in Europe.

5.1.3.1 France

The strict interpretation of the doctrine of limited liability is one of the most significant barriers to accessing effective judicial remedy in France. However, recently courts have ruled that corporate, self-regulatory initiatives, such as codes of conduct, may trigger legal liability. For instance, French courts found the company Total SA criminally and civilly liable for the oil that spilled from the ERIKA oil tanker off the coast of Brittany when it split apart in 1999. French judges found the parent corporation liable partly because of its voluntary practice of vetting oil tankers contracted by its subsidiaries.[16] This holding suggests that voluntary actions by parent corporations that intercede in the operations of their subsidiaries as part of corporate codes or standards may accrue liability.

In recognition of the challenges in achieving parent company accountability, in March 2017 a new law was passed in France which imposes requirements on parent companies to conduct due diligence in relation to the activities of their subsidiaries. The law establishes an obligation of vigilance (*devoir de vigilance*) on companies incorporated or registered in France that employ at least 5,000 people domestically (including through domestic French subsidiaries), or employ at least 10,000 people worldwide.[17] While the obligation under the law is for companies to conduct a "vigilance plan," ordinary tort claims brought against the French (typically parent) companies may use the company's non-compliance with the due diligence obligation to evidence the alleged wrongdoing.[18]

---

[16] *Tribunal correctionnel de Paris*, January 16, 2008; *Cour d'appel de Paris, Pôle 4, 11e ch.*, March 30, 2010, RG n° 08/02278; *Cour de cassation*, No. 3439, September 25, 2012.

[17] Sandra Cossart, Jérôme Chaplier & Tiphaine Beau de Lomenie, *The French Law on Duty of Care: A Historic Step Towards Making Globalization Work for All*, 2 Bus. Hum. Rts. J. 317–23 (2017).

[18] *Id.* at 321. Companies would incur civil liability under the French Civil Code Articles 1240 and 1241.

5.1.3.2 United Kingdom

The law of the United Kingdom now provides that the "domicile" of a business is the relevant test for being able to bring a claim against it. After a claim meets that threshold, the courts will consider the control and duty of care of the parent company. A claimant must show control and/or a direct duty of care. In reality, the complexity of corporate groups can make it difficult to identify which parent corporation has a duty of care. While in some cases, the sole defendant may be the parent company within the forum state, in other instances it may be both the parent and a subsidiary which has been incorporated in another state. There may be still other situations where a number of subsidiaries or other businesses should be sued. For example, in Guerrero v. Monterrico, the plaintiffs initially sued the Peruvian mine operating business as a defendant, along with the parent corporation, but when it became clear that the absence of a treaty between Peru and the United Kingdom would make it difficult to enforce any UK judicial decision, the Peruvian business was removed as a defendant.[19]

Once the proper defendants have been identified (assuming that they can even be found), courts must still assess whether the parent company owed a duty of care to the plaintiffs. The test for determining whether a duty exists was developed by the UK Court of Appeal in Chandler v. Cape plc.[20] The *Chandler* case concerned a claim against a UK parent company for asbestosis contracted as result of exposure to asbestos dust by employees of a subsidiary company. The UK Court of Appeal held that in appropriate circumstances, the law may impose on a parent company a duty of care in relation to the health and safety of its subsidiary's employees. The court held that:

> [I]f a parent company has responsibility towards the employees of a subsidiary there may not be an exact correlation between the responsibilities of the two companies. The parent company is not likely to accept responsibility towards its subsidiary's employees in all respects but only for example in relation to what might be called high-level advice or strategy.[21]

The court outlined a number of factors which could give rise to such a duty:

> [In] appropriate circumstances the law may impose on a parent company responsibility for the health and safety of its subsidiary's employees. Those circumstances include a situation where, as in the present case, (1) the businesses of the parent and subsidiary are in a relevant respect the same; (2) the parent has, or ought to have, superior knowledge on some relevant aspect of health and safety in the particular industry; (3) the subsidiary's system of work is unsafe as the parent company knew,

---

[19] Guerrero v. Monterrico Metals plc [2009] EWHC 2475.
[20] Chandler v. Cape plc [2012] EWCA Civ 525.
[21] *Id.*, § 66.

or ought to have known; and (4) the parent knew or ought to have foreseen that the subsidiary or its employees would rely on its using that superior knowledge for the employees' protection. For the purposes of (4) it is not necessary to show that the parent is in the practice of intervening in the health and safety policies of the subsidiary. The court will look at the relationship between the companies more widely. The court may find that element (4) is established where the evidence shows that the parent has a practice of intervening in the trading operations of the subsidiary, for example production and funding issues.[22]

In *Chandler*, the court found that the parent company did owe a duty of care to the plaintiff employees.[23] The court emphatically rejected any suggestion that it was in any way concerned with what is usually referred to as piercing the corporate veil. A subsidiary and its company are separate entities: "There is no imposition or assumption of responsibility by reason only that a company is the parent company of another company. The question is simply whether what the parent company did amounted to taking on a direct duty to the subsidiary's employees."[24]

The *Chandler* decision demonstrates that in certain situations, a parent company may owe a duty of care to those impacted by the actions of its subsidiary. The decision has been applied in cases concerning extraterritorial actions in Lungowe v. Vedanta[25] and Okpabi v. Royal Dutch Shell. In *Lungowe*, the UK Supreme Court accepted jurisdiction on the basis that it was at least arguable that the parent company, Vedanta, may owe a duty of care to those impacted by the actions of its subsidiary. Faced with different arrangements between parent and subsidiary in *Okpabi*,[26] the Court of Appeal declined jurisdiction on the basis that it was not arguable that the parent company, Royal Dutch Shell, had assumed a direct duty of care to those impacted by the actions of its subsidiary. In the latter case, therefore, the stricture of limited liability and the corporate veil prevailed.

5.1.3.3 Switzerland

Swiss law recognizes the concept of a "group of companies," known as "Konzern," in which different companies, as separate legal entities, are linked to one another by investment or contract, often under a single direction, thus forming an "economic unit."[27] Nonetheless, Swiss law will not impute the conduct of subsidiaries to their parent companies, with an exception for situations in which the parent company interferes in the conduct of its subsidiary, giving direct instructions so as to become,

---

[22] *Id.*, §80.
[23] *Id.*, § 72–76.
[24] *Id.*, §§ 69–70.
[25] Lungowe v. Vedanta Resources Plc [2019] UKSC 20.
[26] His Royal Highness Emere Godwin Bebe Okpabi and Others v. Royal Dutch Shell Plc and Another [2018] EWCA Civ 191.
[27] The notion is defined in art. 663e, al. 1, of the *Code des obligations*.

in fact, an organ of the subsidiary.[28] The interference must be extensive and direct, going beyond the general influence on broad policy decisions and beyond the normal role of the parent company, as a shareholder, in the decisions of the subsidiary.[29]

Relief from the doctrine of parent company liability also comes from Article 2, al. 2 of the Swiss Civil Code, which prohibits taking advantage of the corporate form. Where the corporate form is abused, courts will apply the principle of "transparence" or "looking through," known as "*durchgriff*," and plaintiffs will be permitted to "lift the corporate veil" to reach the parent. However, this is a limited tool as the Federal Tribunal has imposed very strict conditions for the "transparence" doctrine to be invoked.[30] There are indications that the country is moving in the direction of creating liability on the part of the parent company or entire corporate enterprise for subsidiaries' extraterritorial human rights abuses in certain situations under a due diligence approach, akin to that adopted in France.[31] The proposed law, currently under debate in the Swiss parliament, is discussed in section 7.1.

---

[28] Art. 680, al. 1 *Code des obligations*.

[29] Art. 754, *Code des obligations*.

[30] See in particular the following judgments of the Swiss Federal Tribunal: case 5A_404/2008 (judgment of 30 June 2009) and case 4A_263/2010 (judgment of 28 October 2010), in which the Federal Tribunal refused to apply the *durchgriff* doctrine.

[31] *See* Oliver Elgie, *Swiss Parliament Calls for Parent Company Liability for Human Rights Breaches*, HERBERT SMITH FREEHILLS (Nov. 17, 2017), https://www.herbertsmithfreehills.com/latest-thinking/swiss-parliament-calls-for-parent-company-liability-for-human-rights-breaches (last visited January 1, 2020) (describing the launch of the Responsible Business Initiative in Switzerland and its first steps).

6

Lack of *In Personam* Jurisdiction over TNCs and their Affiliates

Another barrier to remedy for victims of human rights abuses is that courts may lack jurisdiction over the defendant in the case. As a threshold matter, for a court to adjudicate a case, it must have jurisdiction over the person who is the defendant, known as *in personam* jurisdiction, or personal jurisdiction. Almost always a court will have personal jurisdiction over an entity (a parent, subsidiary, or other entity) if it is domiciled or incorporated in the court's country. Thus, if a victim of a human rights abuse can bring a claim against the corporate entity involved the harm in the country where the victim lives and the harm occurs, because the entity is domiciled or headquartered there, personal jurisdiction usually exists and will not typically pose a barrier to remedy. Similarly, if a victim is able to bring a claim for extraterritorial harm against the parent company in the parent company's domicile or country where they are headquartered (either because they can "pierce the corporate veil" or because of the availability of an alternative theory allowing the victim to sue the parent), personal jurisdiction typically will not present a problem. Unfortunately, and as discussed above, in the high-risk countries and industries where human rights abuses take place, these situations are comparatively rare. Either the host country does not permit the cause of action, or there is no ability to pierce the corporate veil, or there is another barrier to suit. However, where a victim attempts to sue an entity, whether a parent, subsidiary or other entity, in a country that allows a cause of action for the harm but is not the country of legal domicile, personal jurisdiction may pose an insurmountable obstacle. For example, due to barriers in their own country, a victim might try to seek damages against an offending entity, such as a subsidiary, in the country where its parent is located; similarly, a victim may try to seek damages against a parent company that was involved in the abuse where it conducts substantial business, has offices, or operates through a subsidiary or subsidiaries. It is in these situations, where the country may well provide a cause of action that would allow the victim to bring a claim, that courts might find they do not have personal jurisdiction over the proposed defendant entity, and thus cannot adjudicate the case.

In this way, the legal doctrine of personal jurisdiction greatly limits a victim's ability to seek a remedy against a TNC operating in a host country when the TNC is headquartered elsewhere. Furthermore, the doctrine of personal jurisdiction has been devised with a conception of corporate entities as clearly separate in fact, but as discussed in more detail below, that is no longer accurate. Modern TNCs are complex structures organized amorphously, which exacerbates the problems of personal jurisdiction. These jurisdictional rules that made sense once upon a time no longer do so with regard to modern corporate structures, and are no longer fair.

The United States, Europe, and Canada all have rules that restrict assertions of jurisdiction over TNCs, including those that do business in the country. Until recently, the United States had the most liberal rules, allowing the assertions of jurisdiction over any entity that did "substantial and continuous" business in the United States, even for claims that did not arise out of the entity's business in the United States (known as general personal jurisdiction); the law in the United States also allowed for assertions of jurisdiction over an entity whenever its contacts with the United States gave rise to a claim, i.e., a product that the company had placed into the stream of commerce in the United States caused an injury (known as specific jurisdiction). But both of these bases of jurisdiction have been cut back by the US Supreme Court, greatly narrowing *in personam* jurisdiction in the United States.

Specifically, two recent US Supreme Court cases, Goodyear Dunlop Tires Operations, S.A. v. Brown (2001)[1] and Daimler AG v. Bauman (2013),[2] have greatly limited US courts' ability to assert general personal jurisdiction over TNCs – i.e., personal jurisdiction over claims that do not arise from the contacts with the United States but that would have previously been allowed due to the TNCs "substantial and continuous business" therein. In the decades prior to these cases, the standard for asserting general personal jurisdiction over TNCs was governed by the 1945 case of International Shoe Co. v. Washington,[3] which provided that courts could assert jurisdiction over a foreign corporation whenever it had engaged in "sufficiently substantial continuous activity"[4] in the US state where the claim was brought (forum state). Lower courts have also characterized this standard as "continuous and systematic activity,"[5] justifying the application of general personal jurisdiction on the basis that, since the corporate entity broadly enjoys the protection of United States law, the entity must also be prepared to defend itself against claims that arise

---

[1] 564 U.S. 915 (2011).
[2] 134 S. Ct. 746 (2014).
[3] 326 U.S. 310 (1945).
[4] Id. at 321. The Court also used the phrase "activity so substantial and of such a nature to justify" general personal jurisdiction. Id. at 318.
[5] *Goodyear*, note 1 *supra* at 925. Many courts continued to use the term "system and continuous business," even though *International Shoe* used the term *"so substantial and of such a nature to justify"* general personal jurisdiction. *International Shoe*, note 3 *supra* at 318.

under said law. The recent limitation on such jurisdiction thus represents a limitation on the applicability of US law to non-US corporate entities, and cuts of a major avenue of redress for victims of human rights abuses committed by corporations with substantial business in, but not legally domiciled in, the United States.

6.1 AN OVERVIEW OF IN PERSONAM (ADJUDICATORY) JURISDICTION

6.1.1 The United States: Historical and Current Theories of Personal Jurisdiction

In the United States, personal jurisdiction over a defendant is limited by notions of fairness and "due process" under the Fourteenth Amendment of the Constitution. The rationale for this has evolved over time. Initially, such concerns related directly to courts' desire not to impede on another jurisdiction's sovereignty over a person, especially where the defendant might not have notice that he (or it) could be sued in that jurisdiction.[6] Later, personal jurisdiction grew firmly rooted in these notions of fairness and adequate notice: courts now view assertions of personal jurisdiction as a matter of due process, governed by constitutional notions of "fair play" toward defendants.[7]

Early in American history, a court could exercise personal jurisdiction over an individual defendant as long as it had power over the defendant or his property.[8] Courts could likewise assert jurisdiction over an individual not domiciled in the state, as long as he was found in the state and served there.[9] However, until the mid-1800s, courts could assert jurisdiction over corporations only in their state of incorporation because such entities did not legally exist outside that state's boundaries.[10]

---

[6] See 4 CHARLES ALAN WRIGHT & ARTHUR R. MILLER, FEDERAL PRACTICE AND PROCEDURE § 1066 (4th ed. 2016).

[7] *Goodyear*, note 1 *supra* at 316, *citing* Milliken v. Meyer 311 U.S. 457, 463 (1940). My own view is that because these two concepts – sovereignty and fairness – are interrelated in the manner just described, personal jurisdiction is required for both reasons, matters of sovereignty and due to Constitutional Due Process.

[8] W.F. BAILEY, THE LAW OF JURISDICTION, INCLUDING IMPEACHMENT OF JUDGMENTS, LIABILITY FOR JUDICIAL ACTS, AND SPECIAL REMEDIES (1st ed. 1899); McDonald v. Mabee, 243 U.S. 90, 91–92 (1917) (wherein Justice Holmes famously noted that "[t]he foundation of jurisdiction is physical power … the ground for giving subsequent effect to a judgment is that the court rendering it had acquired power to carry it out"); *International Shoe*, note 3 *supra* at 316 ("[h]istorically the jurisdiction of courts to render judgment in personam is grounded on their de facto power of the defendant's person").

[9] See WRIGHT & MILLER, *supra* note 6. The Supreme Court confirmed this in Pennoyer v. Neff, 95 U.S. 714, 734 (1878), where it held that consistent with due process, a court could only assert jurisdiction over a non-consenting defendant who was either physically residing or domiciled within the state or a noncitizen served while in that state.

[10] See WRIGHT & MILLER, *supra* note 6 ("[A] corporation can have no legal existence out of the boundaries of the sovereignty by which it is created. It exists only in contemplation of law, and

Similarly, service on an individual officer outside the state of incorporation was typically not valid because corporate officers lost their official status as soon as they left the state of incorporation.[11] Thus, unless the corporation owned property in the state and attachment was available,[12] victims were out of luck if they wanted to bring a case in the state where they lived and where the injury occurred if the corporate defendant was not incorporated there.

After the industrial revolution, when corporations began doing business across state lines, these limitations began to seem both unrealistic and unfair.[13] As a solution, the Supreme Court held that a court may assert specific personal jurisdiction over a nonresident corporate defendant where the business has "certain minimum contacts with [the forum] such that the maintenance of the suit does not offend 'traditional notions of fair play and substantial justice.'"[14] With regard to general personal jurisdiction, the Court recognized that contacts may be sufficiently continuous and substantial.[15]

After the ATS was given new life in the 1980 case of Filartiga v. Pena-Irala (discussed in Chapter 4), US courts began relying on *International Shoe* to assert general personal jurisdiction over foreign corporations for human rights abuses. But in Goodyear Dunlop Tires Operations, S.A. v. Brown[16] and Daimler AG v. Bauman,[17] the Supreme Court created a sea change in the law of general personal jurisdiction over foreign corporate defendants. In the decisions, the Court held that

---

by force of the law; and where that law ceases to operate, and is no longer obligatory, the corporation can have no existence. It must dwell in the place of its creation, and cannot migrate to another sovereignty."); RICHARD D. FREER & WENDY COLLINS PERDUE, CIVIL PROCEDURE: CASES, MATERIALS, AND QUESTIONS 32 (5th ed. 2008).

[11] WRIGHT & MILLER, *supra* note 6, *citing* McQueen v. Middletown Mfg. Co., 16 Johns.R. 5, 7 (N.Y. Sup. Ct. 1819).

[12] WRIGHT & MILLER, *supra* note 6.

[13] *See* WRIGHT & MILLER *supra* note 6, *citing* Charles E. Clark, Chief Judge of the Second Circuit, in Deveny v. Rheem Mfg. Co., 319 F.2d 124, 126 (2d Cir. 1963) ("In the late nineteenth century, and continuing on into our own, increased use of the corporate form, together with the greater mobility afforded by modern means of transportation, brought about an expansion of corporate activity to a nationwide scale; corporations simply refused to remain penned up within their own states of incorporation. The existence of corporations which could — and did — do business on a nationwide scale necessitated revision of older, more limited, notions concerning jurisdiction.").

[14] Santa Clara County v. Southern Pacific RR, 118 U.S. 394, 316 (1886), *citing* Milliken v. Meyer 311 U.S. 457, 463 (1940) (in this case, just five years earlier, the Court held that individuals can be sued in the state of their domicile for all claims, even if they were found are served in another state because given their contacts with their domicile, suing them for any claim there satisfied due process – "traditional notions of fair play and substantial justice").

[15] *Id.* at 318 ("[T]here have been instances in which the continuous and corporate operations within a state were thought *so substantial and of such a nature as to justify suit* against it on causes of action arising from dealing entirely distinct from those activities."), *citing* Missouri, K. & T.R. Co. v. Reynolds, 255 U.S. 565 (1921); Tauza v. Susquehanna Coal Co., 220 N.Y. 259 (1917); *and* St. Louis S.W. Co. v. Alexander, 227 U.S. 218 (1913).

[16] 564 U.S. 915 (2011).

[17] 134 S. Ct. 746 (2014).

even where foreign corporations conduct systematic and continuous business in the United States, US courts cannot assert general personal jurisdiction over them unless the corporations' activities are "so continuous and systematic" as to render them essentially "at home" in the forum state.[18] Under *Daimler*, in nearly all circumstances, this will mean that the corporation must be headquartered or incorporated in the forum state.[19] The sum of these developments is that it is now very difficult to assert general personal jurisdiction over a foreign corporation.

Taken as a whole, these limitations create a breathtaking disparity in the treatment of an entity as compared to the treatment of natural persons under the law. Natural persons can be subjected to a court's jurisdiction simply by being served while within the state in which the court sits – even just passing through on one occasion ("transient" or "tag"[20] jurisdiction).[21] Courts have found personal jurisdiction over nonresident individual defendants in human rights cases, such as the self-proclaimed president of Serbia, who was served while he was temporarily in the jurisdiction.[22] However, nearly all courts have found that tag jurisdiction does not apply to corporations.[23] They argue that individuals are on notice that

---

[18] *Goodyear*, note 1 *supra* at 918–19; Daimler AG v. Bauman 34 S. Ct. 746 (2014) at 751.
[19] *Daimler, id.* at 761.
[20] See Martinez v. Aero Corporation, 764 F.3d 1062, 1067 (9th Cir. 2014), (noting that this kind of jurisdiction is often referred to as "tag jurisdiction").
[21] Fed. R. Civ. P. 4(e)(2) specifically authorizes jurisdiction where there has been personal service of a summons and complaint upon an individual physically present within a judicial district of the United States, and the Supreme Court found such complied with due process in Burnham v. Superior Court of California, 495 U.S. 604 (1990). Notably, the same section also allows service of summons on an agent authorized to receive service, but in *Goodyear* and *Daimler*, the Court essentially found that provision does not comply with due process rights of corporations.
[22] See Kadic v. Karadžić, 70 F.3d 232, 247 (2d Cir. 1994) (upholding personal jurisdiction over Defendant Karadžić who was served while visiting New York, on the basis of *Burnham*, and finding that "personal service comports with the requirements of due process for the assertion of personal jurisdiction"), *cert. denied*, 116 S. Ct. 2524 (1996).
[23] See, e.g., *Martinez*, *supra* note 20 at 1067–69 (holding that tag jurisdiction over defendant does not extend jurisdiction to the defendant's corporation, despite the defendant acting on behalf of the corporation at the time of service of process; and that *International Shoe* and all Supreme Court decisions since have assumed that tag jurisdiction does not apply to corporations); Wenche Siemer v. Learjet Acquisition Corp., 966 F.2d 179, 182–83 (5th Cir. 1992) (holding that *Burnham* did not authorize tag jurisdiction based on in-state service on a corporation's registered agent). But see Northern Light Tech., Inc. v. Northern Lights Club, 236 F.3d 57, 63 n.10 (1st Cir. 2001) (stating in a footnote that service on a corporation's president conferred general personal jurisdiction over the corporation, without explaining its decision or citing any supporting case). In First Am. Corp. v. Price Waterhouse LLP, 154 F.3d 16, 23 (2d Cir. 1998), the court held that tag jurisdiction over PW-UK, a "worldwide" company was proper regarding a third-party subpoena because PW-UK's partner was properly served within the forum, relying on the notion that service on one partner is service upon the partnership. It does not appear that the court considered the argument that because Price Waterhouse was a corporation, *Burnham* did not apply. Moreover, this case addressed a third-party subpoena, not service of a summons and complaint. A later opinion in a federal district court within the Second Circuit, Estate of Unger v. Palestinian Authority, 400 F. Supp.2d 541, 553 (2005), clarified that tag jurisdiction did

they could be served while in the state; that those traveling to the state are subjecting themselves to its protection, so that asserting jurisdiction over them is fair; that modern technology makes it less burdensome for nonresident defendants to defend themselves in another state's courts; and that the doctrine of *forum non conveniens* was always available to the defendant.[24] The same is true of corporations. This discrepancy highlights the unfairness of current jurisdictional doctrine.

6.1.2 *Europe*

Most European countries do not treat subject matter and personal jurisdiction as separately as is done in the United States, and *in personam* jurisdiction is not based on constitutional law or theories of "due process," but is completely statutory or regulatory. The focus of Europe's jurisdictional rules is on the claim, not on the particular rights of the defendant. These European jurisdictional rules focus both on the domicile of the defendant and on the type of claim being brought, with different jurisdictional rules applying in different types of cases and depending on who is bringing the claim.[25]

The European Union (EU) has its own regulations providing for jurisdiction over corporations domiciled in an EU country.[26] Although there are no constitutional limitations on personal jurisdiction under EU regulations, the reasons for some jurisdictional limitations are based on notions of fairness, similar to US jurisprudence focus on due process rights of defendants.[27] Generally speaking, the European Union now limits its member countries' courts assertion of general jurisdiction over TNCs to the corporation's place of domicile. Under the EU's Brussels I Regulation on jurisdiction (recast in 2012) ("Brussels I, recast"),[28] which went into effect on January 10, 2015, a member country's courts generally have jurisdiction to hear claims brought against defendants domiciled within that member country,[29] regardless of who is bringing the claim. There is no provision allowing a member

---

  not apply to corporations, noting that although "'tag' jurisdiction—personal service on an individual within the state—remains a valid method of acquiring personal jurisdiction over an individual, though not over a corporation through the persons of its officers," distinguishing *Price Waterhouse*).

[24] *Burnham*, supra note 21 at 632–39 (Brennan).

[25] Regulation 1215/2012 of the European Parliament and of the Council of 12 December 2012 on Jurisdiction and the Recognition and Enforcement of Judgments in Civil and Commercial Matters, 2012 O.J. (L 351) (hereinafter Brussels I, recast) Preamble arts. 13, 15; *id.* at ch. 2, art. 4, § 1.

[26] *Id.* at Preamble at § 14; *id.* at ch. II, § 1, art. 6.

[27] *Id.* at Preamble, §§ 1, 3.

[28] *Id.*, art. 81.

[29] *Id.* at Preamble, arts. 13, 15; ch. 2, § 1, art. 4. There are some exceptions, such as in areas of marital property, probate, bankruptcy, social security. *Id.* at ch. 1, art. 1. A defendant company is domiciled within a member state if its statutory seat, central administration, or principal place of business is located there. *Id.* at art. 63.

country to generally assert jurisdiction over a defendant domiciled within another member country, even where that defendant, such as a corporation, might engage in continuous and systematic economic activity.

The EU, however, provides for jurisdiction over specific cases in a manner similar to US's doctrine specific jurisdiction, although notably, such jurisdiction is often broader than in the United States post-*Nicastro*. There are several provisions that allow a member country's courts to adjudicate claims against defendants domiciled in another member country, depending on the claim.[30] They involve areas of law such as insurance, consumer law and employment, contract, and *in rem* jurisdiction, including claims involving these subjects where a plaintiff is domiciled in that Member State.[31] Similarly, the regulations allow the courts of a member country to hear tort claims against a defendant domiciled in the EU if the "harmful event" occurred in that country.[32]

Nonetheless, a close read of the EU's jurisdictional rules demonstrates that for human rights claims that occur extraterritorially, there are no personal jurisdiction rules that would allow noncitizen victims to bring a claim against a corporate defendant, even an EU-based corporation from another EU country, in an EU member country. This is true even if there were claims that might exist for extraterritorial human rights torts. Unfortunately, no EU country allows for extraterritorial human rights claims at the present; but if there were to be in the future, the EU would need to change its personal jurisdictional rules in order for such victims to bring claims.

However, the EU rule only applies to corporations of EU countries and does not protect corporations that are domiciled outside an EU country from expansive jurisdiction if provided for in the law – each European country's own laws on jurisdiction apply to non-EU corporations.[33] This means that, for corporations not domiciled in an EU country, personal jurisdiction ranges, but can be quite broad – in many instances, even broader than in the United States. For example, Germany allow for assertions of general jurisdiction over parent corporations if they have any property – tangible or intangible – located in those countries, even for cases completely unrelated to the property.[34] This basis for asserting personal jurisdiction is something that the US Supreme Court found unconstitutional early in the US's history.[35] The UK allows

---

[30] *See, generally, id.* at ch. 2, §§ 2–6. Note that, like the general jurisdiction in corporation's domicile, these provisions do not apply to defendants that are domiciled in a country that is not a member of the EU.

[31] *See, generally, id.* at ch. 2, §§ 2–6.

[32] *Id.*, ch. 2, § 2, art. 7(2).

[33] Brussels I, recast, *supra* note 25, at Preamble at § 14; *id.* at ch. II, § 1, art. 6.

[34] Kate Bonacorsi, *Not at Home with "At-Home" Jurisdiction*, 37 FORDHAM INT'L L. J. 1821, 1835, 1846 (2014) (noting that recently, Germany's high court has imposed a requirement for some sort of national connection), citing ZIVILPROZESSORDNUNG [ZPO] [CODE OF CIVIL PROCEDURE], § 23, translation at http://www.gesetze-im-internet.de/englisch_zpo/englisch_zpo.html (Ger.) (last visited January 1, 2020).

[35] *Shaffer v. Heitner* 433 U.S. 186 (1977) (finding quasi-rem jurisdiction unconstitutional).

for general jurisdiction over non-EU businesses that are "doing business," and although courts have stated that some connection to the UK is required, courts have not clearly defined what that entails, and it too could be very broad.[36] Some countries allow for jurisdiction over a parent corporation if it has a subsidiary domiciled within the jurisdiction,[37] something probably no longer available in the United States after *Daimler*, except possibly in unique circumstances equating to the subsidiary acting as the alter ego. And still other countries allow for jurisdiction over all defendants, including foreign corporations which would include a subsidiary, if a court has jurisdiction over any one of them, assuming the claims are closely connected (a jurisdictional rule similar to the idea of joint and several liability in US law).[38] Indeed, the common law countries of England, Ireland, and Malta and Cyprus, for example, allow for tag jurisdiction over defendants similar to the tag jurisdiction under which natural persons can be brought into court in the United States (although it is unclear how or whether it would apply to corporate defendants).[39]

However, despite the potential breadth of personal jurisdiction in at least some European countries, these assertions of personal jurisdiction for nonEU-based companies may make little difference, given the lack of causes of action available for extraterritorial human rights violations. And plaintiffs bringing suit in European countries face additional hurdles. For example, unlike in the United States, there are no contingency fee arrangements, there are loser pays rules, and often the choice of law rules means that damages paid are minimal, thus limiting the ability of victims of human rights abuses to bring a claim to fruition.[40] Thus, changing the jurisdictional rules in the United States will have more of an impact on providing a remedy for human rights violations than amendments to European law.

6.1.3 *Canada*

In Canada, personal jurisdiction over foreign defendants is viewed as a matter of private international law, with constitutional underpinnings primarily related to sovereignty issues.[41] However, fairness is also part of the approach.[42] Much like the United States, it has struggled to determine the underlying theory of assertions of

---

[36] Bonacorsi, *supra* note 34 at 1841.
[37] PETER T. MUCHLINSKI, MULTINATIONAL ENTERPRISES & THE LAW 115–16 n151 (2nd ed. 2007) (generalizing from the facts in the English case of Multinational Gas and Petrochemical Co v. Multinational Gas and Petrochemical Services Ltd [1983] Ch 258, [1983] 2 All ER 563 (CA)).
[38] Linda Silberman, *Jurisdictional Imputation in Daimler Chrysler AG v. Bauman: A Bridge Too Far*, 66 VAND. L. REV. EN BANC 123, 129 (2013).
[39] *See* Gwynne Skinner, *Expanding General Personal Jurisdiction Over Transnational Corporations For Federal Causes of Action*, 121 PENN ST. L. REV. 617, 657 n223 (2017). For the relevant rules in England, see Civil Procedure Rules of 1998, Part 6 Service of Documents, and associated Practice Direction.
[40] *See* Skinner, *supra* note 39 at 662–63.
[41] Club Resorts, Ltd v. Van Breda, 2012 SCC 17, [2012] 1 SCR 572, at 21–29.
[42] *Id*. at 58.

personal jurisdiction, vacillating between sovereignty and other possible constitutional limitations, such as the legitimate exercise of power under its Constitution.[43]

General personal jurisdiction over foreign defendants has been seemingly broader than in the United States,[44] even though it became slightly more restrictive in some ways in 2012. In two cases in the early 1990s, the Canadian Supreme Court held that personal jurisdiction over a foreign defendant was limited by the principles of "order and fairness," and that courts could only assert jurisdiction over a foreign defendant that had a "real and substantial connection."[45] In 2002, the Ontario Court of Appeal issued another decision expanding on personal jurisdiction, Muscutt v. Courcelles,[46] instructing courts to balance numerous factors in determining what constituted a real and substantial connection.[47] These cases gave particular consideration to the complications of asserting personal jurisdiction over defendants that were located outside of Canada, given comity and enforcement of judgment concerns.[48] But the numerous factors set forth by the *Muscutt* case were seen as cumbersome, and too vulnerable to individual judges' discretion.[49]

In 2012, the Canadian court clarified personal jurisdiction, and arguably narrowed it in Club Resorts Ltd. v. Van Breda.[50] The case involved two claims of two individuals killed and injured at two vacation resorts in Cuba, managed by Club Resorts Ltd., a resort management company incorporated in the Cayman Islands. Club Resorts argued that the province, Ontario, did not have jurisdiction over it. In commenting on the current law governing jurisdiction, the court gave a nod to the consideration of fairness to individuals, but also viewed predictability as critical, noting the importance of a "system of principles and rules that ensures predictability in the law governing the assumption of jurisdiction by a court."[51]

The court then set out four factors that would be presumed to be sufficient connecting factors to meet the "real and substantial connection" test. The four

---

[43] *Id.* at 30–33.
[44] See Caroline Davidson, *Tort Au Canadien: A Proposal For Canadian Tort Legislation on Gross Violations of International Human Rights and Humanitarian Law*, 38 VAND. J. TRANSNAT'L L. 1403, 1437 (2005) (noting that the test was "looser" than the "continuous and systematic" test of the United States). See also Linda J. Silberman, *Goodyear and Nicastro: Observations from a Transnational and Comparative Perspective*, 63 S. C. L. REV. 591, 600 (2012) (noting that in the United States, personal jurisdiction emphasizes the connection between the defendant and the forum, where in Canada, there are other factors to take into consideration, potentially leading to broader assertions of personal jurisdiction).
[45] Morguard Investments Ltd. v. De Savoye [1990] 3 S.C.R. 1077 (Can.); Hunt v. T & N plc. [1993] 4 S.C.R. 289 (Can.). However, the concept of "real and substantial connection" was first articulated in the 1975 case of Moran v. Pyle National (Canada) Ltd. [1975] 1 SCR 393.
[46] Muscutt v. Courcells [2002], 60 OR (3d) 20 (Can. Ont.).
[47] Davidson, *supra* note 44 at 1438.
[48] See Silberman, *supra* note 44 at 598–99.
[49] See Club Resorts, Ltd v. Van Breda, 2012 SCC 17, [2012] 1 SCR 572, at ¶ 51, 67. See also Silberman, *supra* note 44 at 599.
[50] See Club Resorts, *supra* note 49; *see also* Davidson, *supra* note 44 at 1437–38.
[51] Club Resorts, *supra* note 49 at 73.

connecting factors included two that in the United States would be seen as giving rise to specific personal jurisdiction: (1) where the tort was committed in the province, and (2) where a contract involved in the dispute was made in the province. The other two were for claims not related to the connections (i.e., general personal jurisdiction): (3) when the defendant was domiciled or resided in the province, or (4) where the defendant "carries on business" in the province.[52] These are presumptive "connecting factors," and the presumption is rebuttable, meaning that a defendant has the opportunity to offer its own evidence to demonstrate that the factor really bears little of a connection to Canada, and therefore should not be subject to personal jurisdiction there.

With regard to the "carries on business" factor (the broadest basis for general personal jurisdiction), the court noted that "carrying on business requires some form of actual, not only virtual, presence in the jurisdiction, such as maintaining an office there or regularly visiting the territory of the particular jurisdiction."[53] The court noted that advertising within a jurisdiction, by itself, would not be enough to create a sufficient connection.[54] The court further noted that it believed its new test gave greater clarity and predictability with the law of personal jurisdiction, allowing the "[p]arties ... to predict with reasonable confidence whether a court will assume jurisdiction in a case with an international or interprovincial aspect."[55]

What is somewhat limiting, however, is that just as the US Supreme Court did in *International Shoe*, the court noted that the booking of the resort, where the plaintiff was injured, occurred in Ontario, the forum of the case.[56] Thus the actual application of general personal jurisdiction under the facts of *Van Breda* is more akin to a looser version of specific jurisdiction in the United States, although it does not require that the harm arose directly from the contacts. Even though the court did not specifically hold that the harm must arise from the contacts in order for Canadian courts to assert jurisdiction over the foreign defendant, it certainly suggests this to be the case. This makes Canadian personal jurisdiction law somewhat similar to what now exists in the United States; at the very least, although broader than what is allowed now in the United States, it is not as expansive as the rules in the United States as they existed before *Daimler* and *Goodyear*. Of course, until more cases address what it means to "do business" in Canada, the degree of doing business sufficient to allow for general personal jurisdiction remains unknown for now.

---

[52] *Id.* at 90. The court did note that additional factors could be identified, but that in "identifying new presumptive factors, a court should look to connections that give rise to a relationship with the forum that is similar in nature to the ones which result from the listed factors." *Id.* at 80, 91.
[53] *Id.* at 87.
[54] *Id.* at 114.
[55] *Id.* at 73.
[56] *Id.* at 120.

PART II

Legal Barriers to Remedy and How to Overcome Them

7

Overcoming Legal Barriers to Remedy

7.1 PROPOSALS TO OVERCOME LIMITED LIABILITY OF PARENT CORPORATIONS

As discussed in Part I, there is increasing international consensus that it is unfair and unjust for parent corporations to receive the immense financial benefits derived from operations of subsidiaries or affiliates while being able to avoid liability when those wholly owned subsidiaries engage in human rights violations, even if the parent corporation is not directly at fault. Indeed, it is clear that the doctrine of limited liability, as applied to corporate parents, should be reconsidered – at least in circumstances such as high-risk industries operating within fragile or high-risk countries where remedies for serious torts are probably unavailable within the legal system of the subsidiary's domicile.

Therefore, the question becomes how to hold parent corporations accountable and liable for a subsidiary's human rights abuses, particularly if the corporate veil cannot be pierced. Scholars in recent years have advanced multiple theories, including enterprise liability, the so-called "due diligence" approach, and general tort-based approach. However, none of these approaches sufficiently addresses the problem. A different approach is needed – one that moves away from the current notion that a parent corporation should only be liable where it has some actual control over a subsidiary, and that moves toward parent corporate liability in appropriate circumstances even absent actual control. Any such approach should serve to create an incentive for parent corporations to assert their influence over subsidiaries or other operations in developing countries, especially when engaging in high-risk industries, in order to engage in processes that would serve to reduce potential violations of international human rights standards.

Such a fundamental change to the notion of limited corporate liability will necessarily require statutory change. In order to enact such an approach, lawmakers would need to enact changes to state limited liability statutes, removing the limitation on liability for parent companies with wholly owned subsidiaries operating abroad, especially where there are tort claims involved. At a minimum, limited liability rules should be changed by statute to create a presumption of parent liability where a corporation's subsidiary has engaged in human rights violations (or all serious tort violations). To overcome such a presumption, a corporation would have the burden to establish either that: (1) it was not aware of its subsidiary's violation even though the company created safe avenues for foreign citizens to complain about such abuses, or (2) they were aware and have taken action to end the abuses and fairly compensate the victim(s).

This is not as radical as it may seem. A similar type of presumption has been created in the area of sexual harassment in the United States, whereby businesses can avoid liability on the part of an employee for sexual harassment if the company can establish that it had an anti-harassment policy, had avenues available for persons subjected to sexual harassment to make complaints, and took actions to end the abuse. As this example shows, corporations' due diligence obligations in many ways are or should be designed to create such mechanisms to ensure that the business is aware of abuses or potential abuses, and takes action to prevent the abuse from occurring. This allows the law to reward (by means of protection from liability) the corporation that takes responsibility for the actions of its subsidiaries while preserving the availability of remedy for victims of corporate bad actors.

Nonetheless, an approach that requires statutory change, especially statutory change in the United States, is not a light undertaking, and may be perceived as an attack on business interests that is unnecessary in the context of other available legal tools. Therefore, I will examine each of the recent competing theories, including enterprise liability, the so-called due diligence approach, and general tort-based approach, and demonstrate why these approaches are insufficient despite providing valuable advances in holding parent corporations accountable for the actions of their subsidiaries. I will then, in section 7.1.4, present my preferred legislative approach, which retains the insights of the previously explored approaches while overcoming the legal limitations of these approaches.[1]

7.1.1 *Enterprise Liability*

The first of the theories for holding parent companies liable for acts of a subsidiary has been enterprise liability, where an enterprise or a parent company is strictly

---

[1] Some have advocated for unlimited liability of shareholders given that the victims of torts are typically nonconsenting victims who are absorbing all the risks of the corporate activity. However, with unlimited liability, all shareholders, even individual shareholders, face liability for a company's acts. Because unlimited liability applies even to individual shareholders it is, in the opinion of the author, not feasible. Thus, I do not explore this approach in any detail. This approach is distinguished from enterprise liability, where only corporate shareholders can be liable.

liable for the actions of its subsidiaries or affiliates if (and only if) the parent functionally controls its subsidiaries or affiliates.[2] The theory of enterprise liability is perhaps the oldest of the theories for holding parent companies liable for acts of any of its enterprise. It first began to appear in the literature in the early 1900s, arising initially as a tort concept, and was furthered in 1947 by Professor Adolf Berle, Jr., with a substantial scholarly piece concerning enterprise liability in which he argued that creditors ought to be able to recover from any member of a group of corporations that constituted an "enterprise."[3]

There are numerous examples of enterprise liability. For example, United States federal regulatory law provides for many types of enterprise liability via statute, especially in the areas of public utilities, the financial sectors, employer-sponsored pension plans, taxes, securities, export controls, and foreign trade.[4] Such legislation explicitly overcomes limited liability of parent corporations in certain situations.

---

[2] *See, e.g.,* Robert B. Thompson, *Unpacking Limited Liability: Direct and Vicarious Liability of Corporate Participants for Torts of the Enterprise*, 47 VAND. L. REV. 1, 12–17 (1994) (considering the theory of enterprise liability and some justifications for its use); Henry Hansmann & Reinier Kraakman, *Toward Unlimited Shareholder Liability for Corporate Torts*, 100 YALE L. J. 1879, at 1916–19 (1991) (discussing enterprise liability theory in light of arguments on whether limited liability or unlimited liability is the best regime for corporations); Phillip I. Blumberg, *The Corporate Entity in an Era of Multinational Corporations*, 15 DEL. J. CORP. L. 283, 298 (1990) (noting the emergence of enterprise theory in areas of law dealing with corporate governance); Christopher D. Stone, *The Place of Enterprise Liability in the Control of Corporate Conduct*, 90 YALE L. J. 1, 1 (1980) (analyzing enterprise liability theory and noting that in some cases the theory is the best option while in others the theory would need to be reinforced by other techniques); Howard Klemme, *The Enterprise Liability Theory of Torts*, 47 U. COLO. L. REV. 153, 157 (1976) (discussing the theory of enterprise liability for torts and suggesting that the logic of tort liability is moving toward enterprise liability). For a more complete discussion of the enterprise law, especially in comparison to entity law, see generally Phillip Blumberg, *The Increasing Recognition of Enterprise Liability Principles In Determining Parent and Subsidiary Corporation Liabilities*, 28 CONN. L. REV. 295 (1996) [hereinafter Blumberg, *Increasing Recognition*].

[3] *See, e.g.,* Leon Green, *The Duty Problem in Negligence Cases: II*, 29 COLUM. L. REV. 255, 273 (1929). For a detailed and helpful description of the early notions of enterprise liability in tort, see Edmund Ursin, *Holmes, Cardozo, and the Legal Realists: Early Incarnations of Legal Pragmatism and Enterprise Liability*, 50 SAN DIEGO L. REV. 537 (2013). The term "enterprise liability" is credited to Albert Ehrenzweig who used it in the book *Negligence Without Fault* in 1951. ALBERT A. EHRENZWEIG, NEGLIGENCE WITHOUT FAULT (The Regents of the Univ. of Cal., 1951) (currently out of print), *reprinted in* 54 CAL. L. REV. 1422, 1424–25 (1966). Before 1951, Leon Green was considered to be influential in the early notions of the theory with regard to tort reform in the 1920s and 30s. *See* Ursin at 559, 572–58 (discussing at length Green's role in the development of the theory). *Also see* Adolf A. Berle, Jr., *The Theory of Enterprise Entity*, 47 COLUM. L. REV. 343, 344 (1947) (discussing the theory of enterprise entities and their liabilities).

[4] *See, e.g.,* Blumberg, *Increasing Recognition*, *supra* note 2 at 303 (mentioning that enterprise principles now govern a wide array of industries); Meredith Dearborn, *Enterprise Liability: Reviewing and Revitalizing Liability for Corporate Groups*, 97 CAL. L. REV. 195, 240–45 (2009) (identifying ERISA, labor law, and bank holding companies as subject to "explicit statutory enterprise liability").

In nearly all instances, the statute requires a finding that the parent "controls" the subsidiary,[5] although the definition of control varies.[6] Additionally, in at least one instance, "control" can be presumed simply from a controlling ownership interest in stock.[7]

The Employee Retirement Income Security Act (ERISA)[8] notes that when a company that is part of a multi-employer-sponsored retirement income plan terminates its plan, thus leaving the possibility of unfunded benefits owed to employees of that single employer, all businesses that are under "common control" are liable for the benefits, plus interests, to all the participants in the terminated plan, regardless of whether any or all related businesses have corporate form.[9] Importantly, the regulations define "common control" as businesses connected through ownership of a controlling interest with a common parent organization; and a controlling interest is presumed at 80 percent ownership.[10] In enacting this section of the statute, Congress essentially pierced the corporate veil for parent corporations owning at least 80 percent of the subsidiary, as one court noted.[11]

---

[5] For a detailed catalogue of legislation and regulations where Congress has statutorily determined when a parent corporation can be liable for obligations of subsidiaries, or enterprises liable for actions of its various businesses, see Blumberg, *Increasing Recognition*, supra note 2, at 303–21. As he notes, however, nearly every one requires that the parent control the subsidiary. *Id.* at 304. Dearborn also discusses various instances, including what she terms the explicit statutory adoption of enterprise law with regard to employee pension law, labor laws, and financial institutions. Dearborn, *supra* note 4 at 240–44. This section of the book relies on both Dearborn's and Blumberg's work.

[6] See PHILLIP I. BLUMBERG, THE MULTINATIONAL CHALLENGE TO CORPORATION LAW: THE SEARCH FOR A NEW CORPORATE PERSONALITY 33–36 (1993) (distinguishing between the different definitions of "control" in the context of the decision-making process of a corporation).

[7] See I.R.C. § 1563 (2012) (defining the term "controlled group of corporations" to mean the group possessing a certain controlling stock ownership).

[8] 29 U.S.C. §§ 1101–461 (2012).

[9] See id. § 1301(b)(1) ("[A]ll employees of trades or businesses (whether or not incorporated) which are under common control shall be treated as employed by a single employer and all such trades or businesses as a single employer.").

[10] I.R.C. § 1563 (2012); Treas. Reg. § 1.414(c)–2(b)(2)(i)(A) (2012). The 80 percent rule is taken from the Internal Revenue Code and Treasury Regulations, as ERISA incorporates both. 29 U.S.C.A. §§ 1301(b)(1), 1302(b)(3) (West 1995). *See also* Blumberg, *Increasing Recognition*, supra note 2 at 313 (noting that the term "under common control" refers to "ownership of stock possessing at least 80 percent of the combined voting power of all classes of stock... or at least 80 percent of the total value of shares of all classes of stock").

[11] This was also noted by the First Circuit in Pension Benefit Guar. Corp. v. Ouimet Corp., 711 F.2d 1085, 1093 (1st Cir. 1983). Blumberg, *Increasing Recognition*, supra note 2 at 313 ("The regulations utilize the concept of the 'controlled group of corporations' as the determining standard for businesses 'under common control' and define the term by reference to one of the 80 percent stock ownership standards of the Internal Revenue Code."). The same is not true of single-employer plans; in those instances, courts have found that corporate parents are not liable for subsidiaries' pension-related liabilities, although, as Professor Phillip Blumberg has noted, in those situations a few courts have opined that piercing standards should be relaxed to further the statutory goals of the statute and plan. *Id.*

Additionally, in the context of financial institution regulations, for over fifty years the Bank Holding Company Act[12] – which protects creditors and places restrictions on mergers and acquisitions – applies to any parent or holding company that controls another covered corporation.[13] There is a presumption of control where the parent or holding company holds 25 percent of the voting shares of the other corporation and controls the election of the majority of directors or trustees, or the company directly or indirectly exercises a controlling influence over the management or policies of the bank or company.[14]

In most other jurisdictions, neither legislation nor case law show widespread acceptance of the concept of enterprise liability. There are a few exceptions however.[15] In competition cases, the EU Commission has asserted jurisdiction over non-EU firms operating through EU subsidiaries "on the basis of the parent/subsidiary relationship."[16] Where an undertaking encompasses a group of companies and an unlawful practice has been committed by a subsidiary, and where the parent company exercises decisive influence over the conduct of the subsidiary, the two entities constitute a "single undertaking" and may thus be held jointly and severally liable for the antitrust violation in question and the imposed fine.[17]

So, at least with statutory support, there is evidence for a workable scheme of enterprise liability. But while enterprise liability is a promising approach, there are important limitations that ultimately diminish its viability as an avenue of redress for individuals damaged by the actions of subsidiary corporations, particularly in the absence of statutory change. As mentioned above, enterprise liability as traditionally conceived is limited to where a parent company functionally and de facto controls the subsidiary; enterprise liability does not compensate those victims who are harmed by a subsidiary or affiliate when there has not been the requisite control, even where the parent corporation greatly benefits from the subsidiary's/affiliate's operations (and even the statutory examples above require a showing of control).[18] But traditional theories of enterprise liability, in requiring proof of functional control, are not that different to piercing the corporate veil (which, if available, removes the need for a theory of enterprise liability), and there is no consistent definition of how much control a parent would need to assert over the subsidiary for enterprise liability to attach. Given that corporate entities are complex and that the enterprise maintains control over documents, being able to determine, let alone

---

[12] The Bank Holding Company Act of 1956, 12 U.S.C. §§ 1841–52 (2012).
[13] Id. § 1841(a)(2).
[14] Id.
[15] PETER T. MUCHLINSKI, MULTINATIONAL ENTERPRISES & THE LAW 318 (2nd ed. 2007).
[16] Id.
[17] Andriani Kalintiri, 'Revisiting Parental Liability in EU Competition Law' 2 (2018) http://eprints.lse.ac.uk/87251/1/Kalintiri_%20Revisiting%20parental%20liability_2018_asuthor.pdf (last visited January 1, 2020).
[18] For similar arguments regarding why functional enterprise liability is limited in its usefulness, see Dearborn, *supra* note 4 at 246–54.

establish control, would prove daunting and simply too burdensome for most victims. Finally, like piercing the corporate veil, the theory incentivizes an arms-length approach of parent to subsidiaries rather than incentivizing working closely with the subsidiary to ensure that it meets its human rights obligations, and therefore does not further the clear policy goal of improving the human rights conduct of large multinational corporations operating through subsidiaries in high-risk environments.

In light of the problems with "control," some scholars have recently argued for a broader enterprise liability, where the enterprise or the parent would be liable regardless of the level of control the parent has over the subsidiary/affiliate.[19] With this type of enterprise liability, ownership of subsidiaries in an integrated economic unit could result in overcoming limited liability of a parent corporation in certain circumstances.[20] Indeed, this is the approach the UNGPs appear to endorse. Principle 22 of the UNGPs, which specifically addresses remedies,[21] states that where *business enterprises* identify that they have caused or contributed to adverse impacts, they should provide for or cooperate in their remediation.[22] The commentary to this principle notes, "Where a business enterprise identifies such a situation, whether through its human rights due diligence process or other means, its responsibility to respect human rights requires active engagement in remediation, by itself or in cooperation with other actors."[23]

The type of enterprise liability where there is economic control rather than mere functional control over a subsidiary or affiliate is an attractive solution, given that it would: (1) provide compensation to victims by the entity most benefiting from the subsidiaries'/affiliates' operations, regardless of having to prove functional control; and (2) incentivize parent companies to ensure that their affiliates were not committing human rights violations. However, this approach also has its limitations. First, similar to the general financial control-based enterprise liability, it is not limited to situations where the victims cannot otherwise obtain a remedy from the subsidiary, either due to underfunding or due to the host country's ineffectual judiciary, and therefore can result, at least hypothetically, in unfair liability for the corporate parent even when a more appropriate remedy is available directly from the subsidiary.

Second, the theory of enterprise liability does not adequately address the practical limitations to application that the Supreme Court imposed in *Kiobel*

---

[19] See, e.g., Dearborn *supra* note 4 at 252 (noting that enterprise liability theory has historically only applied where the parent behaviorally controls the subsidiary, and proposing a new test that would allow enterprise liability for human rights violations when the parent has economic control over the subsidiary).

[20] See *id.* at 252–54 (explaining that the parent corporation should be liable for its subsidiaries when the parent has economic control).

[21] See John Ruggie, *Guiding Principles on Business and Human Rights: Implementing the United Nations "Protect, Respect, and Remedy" Framework*, U.N. Doc A/HRC/17/L.17/31 (June 16, 2011).

[22] See *id.* at princ. 22 (discussing business enterprise remediation guidelines).

[23] See *id.*, at princ. 22, Commentary.

and *Jesner*.[24] *Kiobel* is a barrier to victims who seek a remedy from a corporate parent for violations by a foreign subsidiary in the host country, given that such violations would be unlikely to overcome the presumption of extraterritoriality that *Kiobel* imposed, unless the victims can establish that decisions, which led to the harm, were made in the United States.[25] *Jesner* is an effective bar to ATS claims against foreign corporate defendants. Thus, there does not appear to be a workable application of enterprise liability in the absence of statutory change to reverse or mitigate the *Kiobel* and *Jesner* decisions – and avenues of statutory change can, as I will demonstrate, provide better legal and policy solutions.

7.1.2 *Due Diligence Approach*

Many scholars have begun to argue for an approach I term the due diligence approach.[26] Due diligence in this context means that a parent company is expected to monitor the activities of its subsidiaries and affiliates – indeed any company within its sphere of influence – to ensure that the entities are complying with human rights and other legal obligations. This is consistent with the emerging notion that parent companies have a due diligence obligation to ensure that human rights are complied with within their sphere of influence.[27]

---

[24] *See Kiobel v. Royal Dutch Petroleum Co.*, 133 S. Ct. 1659, 1669 (2013) (concluding that the ATS does not permit claims against corporations for acts occurring outside the United States without "sufficient force to displace the presumption against extraterritorial application").

[25] *See id.* at 1677–78 (Breyer, J., concurring) (analyzing the corporation's contact in the United States as consisting of an office in New York, owned by an affiliate company, and merely being alleged to help the wrongdoers and agreeing with the majority that holding the corporation liable would be "too much"). There has been a very recent court decision allowing cases under the ATS to proceed based on amended complaints, citing substantial allegations of funding and decision-making in the United States by a US corporation. *See generally* Doe v. Exxon, Order, Doe I v. Exxon Mobil Corp., No. 01-CV-1357 (D.D.C. July 6, 2015), ECF No. 512. For a list of the few cases the courts have thus far allowed to proceed under *Kiobel*, usually because of some activity in the United States, and a list of the numerous cases that the courts have dismissed in light of *Kiobel*, as of December 2014, see Gwynne Skinner, *Beyond Kiobel: Providing Access to Judicial Remedies for Corporate Accountability for Violations of International Human Rights Norms by Transnational Corporations in a New (Post-Kiobel) World*, 46 COLUM. HUM. RTS. L. REV. 158, 199–200 (2014).

[26] *See* Lucien J. Dhooge, *Due Diligence as a Defense to Corporate Liability Pursuant to the Alien Tort Statute*, 22 EMORY INT'L L. REV. 455, 457 (2008) (discussing transnational businesses' duty to engage in human rights pursuant to the UNGPs and discussing how businesses can use their due diligence as a defense to human rights claims under the ATS); *see also* Yihe Yang, *Corporate Civil Liability Under the Alien Tort Statute: The Practical Implications from* Kiobel, 40 W. ST. U. L. REV. 195, 207–08 (2013) (advocating that corporations should incorporate due diligence mechanisms for human rights, and discussing how corporations might be able to use due diligence as a defense).

[27] *See* John Ruggie, *Guiding Principles on Business and Human Rights: Implementing the United Nations "Protect, Respect, and Remedy" Framework*, U.N. Doc A/HRC/17/L.17/31 (June 16, 2011) at 17–24 (outlining UN principles on business and human rights); Olivier De Schutter, Anita Ramasastry, Mark B. Taylor, & Robert C. Thompson, *Human Rights Due Diligence: The*

When the subsidiary or affiliate is found to have breached an international human rights obligation, a legal presumption of liability exists on the part of a parent corporation. The parent company can overcome the presumption by showing that: (1) it engaged in due diligence efforts to ensure that its subsidiaries/affiliates operated consistently with human rights standards, and (2) that it was otherwise unaware of the abuses. This approach would incentivize parent companies to engage in preventative measures that would both reduce human rights abuses from happening in the first place and provide for an "early warning system" for such abuses, allowing the parent to prevent them from happening. Moreover, some might argue that this is fairer to the parent corporation than economic control enterprise liability, and more consistent with notions of limited liability of parent corporations.

One European country, France, has incorporated this approach into legislation. The legislation effectively requires parent corporations to engage in due diligence regarding their subsidiaries' and affiliates' actions that might impact international human rights legal norms. The legislation creates a presumption of parent company liability for subsidiaries' torts abroad that the parent corporations can overcome if they had taken preventative measures by implementing a human rights due diligence plan regarding acts of their subsidiaries.[28] The French Constitutional Council removed civil penalties that the law originally imposed in the event that corporations failed to comply with the law, but otherwise upheld the integrity of the law.[29]

Additionally, in Switzerland there are plans to create liability on the part of the parent company or entire corporate enterprise for subsidiaries' extraterritorial human rights abuses in certain situations under a due diligence approach.[30] On September 1, 2014, the Foreign Affairs Committee of Switzerland's Lower Chamber, by motion, called for Swiss companies operating abroad to institute human rights

---

Role of States 7–8 (2012), https://www.icar.ngo/publications/2017/1/4/human-rights-due-diligence-the-role-of-states (last visited January 1, 2020) (follow "Download the full report" hyperlink) (explaining that corporations should use human rights due diligence to address risks and that States should regulate corporations to ensure they conduct human rights due diligence).

[28] *See* Skinner, *supra* note 25 at 260–61 (explaining France's bill). On March 27, 2017, the French Constitutional Council approved the Duty of Vigilance Law. *See* Sandra Cossart, Jérôme Chaplier & Tiphaine Beau de Lomenie, *The French Law on Duty of Care: A Historic Step Towards Making Globalization Work for All*, 2 BUS. HUM. RTS. J. 317 (2017), http://corporate-responsibility.org/wp-content/uploads/2017/08/french_law_on_duty_of_care_a_historic_step_towards_making_globalization_work_for_all.pdf (last visited January 1, 2020); *see also*, Cécile Barbière (Samuel White, trans.), *France Leads EU on Duty of Care requirements for Multinationals*, EURACTIV (last updated Apr. 28, 2017), http://www.euractiv.com/section/global-europe/news/france-leads-eu-on-duty-of-care-requirements-for-multinationals/ (last visited January 1, 2020).

[29] Cossart et al., *supra* note 28.

[30] *See* Oliver Elgie, *Swiss Parliament Calls for Parent Company Liability for Human Rights Breaches*, HERBERT SMITH FREEHILLS (Nov. 17, 2017), https://www.herbertsmithfreehills.com/latest-thinking/swiss-parliament-calls-for-parent-company-liability-for-human-rights-breaches (last visited January 1, 2020) (describing the launch of the Responsible Business Initiative in Switzerland and its first steps).

and environmental due diligence.[31] The motion required that Switzerland's Federal Council "draft a law to implement this requirement—if possible in the context of the upcoming stock corporation law reforms."[32] The Federal Council recommended rejecting the motion on the grounds that it would require more than the current EU regulations, which do not mandate human rights due diligence, and because it would place Switzerland at a disadvantage as a business destination.[33] In March 2015, the Foreign Affairs Committee's motion was narrowly defeated in the Lower Chamber.[34] However, a coalition in Switzerland has gathered over 120,000 signatures for a referendum to be submitted that, similar to the French bill, would require larger companies to engage in due diligence, risk assessment, the development of measures to prevent possible human rights violations and environmental damages, and comprehensive reporting on such policies and actions.[35] The bill met the signature requirement needed to be placed on a ballot, but in late 2017 was

---

[31] *See A Milestone for Human Rights*, CORPORATE JUSTICE (Sept. 2, 2014), https://www.business-humanrights.org/en/swiss-foreign-affairs-committee-calls-for-mandatory-human-rights-due-diligence-for-companies-o (last visited January 1, 2020) (follow "Swiss Foreign Affairs Committee calls for mandatory human rights due diligence for companies" hyperlink) (describing developments in Switzerland to improve in corporate social responsibility).

[32] *Id.*, *see* Motion 14.3671: Mise en oeuvre du rapport de droit comparé du Conseil fédéral sur la responsabilité des entreprises en matière de droits humains et d'environnement [Implementation of the Federal Council Comparative Law Report on the Responsibility of Businesses in Human Rights and the Environment], THE FED. ASSEMBLY – THE SWISS PARLIAMENT (Sept. 1, 2014) https://www.parlament.ch/fr/ratsbetrieb/suche-curia-vista/geschaeft?AffairId=20143671 (Switz.) (last visited January 1, 2020).

[33] *See* CORPORATE JUSTICE, *supra* note 31 (describing the Council's desire to appease corporations who use Switzerland as a home state).

[34] *See* Press Release, Swiss Coalition for Corp. Just., *Conservative Backlash Blocks Increased Corporate Accountability* (Mar. 13, 2015), http://corporatejustice.ch/conservative-backlash-blocks-increased-corporate-accountability/ (last visited January 1, 2020) (explaining that the motion for increased corporate accountability failed on a re-vote, losing by nine votes).

[35] *See* Press Release, Swiss Coal. of Corp. Just., *Global Business? Global Responsibility!* (Apr. 21, 2015), http://corporatejustice.ch/global-business-global-responsibility/ (last visited January 1, 2020) (discussing that sixty-six organizations are collecting signatures to require Swiss companies to carry out human rights due diligence); *see also* Leon Kaye, *Citizens Demand Swiss Firms be Held Accountable for Human Rights, Environmental Policies*, TRIPLE PUNDIT (Oct. 13, 2016), http://www.triplepundit.com/2016/10/citizens-demand-swiss-firms-held-accountable-human-rights-environmental-policies/ (last visited January 1, 2020) (reporting that the 120,000 signatures needed have been obtained); *The Initiative Text with Explanations*, SWISS COAL. OF CORP. JUST., http://corporatejustice.ch/wp-content/uploads/2017/11/The-initiative-text-with-explanations.pdf (last visited July 3, 2018) (describing the Swiss Coalition of Corporate Justice's campaign). The Coalition notes that at the heart of the initiative is mandatory due diligence regarding human rights and the environment. *Id.* It further notes that due diligence in this context includes a risk assessment, measures to prevent and eliminate possible human rights violations and environmental damage, as well as comprehensive reporting on the policies in place and the action taken. *Id.* According to its material, the duty to carry out due diligence extends through all business operations and is based on the UNGPs on Business and Human Rights. *Id.* Moreover, the scale and complexity of the due diligence depends on the specific risks of the corporation – small and medium-sized enterprises will remain largely unaffected by the initiative. *Id.* The text of the initiative is currently under review at the Federal Chancellery. *Id.*

rejected (by Switzerland's Federal Council), subsequently modified (by the Lower Chamber), and sent back to the Legal Affairs Committee for approval.[36] In 2019, the Federal Council, with a vote of 22 to 20, rejected discussion of the counter-proposal on responsible business put forward by the Lower Chamber. It also rejected the popular initiative launched last year by a coalition of non-governmental organizations (NGOs) by a vote of 25 to 14. With this decision, the counter-proposal goes back to the Lower Chamber. The next steps are unclear, but it is likely that the initiative could go to a nationwide public vote.[37]

Although the due diligence approach has its advantages as discussed above – such as an incentive to prevent harm – it also has its limitations. Like the control-based enterprise liability, it would only require parent corporations to provide a remedy to victims who have been harmed if the company failed to engage in its due diligence approach. Thus, even where a human rights violation occurs and victims suffer death or serious injuries, a parent company can still reap all the financial benefits of its subsidiaries and affiliates, while the victims, who bear all the costs, are left remediless. Second, there is a real fear that the due diligence process will simply become a "box-checking" exercise on the part of the parent instead of real, substantial human rights preventative measures, ultimately leading to non-liability on the part of the parent company for simply engaging in mechanical reviews. Third, there is a lack of clarity about what due diligence really means, or what activities a parent company should engage in for there to be real due diligence.[38] The French law, for example, does not define due diligence. These weaknesses demonstrate that due diligence is not a complete solution to either preventing human rights abuses or ensuring that victims of such abuses have a remedy. Finally, although such an approach would be an important step in Europe, this approach (like the enterprise liability approach) does not address the barriers in the United States that *Kiobel* and *Jesner* erected.

7.1.3 *Parent Corporation Duty of Care for its Own Assumptions of Obligations*

Another somewhat recent approach arises from the theory of a parent corporation's "duty of care." Commentators and advocates who favor this approach have taken the

---

[36] Julianne Hughes-Jennett, Peter Hood & Marie Davoise, *Switzerland: The Next Frontier for Mandatory Human Rights Due Diligence?* HOGAN LOVELLS (Dec. 1, 2017), https://www.hlregulation.com/2017/12/01/switzerland-the-next-frontier-for-mandatory-human-rights-due-diligence/ (last visited January 1, 2020).

[37] Jessica Davis Plüss & Andrea Tognina, *Responsible Business Initiative Heads Closer to a National Vote*, SWISSINFO.CH (Mar. 9, 2019), https://www.swissinfo.ch/eng/corporate-responsibility_responsible-business-initiative-heads-closer-to-a-national-vote/44818824 (last visited January 1, 2020).

[38] OECD, *Due Diligence Guidance for Responsible Business Conduct* (2018), and the UN WORKING GROUP ON BUSINESS AND HUMAN RIGHTS, *Corporate Human Rights Due Diligence – Emerging Practices, Challenges and Ways Forward* (2018).

traditional idea of a parent corporation being held liable for its own breach of duties owed to third parties,[39] and have argued that such a legal duty is created where the parent owns, creates, or allows a subsidiary to operate in a fashion that creates foreseeable harm to nonconsenting third parties.[40] This approach is illustrated in the case law, with two leading cases (from the UK and Canada) demonstrating its applicability to transnational corporations. These cases were welcomed in certain quarters as offering a way forward to hold parent corporations liable when their subsidiaries cause injury abroad.[41] However, the reality is that, although these cases

---

[39] As early as 1929, Professors Douglas and Shanks noted that there were situations where, even though subsidiaries maintained their separateness from parent corporations, parent corporations were seemingly found liable in tort for acts of their subsidiaries. *See* William Douglas & Carol Shanks, *Insulation from Liability Through Subsidiary Corporations*, 39 YALE L. J. 193, 205–10 (1929) (noting the circumstances under which the parent corporation is traditionally found liable for its subsidiary's tortious conduct). However, they closely reviewed the cases and noted that the liability was either due to the parent's direct role in the tort or the subsidiary was acting specifically as an agent for the parent in carrying out a decision of the parent. *See id.* (pointing to instances of the parent's agency or direct involvement in the subsidiary's conduct). In more recent cases, the courts have found that under the "third party" theory, an action for a breach of a duty of care against a parent company is available only if the employee can establish that the parent company assumed, either by express agreement or by implication, the "primary responsibility" for providing safety of others. *See* Mendez-Laboy v. Abbott Labs., Inc., 424 F.3d 35, 37 (1st Cir. 2005) (ruling that the plaintiff must show that the parent/employer exerted a notable level of control over the factors leading to the injury) (internal citations omitted).

[40] *See* Radu Mares, *Responsibility to Respect: Why the Core Company Should Act When Affiliates Infringe Rights*, in THE UN GUIDING PRINCIPLES ON BUSINESS AND HUMAN RIGHTS: FOUNDATION AND IMPLEMENTATION 169–92 (Radu Mares ed. 2012) (advocating for a duty of care approach to hold parent corporations liable for the acts they take in creating subsidiaries in high-risk environments); Nora Mardirossian, *Direct Parental Negligence Liability: An Expanding Means to Hold Parent Companies Accountable for the Human Rights Impacts of Their Foreign Subsidiaries* 4 (2015), http://ssrn.com/abstract=2607592 (last visited January 1, 2020) (follow "Download This Paper" hyperlink) (arguing "that parent companies with high levels of control or supervision of their subsidiaries owe a direct duty of care to those whose risk of injury is foreseeable" and that "[w]hen these parents act negligently...controlling the actions of their subsidiaries, they should be held directly liable"); Nicola M.C.P. Jägers & Marie-José van der Heijden, *Corporate Human Rights Violations: The Feasibility of Civil Recourse in the Netherlands*, 33 BROOK. J. INT'L L. 833, 843 (2008) (noting that "plaintiffs in transnational human rights litigation may rely on ... direct liability of the *parent* for an act or omission by the parent in violation of its duty to exercise due diligence in the relationship towards the subsidiary") (emphasis in original). In this situation, the parent company's conduct and omissions defy a domestic liability standard. This mechanism has some advantages for transnational human rights litigation as it will encourage rather than discourage "more active involvement by the parent company towards its subsidiaries." Jodie Kirshner, *Why is the U.S. Abdicating the Policing of Multinational Corporations to Europe?: Extraterritoriality, Sovereignty, and the Alien Tort Statute*, 30 BERKELEY J. INT'L L. 259, 279–81 (2012) (noting a similar approach). In addition, the possibility of this theory was discussed at length during several sessions of the Third Annual Forum on Business and Human Rights. *See* Third United Nations Forum on Business and Human Rights, Dec. 1–3, 2014 (notes on file with author).

[41] Numerous participants in forums at the Third Annual Forum discussed these cases and the potential new "duty of care approach." *See* Third Annual Forum on Business and Human Rights, Geneva, Switz., December 1–3, 2014.

are important models when considering whether a parent is liable for acts of its subsidiaries in certain circumstances, the decisions do not suggest a duty occurs simply because a parent creates or purchases a subsidiary and knows it will engage in operations that might pose a risk to third parties.[42]

The two cases fueling the discussion of a parent corporation's liability under a direct duty of care approach for a subsidiary's actions are a 2012 United Kingdom case, Chandler v. Cape PLC,[43] and a 2013 Canadian case, Choc v. Hudbay Minerals.[44] Both cases are significant because for the first time courts in the UK and Canada found that apart from piercing the corporate veil or agency, parent corporations could be directly liable for their subsidiaries' actions based on the parent owing its own "duty of care" to third parties.[45]

Chandler was based on a claim against a UK parent company for injury (asbestosis contracted as result of exposure to asbestos dust) suffered by employees of a subsidiary company.[46] In *Chandler*, the English Court of Appeal held that in appropriate circumstances, the law may impose on a parent company a duty of care in relation to the health and safety of third parties (in that case, of its employees), and that there had been an assumption of responsibility for the health and safety of the subsidiary's employees under the facts of that case.[47]

The facts of the case are important in understanding the assumption of duty. The lower court, whose decision the higher court affirmed,[48] found that the defendant employed a scientific officer and a medical officer who together were responsible for

---

[42] See Chandler v. Cape PLC [2012] EWCA (Civ) 525 [69] (Eng.) ("A subsidiary and its company are separate entities. There is no imposition or assumption of responsibility by reason only that a company is the parent company of another company.").

[43] See Chandler v. Cape PLC [2012] EWCA (Civ) 525 [80] (Eng.) (determining that a parent company may be held liable for injuries sustained by employees of a subsidiary if the parent company knew or should have foreseen that unsafe workplace conditions would cause harm).

[44] See Choc v. Hudbay Minerals, Inc., 2013 ONSC 1414, para. 75 (Can.) (ruling that the plaintiffs could pursue a claim for direct negligence against the parent corporation for human rights violations, including murder and rape, perpetrated against indigenous people at the subsidiary's mining site in South America).

[45] See id. at 75 (noting that it is not plain and obvious that there is no negligence claim possible against the parent subsidiary, so the claim may continue to trial); Chandler v. Cape PLC, *supra* note 43 (concluding "the law may impose on a parent company responsibility for health and safety of its subsidiary's employees"); see also Michael Goldhaber, *Corporate Human Rights Litigation in Non-U.S. Courts: A Comparative Scorecard*, 3 U. C. IRVINE L. REV. 127, 133 (2013) (noting that the UK Court of Appeal "resoundingly endorsed" parent corporation liability in *Chandler*).

[46] See Chandler v. Cape PLC, *supra* note 43 at paras. 1, 3 (noting the plaintiff contracted asbestosis after working for the subsidiary loading bricks at the same factory site as the asbestos production).

[47] See id. at paras. 62–78 (noting that, given the parent corporation's "superior knowledge about the nature and management of asbestos risks... it is appropriate to find that Cape assumed a duty of care").

[48] See id. at para. 79 ("Moreover, while I have reached my conclusion in my own words and following my own route, it turns out that, in all essential respects, my reasoning follows the analysis of the judge in... his judgment.").

health and safety of all the employees within the defendant's subsidiaries; that the evidence demonstrated that it was the defendant and not the subsidiary companies who "dictated policy in relation to health and safety" of the employees; that the parent company "retained responsibility for ensuring that its...employees...were not exposed to the risk of harm through exposure to asbestos"; and the evidence conclusively showed that the defendant retained "overall responsibility."[49] This meant, according to the higher court, that a duty could arise on the part of the parent because of its "superior knowledge about the nature and management of asbestos risks," and that "Cape could, and did on other matters, give Cape Products instructions as to how it was to operate with which, so far as we know, it duly complied."[50] Therefore, the parent could be held to have breached its duties to the subsidiary's employees, for whom it had retained responsibility.

The significance of *Chandler* was that the court held that a parent corporation could be liable for acts of a subsidiary even where it might not have actual control over the *specific* operation at issue.[51] In this way, it was a ground-breaking decision because it indicates that a parent company may have a duty of care depending on the particular facts. But it is a limited decision, all the same. First, it is limited to appropriate circumstances. The holding, narrowly formed, is that a parent corporation may be responsible for the health and safety of subsidiary employees if: (1) the businesses of the parent and subsidiary are in a relevant respect the same; (2) the parent has, or ought to have, superior knowledge on some relevant aspect of health and safety in the particular industry; (3) the subsidiary's system of work is unsafe as the parent company knew, or ought to have known; and (4) the parent knew or *ought to have foreseen that the subsidiary or its employees would rely on its using that superior knowledge for the employees' protection*. For the purposes of (4), it is not necessary to show that the parent is in the practice of intervening in the health and safety policies of the subsidiary. The court will look at the relationship between the companies more widely. The court may find that element (4) is established where the evidence shows that the parent has a practice of intervening in the trading operations of the subsidiary, for example, production and funding issues.[52]

Before *Chandler*, several other UK plaintiff cases relied on the same duty of care theory, although *Chandler* was the first case to accept the theory in the English

---

[49] See id. at para. 31 (providing the trial court judge's reasoning for his conclusion that "[t]his was no failure in day-to-day management; this was a systemic failure of which the Defendant was fully aware").

[50] Id. at para. 78.

[51] See id. at para. 74 (noting that, while the parent corporation "was not responsible for the actual implementation of health and safety measures" at the subsidiary, the case arose from issues of overall omissions of care by the parent and not from noncompliance with specific health and safety procedures).

[52] Id. at para. 80 (emphasis added).

Court of Appeal.[53] As one commentator has noted, under this theory, the parent corporation may be "held liable for harm flowing from its failure to competently perform the functions it controls, or to give foreign subsidiaries sound advice on environmental, worker safety, and human rights policies."[54] Broadly speaking, the theory is "that when a parent company is *directly involved in its subsidiary's operations or exercises de facto control*, then it owes a duty of care to ... anyone affected by the subsidiary's operations."[55] However, such theories of liability exist only where there is "*sufficient involvement in, control over and knowledge of the subsidiary operations* by the parent such that there is no reason why the general principles of duty creation and negligence should not apply."[56] In addition, in looking at the elements, it is clear that, for there to be liability under this theory, the parent must or should have had superior knowledge of the problem at hand, and it must have been foreseeable that the subsidiary or third parties (in this case, employees) would rely on the parent's superior knowledge for the protection of the third parties.[57]

The 2013 Ontario Superior Court of Justice decision in *Choc* has a similar holding.[58] In *Choc*, a Canadian Court found that a Canadian parent company may have owed a direct duty of care to a Guatemalan indigenous community whose rights were violated when a subsidiary of the parent company hired security forces to forcibly evict Mayan community members.[59] The plaintiffs in the case alleged that the security personnel at Hudbay Minerals' former mining project in Guatemala engaged in numerous abuses – including the killing of an outspoken critic, the shooting of another man, and rape of numerous women during their removal from their ancestral village by security personnel, police, and the military.[60]

Significantly, the court rejected Hudbay Minerals' argument that the case should be dismissed because of its limited liability regarding its Guatemala

---

[53] See Goldhaber, *supra* note 45 at 130–32 (discussing the success of precedential cases brought by local inhabitants under English common law against parent corporations in the English courts for human rights violations by subsidiary companies in comparison to claims brought under the ATS in the United States).
[54] *Id.* at 132.
[55] *Id.* (emphasis added).
[56] Richard Meeran, *Litigation of Multinational Corporations: A Critical Stage in the UK*, in LIABILITY OF MULTINATIONAL CORPORATIONS UNDER INTERNATIONAL LAW 251, 261 (Menno T. Kamminga & Saman Zia-Zarifi eds. 2000).
[57] See Chandler v. Cape PLC *supra* note 43 (discussing parent liability where "the parent has, or ought to have, superior knowledge" and "the parent knew or ought to have foreseen that the subsidiary or its employees would rely on its using that superior knowledge").
[58] See Choc v. Hudbay Minerals, *supra* note 44, para. 75 (determining that the plaintiffs may pursue a claim of direct negligence against the parent corporation for human rights abuses that the subsidiary company committed).
[59] See *id.* at paras. 4–7, 75 (ruling that the plaintiffs made a prima facie showing that the parent corporation could owe a duty of care to the native people victimized by the subsidiary).
[60] See *id.* at paras. 4–7 (discussing the basis of the human rights abuses in the consolidated claims as being various types of gross violations against the Mayan people).

subsidiary's action.[61] Among other findings, the court found that plaintiffs had properly pled a direct liability case against Hudbay under local tort law.[62] Specifically, the court found that the plaintiffs could proceed with their case if they adequately pled a "novel" duty of care, given that they did not plead a duty of care already recognized by law.[63] The court set forth the three elements the plaintiffs would have to plead to adequately plead such a duty of care:

1. that the harm complained of is a reasonably foreseeable consequence of the alleged breach;
2. that there is sufficient proximity between the parties that it would not be unjust or unfair to impose a duty of care on the defendants; and
3. that there exist no policy reasons to negative or otherwise restrict that duty.[64]

The court then applied Canadian law on each of these issues, holding that, under Canadian law, harm is foreseeable for purposes of duty if it is foreseeable that harm might occur in a general way and the type of damage was foreseeable.[65]

The court found that the plaintiffs adequately pleaded foreseeability because they had pled specifically that Hudbay knew or should have known that security forces frequently used violence to evict members of the specific community, and that the defendant's executives knew that: violence had been used in previous evictions they had requested; there was a higher risk of extreme violence against this community; security personnel were inadequately trained and possessed illegal firearms; rape against women in Guatemala occurred at a high rate; Guatemala's justice system had serious problems and the vast majority of violence went unpunished.[66] Thus, the court found that the plaintiffs had made very specific allegations about the level of knowledge the parent corporation and its executives had of the human rights damages likely from the relocation action.[67]

---

[61] *See id.* at paras. 17–23, 49 (providing that the argument for piercing the corporate veil should be allowed to proceed to trial because the plaintiffs sufficiently pled that subsidiary was an agent of Hudbay Minerals).

[62] *See id.* at para. 54 (stating that the plaintiffs sufficiently pled "all material facts to establish the constituent elements of their claim of direct negligence against Hudbay").

[63] *See id.* at paras. 56, 58 (noting that the plaintiffs did not attempt to prove that the facts of their case fit under a duty of care already established in a certain category of cases, so it becomes "necessary to apply the test for establishing a novel duty of care") (internal citation omitted).

[64] *Id.* at para 57.

[65] *See id.* at para. 59 (explaining that the court first must ask whether the harm was a "reasonably foreseeable consequence of the defendant's act").

[66] *See id.* at paras. 60–65 (describing the acts committed by the security forces during the forceful eviction of the local inhabitants).

[67] *See id.* at para. 65 ("The plaintiffs have pleaded facts which, if proven at trial, could establish that the harm complained of was the reasonably foreseeable consequence of the defendants' conduct.").

Moreover, the court found that the plaintiffs had sufficiently pled proximity, which under Canadian law exists if "the circumstances of the relationship inhering between the plaintiff and the defendant are of such a nature that the defendant may be said to be under an obligation to be mindful of the plaintiff's legitimate interests in conducting his or her affairs."[68] The court noted that the plaintiffs pleaded that: the parent corporation paid specific attention to the problems of the land conflict between its subsidiary and the Mayan village; the CEO publicly stated that the parent did everything in its power to ensure that the evictions were carried out in accordance with human rights; the parent made public statements regarding its relationship with the Mayan villages; the parent was directly in charge of the operations; and that it assumed direct control over the security personnel.[69] Finally, the court also found there was no obvious policy reason to restrict the duty.[70]

Similar to the UK cases, this case is significant, but its application is still fairly limited given the proximity element.[71] In the case, the plaintiffs alleged significant facts establishing a relationship between the parent and the community, and that the parent had assumed control over security personnel.[72] Thus, the cases have application and promise in certain, limited situations, but they do not stand for the proposition of a general duty of care based on establishing a subsidiary in a high-risk environment. Thus, the duty of care theory is limited to where a parent legally assumes a direct obligation toward employees, or, possibly toward others, such as community members. The parent *assumes* these obligations through its level of knowledge and involvement or apparent involvement or responsibility in the subsidiary's actions. There has to be a fair amount of knowledge or involvement on the part of the parent for a direct duty of care to be established, albeit not the amount often required to pierce the corporate veil.[73] Thus, although this approach does present a way forward for victims to hold a parent liable when the parent has some direct knowledge and some level of involvement, it does not address the problem of victims left without a remedy where the parent has a more separate relationship from

---

[68] *Id.* at para. 66 (internal citations omitted).
[69] *See id.* at para. 67 (discussing how the parent corporation's conduct satisfies factors that indicate a relationship of sufficient proximity with the subsidiary).
[70] *See id.* at para. 74 ("A court should be reluctant to dismiss a claim as disclosing no reasonable cause of action based on policy reasons at the motion stage before there is a record on which a court can analyze the strength and weaknesses of the policy arguments.") (internal citation omitted).
[71] *See id.* (emphasizing the proximity issue).
[72] *See id.* at para. 75 (finding that plaintiffs sufficiently pleaded the elements required for a novel duty of care, that defendants breached that duty of care, that defendants' breach caused, and that it was not plain and obvious that the complaint did not disclose a claim in negligence).
[73] *See Choc v. Hudbay Minerals, supra* note 44, para. 45 (discussing the three situations where the corporate veil may be pierced as "(a) where the corporation is completely dominated and controlled and being used as a shield for fraud or improper conduct; (b) where the corporation has acted as the authorized agent of its controllers, corporate or human; and (c) where a statute or contract requires it") (internal citations and quotation marks omitted).

the subsidiary but still greatly benefits financially from the fact that it created a subsidiary in a high-risk environment.[74]

7.1.4 Expanded Tort Law Approach Toward Parental Duty of Care to Foreseeable Victims

Another similar approach is based on general tort law, and argues that a parent corporation has a duty to foreseeable victims of harm by its subsidiary, especially where the subsidiary operates in a high-risk industry, or in a country known to pose business-related human rights risks. This approach should not be confused with the approach discussed in the prior section, where parent corporations have been held liable for their *own* actions, such as where they have assumed responsibilities of a subsidiary or affiliate but failed in those responsibilities, where the parent exercises de facto control over an operation that results in injury, or where the parent has breached a duty it owed directly to certain stakeholders, such as employees. Rather, the tort-based approach holds the potential of ensuring that parent corporations are responsible for the harm of *subsidiaries'* human rights violations. Under this theory, the parent corporation would owe a duty of care to foreseeable victims of a subsidiary's actions.

The scholar that appears to have taken this parental "duty of care" approach the furthest is Professor Radu Mares of the Netherlands.[75] Professor Mares has suggested holding a company liable for acts of its subsidiaries based on the behavior and actions of the parent in creating a subsidiary to operate in a "high risk" country – one that does not have effective legal mechanisms.[76] Specifically, he argues that, where a core company sets up a separate entity for the purpose of making a profit, the core company should be held responsible for the subsidiary's torts under notions of due diligence, and that doing so without due diligence creates an unreasonable risk, which should be considered an affirmative wrong under the law.[77] His theory would require core companies to retain some responsibility in "initial structuring and ongoing oversight."[78]

---

[74] See Mares, *supra* note 40 at 169, 177 (introducing the conceptual and pragmatic questions that arise when determining a standard for due diligence).

[75] See generally id.

[76] See id. at 176–78 (arguing that the core company's decision to establish a "separated entity in a dangerous environment (poorly governed developing country)" and to let "it loose with a certain mandate (profit-making) without any checks and oversight over subsidiary activities" earns the core company responsibility under the due diligence standard).

[77] See id. at 176–77 (discussing how the parent corporation injures the subsidiary through its own conduct when it instructs the subsidiary to commit wrongful actions).

[78] See id. at 177 (noting that, under the due diligence approach, a "duly diligent company would be free to set up subsidiaries but should retain some responsibility" regarding the original set-up, as well as the long-term supervision of the work).

Mares notes that the vulnerability of rights holders in less developed countries justifies a responsibility to act where there are not effective remedies available.[79] Mares uses classic tort theory to justify his approach, noting that the Restatement of Torts supports an actor being found negligent where its actions involve "an unreasonable risk of harm to another through the foreseeable action of a third person."[80] He notes that such foreseeability could occur especially with subsidiaries in the extraction industries in countries where the legal framework is weak.[81] This is because the Restatement of Torts supports liability for negligent selection of a contractor which poses foreseeable risks;[82] and supports liability for the company to take "special precautions" to maintain safety where a contractor relationship evinces a "peculiar risk of harm," i.e., abnormally dangerous activities.[83] So, by analogy, extractive industries in countries with weak legal frameworks would be considered inherently high risk or abnormally dangerous – at least foreseeably so – and a duty to prevent such foreseeable harm would then attach.

This approach holds great promise, and shares many similarities with the statutory approach I advocate in this book. First, it would provide a remedy to victims in those situations where parent corporations operate through a subsidiary or affiliate where the parent knew or should have known that operations through the subsidiary or affiliate put individuals at risk of human rights violations. This would be true regardless of the level of actual control the parent company asserted over the subsidiary or affiliate. Second, in cases brought in the United States, because this approach focuses on the parent's actions rather than the subsidiary's actions, it might be able to overcome any barrier that *Kiobel* created.

But it, too, has its limitations. First, this tort-based duty of care approach "has an uneasy co-existence with the separation of entities principle."[84] It underestimates this "uneasy co-existence," given how entrenched are the notions of limited liability

---

[79] See id. at 180 (explaining that the vulnerability of citizens in underdeveloped countries is not caused by poverty or the threat of harm by businesses, but by the lack of effective remedies available).

[80] See id. at 181 (citing Restatement (Second) of Torts § 302 (AM. LAW. INST. 1965)) (providing that §302 applies to third-party conduct, whether it is negligent or intentional).

[81] See id. (discussing an example in the instance of setting up a mining site, in that the "undeniable fact is that setting up a mining operations does create risks of harm for local communities, risks that are more likely and severe when the legal frameworks are weak").

[82] See id. at 182 ("So an employer can be held liable for the actions of an independent contractor if the employer was negligent in hiring or retaining that contractor, if the employer knew, or should have known with reasonable care, that the contractor was reckless or incompetent.").

[83] See id. at 182–83 (noting that "special precautions" are required when "an independent contractor poses a peculiar risk of harm," and that in "tort it seems that 'peculiar' risks arise out of 'inherently dangerous' activities") (internal citation omitted).

[84] See id. at 192 (concluding that the responsibility for parent companies to take action to prevent human rights abuses in subsidiary work abroad is at tension with the traditional accepted separation of entities principle, which restricts the piercing of the corporate veil).

in the law.[85] In fact, the doctrine of limited liability exists specifically to shield parent companies from liability for the actions of their subsidiaries; the principle recognizes that parents will create subsidiaries in order to (at least in part) limit liability for economic activity.[86]

Furthermore, although it is possible under tort theory to establish a duty and breach on the part of the parent for its own actions (or inactions), the theory also underestimates both the difficulty of establishing a duty of care for third-party actions under traditional tort law given the conventionally narrow exceptions that apply for non-liability of third-party conduct, and establishing a breach – that the actor acted in a way that was not in line with what a reasonable person (or corporation) would do.[87] For example, deciding whether the parent "breached" its duty (assuming such a duty can be established, itself a possible but difficult exercise) will likely depend on whether the parent company was negligent in establishing the subsidiary or affiliate. But both accessing and proving the facts necessary to establish a duty of care or a breach may be very difficult, especially given that the corporation will have control over the information.

Even assuming that the practical barriers can be overcome, and a duty of care established, one must still show there was negligence in the breach of said duty – which is to say, the question becomes whether the corporation acted in a manner which a reasonable corporation would not have done.[88] Questions of negligence in such suits typically depend on what a "reasonable" corporation would do, which, in turn, may depend on what is typical in the industry. Courts have historically held that a breach of duty cannot be found when the defendant has adhered to normal business practices,[89] and this might be difficult to overcome where the corporation is simply engaging in the type of activity in which other corporations engage by creating subsidiaries to operate abroad.[90] The factual pattern required to establish both a duty and breach will therefore be unique and limited. It may be, for example,

---

[85] *See* Case Comment, *F. Corporations: Perpetual Real Estate v. Michaelson Properties*, 50 WASH. & LEE L. REV. 285, 286 (1993) ("Courts have been willing to depart from the principle of the corporation as a separate entity only under certain circumstances.").

[86] *See id.* (describing the purposes of limited liability – to stimulate business investment and protect certain entities from the actions of others).

[87] *See* Restatement (Second) of Torts § 283 (1965) ("Unless the actor is a child, the standard of conduct to which he must conform to avoid being negligent is that of a reasonable man under like circumstances.").

[88] *Id.* (stating the standard of the reasonable man).

[89] *See Texas & Pac. Ry., Co. v. Behymer*, 189 U.S. 468, 470 (1903) ("What usually is done may be evidence of what ought to be done, but what ought to be done is fixed by a standard of reasonable prudence, whether it usually is complied with or not.") (internal citation omitted); *Shandrew v. Chi. St. P., M. & O. Ry. Co.*, 142 F. 320, 325–26 (8th Cir. 1905) (citing *Behymer* at 470) (noting that the defendant company's negligence is determined by comparison to the conduct of other prudent railway companies).

[90] *See* Mares, *supra* note 40 at 178 (elaborating on the various types of conduct for which core corporations are liable abroad, including the "risks for driving, of medical care, of handling weapons, of manufacturing goods").

only found in those cases where the plaintiff can establish that the parent corporation, either overtly or through its conduct, undertook a responsibility for protection of the plaintiff[91] (the UK and Canadian cases appear to fall into this description).[92] Only in those rare situations where plaintiffs can actually *establish* a duty of care or breach will there be potential for recovery.

Other limitations include many of those relevant to all tort-based theories that involve extraterritorial conduct. One significant limitation in the United States and Canada is the doctrine of *forum non conveniens*, which allows judges to dismiss an extraterritorial-based case on the grounds that another court is more appropriate and convenient for the parties and the fact-finders, given that evidence and witnesses are easier to access in the place where the harm occurred – i.e., in the host country. Although courts are typically not supposed to invoke this doctrine where a plaintiff can establish that no remedy exists in the forum or the action would otherwise be futile, courts often do dismiss such a case on this basis. And when cases are dismissed on the basis of *forum non conveniens*, 98 percent of them are not refiled in the host country – meaning that the obstacles discussed in Chapter 3 have probably prevented the victims from refiling the suit in the host country.[93]

Another limitation is what is referred to as "choice of law" determinations. When a court is adjudicating a tort that has occurred abroad, it has to decide what law to apply – the law of the country (or for the United States, the state) where the case has been brought or the law of the country where the tort occurred. If the law is the same in both places, it does not matter. But typically, in human rights cases, the law is not the same. The elements of the tort may vary – if a cause of action even exists – but it is also likely that there are differences in statutes of limitation, immunity, and other doctrines. For example, recent UK legislation requires that any damages not be based on the value of currency in the UK but the value of currency in the host state, often resulting in smaller damage awards and limiting redress.

---

[91] *See id.* § 324(A) (describing that a person is liable to render services to another third person for harm resulting from his failure to exercise reasonable care, if "(a) his failure increases the risk of harm, or (b) he performs a duty owed by the other to the third person, or (c) harm is suffered because of reliance"); *id.* at cmt. a ("The rule stated in this Section parallels the one stated in § 323, as to the liability of the actor to the one to whom he has undertaken to render services. This Section deals with the liability to third persons.").

[92] *See* Gwynne Skinner, *Rethinking Limited Liability of Parent Corporations for Foreign Subsidiaries' Violations of International Human Rights Law*, 72 WASH. & LEE L. REV. 1769, n241–90 (2015) (analyzing the liability of parent corporations to third party human rights abuses in *Choc* and *Chandler*).

[93] *Forum non conveniens* is not as great of a problem in Europe given that under EU regulations, a court is supposed to allow a case to proceed, even if the abuse and harm occurred extraterritorially, as long as the defendant corporation is domiciled in the EU country. However, there are other limitations to bringing tort claims that affect Europe in particular, including the robust regulatory state and limitations on tort claims, as well as limitations on discovery that may create barriers to establishing the necessary factual basis for negligence claims.

Where the law differs, a court typically applies the law of the forum where the harm occurred – the host state. Often, the law of host states is not favorable to plaintiffs. Applications of a host country's laws in tort actions has resulted in cases being dismissed; for example, a court in the Netherlands ruled that under Nigerian law, a parent company had no obligation to prevent its subsidiary from harming third parties.[94] The few negligence-based claims against US parent companies for actions of subsidiaries abroad have thus far been dismissed because courts have demurred in taking jurisdiction over claims based on foreign tort law due to the complex and novel tort claims associated with such actions.[95]

Finally, unfortunately, some courts in the United States have rejected this theory outright, noting that limited liability of parent corporations trumps such a duty of care for a subsidiary's actions, and one would think that other courts might find similarly.[96] But even though legal duties of parent corporations might not naturally arise in tort under most states' laws in the United States, the reasons behind the

---

[94] See Geert van Calster, *No Big Surprises in Dutch Shell Nigeria/Royal Dutch Shell ruling*, GAVC Law (Jan. 31, 2013), http://gavclaw.com/2013/01/31/no-big-surprises-in-dutch-shell-nigeria-royal-dutch-shell-ruling/ (last visited January 1, 2020) (reporting on the Dutch court ruling that Nigerian law applied in the suit brought by a Dutch environment NGO against Shell corporation and other similar holding companies for environmental damages sustained in Nigeria); *see also* Akpan v. Royal Dutch Shell, No. 337050/HA ZA 09-1580 (District Court of the Hague, Jan. 30, 2013) (the district court dismissed all claims against the parent companies, finding no reason to depart from the principle in Nigerian tort law that there is no general duty of care to prevent others from suffering harm as a result of the activities of third parties).

[95] See Romero v. Drummond Co., 552 F.3d 1303, 1318 (11th Cir. 2008) (affirming dismissal of the plaintiffs' claims for intentional torts and negligence because "Alabama law does not apply to injuries that occurred outside the state"); In re Chiquita Brands Int'l, Inc., Alien Tort Statute and S'holder Derivative Litig., 792 F. Supp. 2d 1301, 1355–56 (S.D. Fl. 2011) (dismissing negligence claims the plaintiffs brought under various US state law due to the extraterritorial nature of the conduct at issue); Roe I v. Bridgestone Corp., 492 F. Supp. 2d 988, 1024 (S.D. Ind. 2007) (dismissing state law claims because "[p]laintiffs have not yet articulated a viable basis for applying California law or Indiana law to the management of a Plantation in Liberia").

[96] See Gwynne Skinner, Robert McCorquodale, Olivier de Schutter, & Andie Lambe, THE THIRD PILLAR: ACCESS TO JUDICIAL REMEDIES FOR HUMAN RIGHTS VIOLATIONS BY TRANSNATIONAL BUSINESSES n482 (2013) (citing Bowoto v. Chevron Texaco Co., 312 F. Supp. 2d 1229, 1235-40 (N.D. Cal. 2004) (refusing to pierce the corporate veil, but holding that the case could proceed under agency law) (A jury trial subsequently resulted in a verdict for defendants). Bowoto v. Chevron Corp., 2009 U.S. Dist. LEXIS 21944 (N.D. Cal. 2009); In re South African Apartheid Litigation, 633 F. Supp. 2d 117 (S.D.N.Y. 2009) (classes of South Africans failed to state a claim against a parent company for acts of its subsidiary; although the parent allegedly maintained a preferential supply agreement with the subsidiary and monitored the use of the parent's technology, a principal-agent relationship was not sufficiently alleged with respect to the design and maintenance of computer systems that predated the parent's collaborative relationship with the subsidiary, and the plaintiffs did not allege that the parent had the right to command subsidiary to sever the subsidiary's long-term preexisting relationship with the South African government); Exxon Mobil Corp., 573 F. Supp. 2d at 30 (finding Exxon Mobil could be liable under an agency theory, but rejecting other theories of liability); Sinaltrainal v. Coca-Cola Co., 256 F. Supp. 2d 1345, 1354 (S.D. Fla. 2003), *aff'd*, 578 F.3d 1252 (11th Cir. 2009) (rejecting agency theories on the grounds that the parent company had nothing more than a franchise-type relationship with the Colombian entity accused of wrongdoing).

tort-based parental duty of care approach support enactment of statutory duties and liability in certain situations to ensure that victims of businesses' human rights violations are not left remediless.

7.2 ENSURING PARENT CORPORATION LIABILITY THROUGH LEGISLATION

Given the limitations of the various theories for holding parent corporations liable for acts of their subsidiaries and affiliates, and given the limitations of the tort-based approach, the best method to ensure redress for international victims of human rights abuses by TNCs would be statutory. Policymakers should consider enacting legislation to create liability on the part of parent companies for acts of their subsidiaries and affiliates which result in harm overseas. There are several options for such legislation. One option, and the one that I advocate, is simply to legislate that parent corporations are strictly liable for any harm resulting from the extraterritorial acts of majority-owned subsidiaries and other affiliates they control which breach international human rights law, at least in those instances where the plaintiffs cannot realistically obtain a remedy from the subsidiary or affiliate in the host country. Under this strict liability approach, the parent corporation would not have the opportunity to avoid liability under any specific affirmative defense such as due diligence.

Other similar options exist, and could be considered as well. For example, one option would be to provide for liability only in certain high-risk industries and/or when operating in high-risk or fragile countries with known problems in their judiciary. However, this approach is complicated given that many believe that designation of certain countries as fragile or high-risk is too political and problematic (and indeed, the designation of countries as high-risk by US or European judicial bodies would be likely be fraught and politically untenable).[97] Alternatively, policymakers could limit liability for only those extraterritorial actions that violate international human rights law. The argument here would be that TNCs operating internationally through subsidiaries and affiliates have a special obligation to provide a remedy to victims when those subsidiaries and affiliates violate international human rights legal norms.

Alternatively, rather than requiring that parent corporations be strictly liable for harms arising from the extraterritorial acts of their subsidiaries or affiliates they control, policy-makers could create a statutory duty of care on the part of parent corporations toward employees and members of the community, to be applied when the parent corporation acts extraterritorially through a subsidiary. The victims would

---

[97] I recommended this approach in a prior article, but during many presentations and discussions, many academics and practitioners voiced their concern with designating certain countries as "high-risk" or fragile, noting that such would prove to be too political to be practical.

not have to establish that such a duty exists under the law, which can be a legal obstacle. In particular, enacting such a statute would address the limitations that some courts in the United States have imposed when finding that parent corporations do not owe a duty of care to anyone for the acts of their subsidiaries, given the doctrine of limited liability.

However, under this approach the victims would still need to establish that the parent corporations breached the statutory duty of care. As mentioned above, establishing a breach because a parent created or allowed a subsidiary to operate in a fragile country might still prove to be difficult, given that the victims would have to establish that the corporation acted outside industry standards. Moreover, all of the barriers associated with tort theory generally do not make this option very satisfactory – including limited access to information, difficulties with transnational application of discovery, and the hurdle of proving causation.

Holding parent corporations strictly liable for the harm resulting from human rights violations of their majority-owned subsidiaries and affiliates they control is the best approach for a variety of reasons. First, with this approach, victims are entitled to receive a remedy for their harm resulting from international human rights violations of a majority-owned company, without the need to establish that the parent corporation had control over the subsidiary. I believe this is appropriate given that the parent derives direct economic benefits from the operations of their subsidiary, while victims absorb the cost. This solution simply shifts to the entity receiving the direct benefit the costs from the subsidiary's operations, much like product liability does in the United States. As a matter of public policy, it should be those entities that derive the benefits that absorb the costs.[98] In addition, a parent corporation has the ability, at least in theory, to control a majority-owned subsidiary. Requiring automatic liability also creates the incentive for the parent corporation to engage in real, substantial due diligence to prevent human rights abuses to minimize the risk of a lawsuit.

This statutory strict liability approach is not as untested as it may seem. In the area of environmental law in the United States, for example, the Comprehensive Environmental Response, Compensation, and Liability Act (CERCLA, a.k.a. Superfund)[99] was enacted as a strict liability statute, with the novel application of strict, retroactive, joint and several liability on potentially responsible parties ("PRPs") who at any point owned or controlled a hazardous waste site or generated or disposed of hazardous materials at the site.[100] Drawing upon the theories of strict liability for abnormally

---

[98] Where a state actor is also involved, a corporation could legitimately argue that the state should also be responsible for the cost of the harm. In such situations, a parent corporation could join the state in the lawsuit, could seek remedy from the state through its negotiations, or could ask a court to attribute to it only the percentage of the harm it is responsible for.
[99] 42 U.S.C. § 9601 et seq. (1980).
[100] Id., see generally Enforcement: Superfund Liability, UNITED STATES ENVIRONMENTAL PROTECTION AGENCY, https://www.epa.gov/enforcement/superfund-liability (last accessed July 2, 2018).

hazardous activities and products liability,[101] Congress, in drafting CERCLA, chose strict liability as the theory that best ensured the public policy goals of appropriate distribution of risks from privately profitable but publicly harmful activities. Congress further recognized that strict liability also incentivizes high levels of due diligence among corporate entities to prevent harms, and overcomes the real practical barriers to demonstrating negligence in complex situations where the duty, breach, and causation are ambiguous but the damages to victims are clear.[102]

Some might argue that it is not efficient from an economic point of view to hold parent corporations liable for "unforeseeable" harm of a subsidiary, even if wholly owned. However, it is highly unlikely that a subsidiary's violation of an international human rights standard would be truly unforeseeable, given that many business-related human rights violations occur in high-risk industries, in post-conflict areas, in countries where the entity is partially owned by a state that has had known problems with use of security forces, and the like. Rather, this would incentivize parent corporations to invest resources into their due diligence processes, to prevent human rights abuses, and to create early warning systems.

Conversely, some might argue that while redress for victims is important, allowing for strict liability in this situation would create a disincentive for corporations to invest in developing countries. But there are no studies that support this notion. In fact, given the benefits which parent corporations receive from the operations of subsidiaries, and the fact that this arrangement would incentivize parent corporations to engage in substantial risk assessment and due diligence to prevent human rights abuses, it is unlikely that requiring such liability would result in parent corporations stopping operations abroad. However, it is quite possible that requiring such liability might incentivize corporations to move operations from a subsidiary to other affiliates, such as contractors (who may then be liable in their own right for violations of human rights law, if domiciled in a state with strict liability legislation).

Thus, under the approach I recommend, a corporation would also be strictly liable for the human rights breaches of its affiliates that it does control. Despite the potential difficulties (discussed above) of a victim's establishing the requisite "control," I would require actual control in the case of affiliates given that the parent corporation does not directly benefit from the operations of an affiliate in the way it does from a subsidiary. Moreover, requiring a corporation to be liable for acts of an affiliate it does not control would likely not be feasible. Such expansive application could open up a

---

[101] See S. REP. No. 848, 96th Cong., 2d Sess. 14 (1980), reprinted in 1 U.S. SENATE COMNI. ON ENV'T & PUBLIC WORKS, A LEGISLATIVE HISTORY OF THE COMPREHENSIVE ENVTL. RESPONSE, COMPENSATION, AND LIABILITY OF 1980 (SUPERFUND), PUBLIC LAW 96–510, 97th Cong., 2d Sess. 321 (1983) ("The most analogous areas of the law are product liability and liability for abnormally dangerous activities.").

[102] See Lynda J. Oswald, *Strict Liability of Individuals Under CERCLA: A Normative Analysis*, 20 B. C. ENVT'L. AFF. L. REV. 579, 598–603 (1993), https://lawdigitalcommons.bc.edu/cgi/viewcontent.cgi?article=1436&context=ealr (last visited January 1, 2020).

corporation to significant liability that may in fact create a disincentive for corporations to investing abroad. The balancing of public policy goals thus weighs toward strict liability strictly applied for subsidiaries of TNCs who are responsible for human rights abuses, but limited application of strict liability to affiliates who are actually controlled by the TNC. While this is a potential loophole in some instances (such as use of local contractors to engage in the conduct that would otherwise give rise to liability), the overall statutory scheme should incentivize a strong culture of due diligence and care on the part of the TNC and appropriately distribute the harms of economically significant activity with human rights impacts to the entity profiting from such activity and away from the victims of such abuse.

7.3 PROPOSALS FOR ADDRESSING LIMITS TO SUBJECT MATTER JURISDICTION

Dealing with extraterritorial human rights violations by businesses is an issue in all jurisdictions. In the United States, the Supreme Court's decision in Kiobel v. Royal Dutch Petroleum has further confused matters. In Europe, by contrast, the Brussels Regulation, recast mandates the national courts of the EU Member States to accept jurisdiction in civil liability cases filed against defendants domiciled in the forum state. The situation in Switzerland is similar. However, the issue of courts' jurisdiction over businesses not domiciled in the European Union (such as foreign subsidiaries of European businesses) is not currently addressed in the Brussels Regulation, recast. National legal systems take a variety of approaches to this issue. Given such divergence, minimum rules should be defined in this area. Actions by all these states, recommended in further detail below, would ensure a greater degree of coherence across home states to enable victims of violations that occurred outside the forum state to bring a case in these states. This would give stability and certainty for business, governments, and civil society.

7.3.1 *Expand Subject Matter Jurisdiction by Statute*

The proposal I advance for ensuring that courts have subject matter jurisdiction over extraterritorial violations of international human rights law is fairly simple – legislative bodies should enact statutes that provide causes of actions for extraterritorial claims for violations of international human rights. Countries, especially countries where TNCs are domiciled or do substantial business, should provide for more expansive subject matter jurisdiction, including for extraterritorial harm. All countries should ensure that causes of actions exist which will allow victims to bring claims, not just for "garden-variety torts," but for torts in violation of CIL. Many countries in Europe already allow subject matter jurisdiction for certain extraterritorial torts against corporations over whom they have personal jurisdiction, and both the United States and Canada should move in this direction.

7.3.1.1 United States

In the United States, Congress should take legislative action to ensure that victims of business-related human rights abuse have access to avenues that will enable access to effective remedy. Specifically, Congress should do the following:

AMEND THE ATS TO CLARIFY THAT IT APPLIES TO EXTRATERRITORIAL CONDUCT IN ORDER TO OVERCOME THE BARRIER *KIOBEL* HAS ERECTED There is precedent for such legislation, most similarly, the Foreign Corrupt Practices Act (FCPA). Moreover, Congress should amend the TVPA to provide that corporations, and not just individuals, be vicariously liability for torture and extrajudicial killing.

Amending the ATS to clarify that it pertains to conduct occurring abroad is the clearest way to move forward in reducing the barrier *Kiobel* has erected. Although such legislation may be very difficult to achieve, arguments for such legislative changes do exist. For example, even those policy-makers who are sympathetic to corporate interests may also want to portray themselves as pro-human rights. Thus, proposed legislation that is characterized as pro-human rights may stand a better chance of succeeding than expected. There have been examples of this occurring, such as section 1502 (conflict minerals section) of the Dodd-Frank Act.

Second, since *Kiobel*'s touch and concern requirement and the decision in *Jesner* result in US businesses being the only feasible defendants in ATS litigation, as opposed to other businesses over which US courts have personal jurisdiction, an argument exists that the ATS should apply to extraterritorial conduct generally, and that it allows claims against foreign corporations so as to create a level playing field for US corporations among corporations doing work abroad.

Some may question whether allowing such claims in US courts is proper under notions of comity, and could affect the US's foreign relations.[103] But US courts adjudicated such extraterritorial human rights violations under the ATS for decades without any serious foreign relations implications. And there are other doctrines to alleviate any such concerns, such as the *forum non conveniens* doctrine, which allows courts to dismiss the case when they believe an alternative jurisdiction is available and more convenient. Moreover, the State Department has available to it the ability to weigh in on such cases before court, and indeed has done so on numerous occasions in the past.[104]

AMEND THE TORTURE VICTIM PROTECTION ACT TO APPLY TO LEGAL PERSONS AND EXPAND THE TYPE OF CLAIMS ALLOWED Amending the TVPA so that legal persons (including businesses) can be defendants, as opposed to "individuals,"

---

[103] Elliot Schrage, *Judging Corporate Accountability in the Global Economy*, 42 COLUM. J. INT'L L. 153 (2003).
[104] *See id.* Equally, there are numerous cases that the State Department has chosen not to intervene in.

would rectify many of the barriers regarding extraterritoriality. The TVPA is a specific cause of action for extraterritorial human rights violations that Congress has enacted. This might be palatable to some policy-makers because there already exists an inherent limitation to TVPA claims, given that the TVPA applies only to those "acting under actual or apparent authority, or color of law, of any foreign nation," as opposed to any corporation working abroad. Thus, even if such a change were made, only those corporations which are actively working under authority of a foreign state and engaging in human rights violations while doing so could be potential defendants. In addition, ideally, any such amendment should also clarify that legal persons can be defendants in such cases where they have conspired with, aided and abetted, or are otherwise complicit in, such actions along with foreign governments. Finally, in order to rectify the limitation on human rights cases for extraterritorial conduct post-*Kiobel*, any amendment expanding the TVPA to allow for legal persons to be defendants should also include more types of violations than those currently allowed under the TVPA, namely torture and extrajudicial killing. For example, the TVPA should be expanded to allow for violations such as war crimes, forced disappearance, ethnic cleansing, and cruel, inhuman, and degrading treatment.

A note of caution must be made regarding any new potential amendments. Advocates must be careful to ensure that any possible new legislation does not affect victims' rights under other statutes. When the TVPA was enacted in 1991, its legislative history made clear that Congress did not intend the TVPA to supplant the ATS or the claims brought thereunder, and that Congress believes it is appropriate for federal courts to adjudicate human rights claims that occur abroad under the ATS. Any attempts to amend the TVPA or enact any new legislation should be sure to include appropriate legislative history indicating that such amendments are not meant to limit rights under the ATS or other statutes.

ENACT STATE LAWS CRIMINALIZING VIOLATIONS OF INTERNATIONAL HUMAN RIGHTS LAW AND PROVIDING PRIVATE RIGHTS OF ACTION FOR SUCH VIOLATIONS Given that most corporate legal matters are addressed by the individual states, state legislatures should enact or amend existing state statutes both to criminalize extraterritorial violations of international human rights law by businesses, and also to provide for parallel private rights of action against such businesses for the violations.[105] States should also ensure that with the private rights of action, the choice of law – the applicable law – in these cases should be CIL for purposes of the underlying violation, and the law of the forum state with regard to other matters.

---

[105] There likely is no need to enact legislation at the state level to clarify that state courts' common law torts apply abroad because (1) state common law already assumes such is the case for violations of state law, if state law applies, and (2) states already have choice of law analysis they would apply to transitory tort violations.

7.3.1.2 Canada

Canada should enact legislation providing for jurisdiction over extraterritorial violations of human rights norms; indeed, Canada has had such legislation pending for many years. Enacting such a statute is critical, given Canada's large extraterritorial extraction industry. Neither Canada as a whole nor its provinces have a statute that allows plaintiffs to bring a cause of action directly for violations of CIL. Although there is some case law suggesting that CIL is part of Canada's common law, a private cause of action does not yet clearly exist in the manner that such exists in the United States. There have been attempts at introducing a bill that would provide jurisdiction over such claims, but such attempts have not yet succeeded. Given the number of businesses in Canada that engage in activity abroad, some of which have resulted in cases alleging violations of human rights, advocates should engage in new efforts for the enactment of such legislation, either at the national level or at the provincial level. Recommendations for limitations and ways to narrow the causes of action, if such would be needed to be palatable, should include elements of the above regarding the ATS and TVPA in the United States.

7.3.1.3 Europe

Most European countries, as well as the European Union generally, provide that the home country where a corporation is domiciled, as long as it is in the European Union, should hear claims that take place abroad. However, these cases are for breaches of tort law. Because it matters to victims to be able to identify a harm as a human rights harm, versus a general tort, and because of the limitations of bringing general tort claims, the European Union should require EU countries to enact legislation which enables claims alleging human rights harms to be brought.

Additionally, the European Commission should reintroduce its proposal (which it considered making as part of the 2011 recast of Brussels I Regulation) to add a *"forum necessitatis"* provision to the Brussels I Regulation. This would require the courts of those Member States which do not already have this provision, to exercise jurisdiction if no other forum guaranteeing the right to a fair trial is available, and the dispute has a sufficient connection with the Member State concerned. This would be an additional means by which EU Member States could discharge their duty to provide effective access to justice for victims of human rights violations linked to corporations domiciled in their territory.

As a note of caution regarding future revisions of jurisdictional rules in Europe, any proposed reform should be carefully evaluated to ensure that they will not limit access to the courts for extraterritorial cases that is currently available in some EU Member States.

More in-depth discussion of forum of necessity follows in the next section.

7.4 ADOPTION OF JURISDICTION/FORUM BY NECESSITY

Policymakers could enact policies to ensure that their courts assert subject matter jurisdiction over a TNC when a person bringing the claim can establish either that: (1) there is no other forum available; or (2) there is no chance that the victim could achieve a remedy in any country that might be able to assert personal jurisdiction over the TNC. This is referred to as "jurisdiction by necessity," "forum of necessity," or "*forum necessitatis.*" Forum of necessity is similar to *forum non conveniens*, but has the effect of the court asserting jurisdiction rather than dismissing it. One author has described jurisdiction by necessity as the "mirror image" of *forum non conveniens*, noting that *forum non conveniens* "gives defendants an extra chance to kill a case, whereas forum of necessity gives plaintiffs an extra chance to save it."[106]

Canadian courts have considered jurisdiction by necessity on at least one occasion in a corporate accountability case. However, the court in Association Canadienne Contre L'Impunité (ACCI) v. Anvil Mining Ltd, which involved human rights violations related to mining in the DRC, found that it had jurisdiction on a different basis, meaning it did not need to consider the *forum necessitatis* argument.[107] An appellate court later overturned the decision to accept jurisdiction. It went on to consider and reject the alternative argument of *forum necessitatis*.[108]

Several European countries also provide for jurisdiction by necessity in certain circumstances.[109] In fact, *forum necessitatis* is an autonomous ground of jurisdiction available in ten EU Member States in order to prevent a denial of justice – six based on statutory provisions and the others based on case law. Because most European countries do not distinguish between subject matter and personal jurisdiction in the way the United States does, the doctrine has been used for establishing both subject matter and personal jurisdiction simultaneously in the event that the country could not otherwise assert jurisdiction over the claim or person. For example, Swiss law provides for *forum necessitatis* in Swiss courts for victims of extraterritorial conduct where there is no other reasonable or competent forum; however, the claim must present some relationship to Switzerland.[110] In the Netherlands, the doctrine is broader, with a court being able to assert civil jurisdiction over claims that would

---

[106] Goldhaber, *supra* note 45 at 135.
[107] Ass'n Canadienne Contre L'Impunité (A.C.C.I.) v. Anvil Mining Ltd., 2011 QCSC 1966 (Can. Que.).
[108] Anvil Mining Ltd. v. Ass'n Canadienne Contre L'Impunité [2012] QCCA 117.
[109] In addition, there has been a proposal before the European Parliament, at least for jurisdiction by necessity in order to enforce a judgment. See *Proposal for a Regulation of the European Parliament and of the Council on Jurisdiction and the Regulation and Enforcement of Judgments in Civil and Commercial Matters*, at 8, COM (2010) 748 final (Dec. 14, 2010) (noting that the jurisdiction by necessity doctrine "currently exists in a sizeable group of Member States and has the advantage of ensuring that a judgment can be enforced in the State where it was issued"). This proposal was not taken up when the Brussels Regulation was recast.
[110] Swiss Law on Private International Law, Loi federate sur le droit international privé [LDIP] Dec. 18, 1987, RS 291 (Switz.), art. 3.

not fall within another basis for jurisdiction if those claims cannot effectively be brought in the host country.[111] French courts, too, have cited Article 6 of the European Convention on Human Rights as the rationale for what they term "exceptional jurisdiction" where no other court could offer a forum, in a dispute between an Iranian company and the State of Israel, as well as in an employment claim against an international organization.[112]

The United States has not yet allowed jurisdiction or forum by necessity. The Supreme Court considered the possibility of invoking the doctrine of "jurisdiction by necessity" in the context of personal jurisdiction (not subject matter jurisdiction) in Helicopteros Nacionales de Colom., S.A. v. Hall[113] but did not discuss the doctrine in any detail.

All countries that have not done so should consider providing for jurisdiction or forum by necessity where victims of TNC-related human rights abuses cannot otherwise find an available forum able to assert jurisdiction, or where bringing a claim in a particular jurisdiction would be futile. Many scholars have advocated for a similar approach.[114]

---

[111] See Cass. Civ. lère, 19 November 1985, Cognacs and Brandies, JDI 1986; Cass. Civ. lère, 23 May 2013, Prieur. For Dutch cases invoking the doctrine, see e.g., Ktg. Amsterdam 27 April 2000, 18 Nederlands Internationaal Privaatrecht No. 315, at 472 (2000) (Saloum/Kuwait Airways Corp.) (Neth.); Ktg. Amsterdam 5 January 1996, 14 Nederlands Internationaal Privaatrecht No. 145, at 222 (1996) (Abood/Kuwait Airways Corp.) (Neth.) (assuming jurisdiction over civil claims brought by Iraqi pilots who asserted that they could not receive a fair trial if forced to bring their claims before the courts in Kuwait); Rb's-Gravenhage 21 March 2012, ECLI:NL:RBSGR:2012:BV9748, https://uitspraken.rechtspraak.nl/inziendocument?id=ECLI:NL:RBSGR:2012:BV9748&showbutton=true&keyword=BV9748 (last visited January 1, 2020) (El-Hojouj/Unnamed Libyan Officials) (Neth.) (relying on *forum necessitatis*, the Dutch district court asserted jurisdiction over a civil claim brought by a foreign plaintiff in relation to his unlawful imprisonment and torture in Libya even though the only connection to the Netherlands was the plaintiff's presence in the Netherlands. The place of residence of the defendants was unknown. The court relied on the rule that allows Dutch courts to exercise jurisdiction over civil claims that would not normally fall under the ordinary bases for jurisdiction but where bringing those claims outside the Netherlands is simply impossible, either legally or practically).

[112] See Jodie A. Kirshner, *A Call for the EU to Assume Jurisdiction over Extraterritorial Corporate Human Rights Abuses*, 13 Nw. J. Int'l Hum. Rts. 1, 25 (2015), citing Council Regulation 4-2009, 2008 O.J.E.U. (L7/1) (on jurisdiction, applicable law, recognition and enforcement of decisions and cooperation in matters relating to maintenance obligations).

[113] 466 U.S. 408, 419 n.13 (1984).

[114] See, e.g., Kirshner, *supra* note 112; John Drobak, *Personal Jurisdiction in a Global World: The Impact of the Supreme Court's Decisions in Goodyear Dunlop Tires and Nicastro*, 90 Wash. U. L. Rev. 1707, 1748–49 (2013). See also Benedetta Ubertazzi, *Intellectual Property Rights and Exclusive (Subject Matter) Jurisdiction: Between Private and Public International Law*, 15 Marq. Intell. Prop. L. Rev. 357 (2011). For an in-depth review of the doctrine and how it might be used in the United States, see generally Tracy Lee Troutman, *Jurisdiction by Necessity: Examining One Proposal for Unbarring the Doors of Our Courts*, 21 Vand. J. Transnat'l L. 401 (1988) (proposing the development of a jurisdiction by necessity doctrine to promote fair play and justice for aggrieved plaintiffs who have no alternative ways to seek remedies).

7.5 MORE EXPANSIVE PERSONAL JURISDICTION OVER TNCS

Given the complex issue of personal jurisdiction and the barriers it creates to remedy, the United States, Europe, and Canada should move toward more expansive personal jurisdiction over TNCs that do business in their countries. Every country's courts should be able to assert general personal jurisdiction over a TNC whenever it does business in that country, including through a subsidiary, as long as there is subject matter jurisdiction (such as where a cause of action for extraterritorial conduct exists) over the claim. Given that TNCs profit tremendously from operations in Western countries, it is only fair that they be subjected to general jurisdiction, especially where victims of their subsidiaries' human rights violations cannot otherwise obtain a remedy in the host country. The Institute of International Law, a well-respected and Nobel Prize-winning international legal organization, enacted a resolution in 2015 providing for universal civil jurisdiction over TNCs where victims do not have available remedies in the courts of any other country.[115]

In Europe, because subject matter and personal jurisdiction are intertwined, I propose that the European Union enact legislation requiring that any EU Member State's courts should be able to assert jurisdiction over a foreign corporation for violations of international human rights law in a host state, as long as the foreign corporation conducts business in the EU country. Similarly, I propose that individual European countries enact similar legislation.

7.5.1 Current Jurisdictional Rules do not Reflect how TNCs Are Structured and Operate

Rules restricting assertions of personal jurisdiction over TNCs do not reflect how TNCs are structured and operate in today's world. Indeed, "a classic obstacle involving litigation against transnational businesses is that corporate groups are organized as a network of distinct legal entities."[116] Not only are such entities extremely complex and often lack transparency regarding their structure, they are increasingly amorphous. In today's global world, related legal entities within a transnational business enterprise are frequently without clear definitions, and often exist without obvious "parent" entities whose domicile or place of incorporation can

---

[115] See Skinner, *supra* note 40 at 677 n312 (2017); *see also* INST. OF INT'L L., 1 Res. En., *Universal Civil Jurisdiction with Regard to Reparation for International Crimes* (Aug. 30, 2015), http://www.andreasbucher-law.ch/images/stories/res_iil_en_universal_civil_jurisdiction.pdf (last visited February 24, 2020).

[116] *Id.* at 215; Kirshner, *supra* note 112 at 266–67 (noting how multinational corporations structure themselves to avoid a court's jurisdiction, and how they can shift financial assets within a corporate group); *see also* Virginia Harper Ho, *Of Enterprise Principles and Corporate Groups: Does Corporate Law Reach Human Rights?* 52 COLUM. J. TRANSNAT'L L. 113, 116–17 (2013) ("At its core, state corporate law governs the formation and 'internal affairs' of discrete legal entities, each with limited liability. It says little about the corporate group as an economic enterprise.").

easily be determined by even the most sophisticated actors. In fact, many organizations addressing similar problems with TNCs are beginning to drop the term "parent company" altogether, using other terms such as "lead company," given this reality. Most countries' legal systems are simply no match for these increasingly massive, complex, and amorphous legal structures.

Current jurisdictional paradigms based on a place of domicile or "home" simply do not match how TNCs are structured and operate today. Thus, expansion of personal jurisdiction over TNCs is both reasonable and fair.

7.6 LEGISLATION NEEDED TO EXPAND PERSONAL JURISDICTION

7.6.1 *The United States Should Require TNCs doing Business in the United States to Consent to General Personal Jurisdiction for Federal Causes of Action*

For the proposals set forth in this section to be effective for ATS claims, the *Jesner* prohibition on ATS claims against foreign corporations would need to be legislatively reversed. As discussed previously, general personal jurisdiction in the United States is limited as a matter of constitutional law, and post-*Daimler*, courts can only assert personal jurisdiction over a corporation "at home" in the jurisdiction, either due to being incorporated there or having its principal place of business there.[117] Thus there are limited options in the United States for expanding the scope of general personal jurisdiction over TNCs. My proposal is that Congress require any TNC doing business in the United States to consent to personal jurisdiction in the jurisdiction in which they conduct such business in those situations where Congress has provided a cause of action. Although individual states may be able to constitutionally require such consent, there are obstacles they face in doing so, primarily under the Commerce Clause. However, there is nothing that prevents the federal government from so requiring, and in fact, the Commerce Clause specifically allows the federal government to do so. Alternatively, Congress could require TNCs doing business in the United States to consent to personal jurisdiction if there is no other forum in which victims can achieve a remedy – statutorily setting forth "jurisdiction by necessity."

Given the complex corporate structure of TNCs, *Daimler* and *Goodyear*'s limitation of a court's assertion of personal jurisdiction over a corporate defendant will limit victims' ability to hold TNCs accountable and obtain a remedy even where Congress has provided one, because in many cases, courts will not be able to assert personal jurisdiction over the corporate entity responsible for the harm. Such is true

---

[117] The position is different for claims under the Trafficking Victims Protection Act; see Yem Ban, Sophea Bun, Sem Kosal, Nol Nakry, Keo Ratha, Sok Sang and Phan Sophea v. Doe Corporations, Phatthana Seafood Co., Ltd., Rubicon Resources, LLC, S.S. Frozen Food Co., Ltd. and Wales and Co. Universe Ltd. No. 2:16-CV-04271, (C.D. Cal, June 15, 2016), currently being litigated in the Ninth Circuit.

even though the responsible corporate entity has significant presence in the United States and engages in significant economic activity within the United States. As has already been discussed, TNCs with headquarters abroad do business in the United States more than in any country in the world.[118]

Given the above, just as US courts responded to changes in corporate structure and operations by expanding jurisdiction in the late 1800s and early 1900s, Congress should do the same now to account for analogous changes in TNCs and their operations. However, because *Daimler* and *Goodyear* are decisions based on the Constitution, Congress' actions are limited. For example, Congress cannot simply enact a statute providing that all corporations that do substantial and continuous business in the United States are subject to the personal jurisdiction of US courts. Such would likely be considered unconstitutional legislation. Therefore, Congress will necessarily need to accomplish the expanded personal jurisdiction by requiring the consent of TNCs doing business in the United States.[119]

Specifically, Congress should respond to *Daimler* and *Goodyear* by expanding jurisdiction, requiring any transnational businesses "doing business" in the United States to explicitly consent to general personal jurisdiction of US courts where Congress has provided for a cause of action for extraterritorial conduct. Although Congress could then statutorily determine what constitutes "doing business," it should include conducting business through the existence of a US subsidiary – essentially addressing the limitation set forth in *Daimler*. Although a full analysis is outside the scope of this book, the European Union, European countries, and Canada should also similarly expand personal jurisdiction over TNCs.[120] This is both because doing so would create a more even playing field for each region's

---

[118] *Foreign Direct Investment in the United States 2017*, ORGANIZATION FOR INTERNATIONAL INVESTMENT 2, https://ofii.org/sites/default/files/FDIUS%202017.pdf (last visited July 3, 2018). This is true on a cumulative basis, and has been true every year but for 2014, when flows into China and Hong Kong exceeded the United States. This was primarily due to the disinvestment of Vodafone (UK business). *Id.* at 3. *See* Deborah Orr, *The Largest Foreign Investments in the U.S.*, FORBES (Apr. 10, 2008), http://www.forbes.com/2008/04/10/foreign-investment-stocks-2000globalo8-biz-cx_do_0410investments.html (last visited January 1, 2020).

[119] At least two scholars have recently recommended that individual states could and should take this course of action where the state has some interest, such as where the harm occurs in the state or the plaintiffs reside in the state. Cassandra Burke Robertson & Charles W. "Rocky" Rhodes, *A Shifting Equilibrium: Personal Jurisdiction, Transnational Litigation, and the Problem of Nonparties*, 19 LEWIS & CLARK L. REV. 643, 661–66 (2015).

[120] Specifically, the EU to revise its regulations regarding jurisdiction to ensure that it has jurisdiction over any entity that does substantial business in an EU state so that where causes of action for extraterritorial conduct exist, EU state courts have the ability to hear and adjudicate the claim. Similarly, European countries should also ensure they have jurisdiction over transnational corporations that do significant business within them. Canada has more expansive jurisdiction than the United States does now post-*Daimler*. *See supra* notes 42–57, discussing jurisdiction in Canada. However, Canada should expand even this broader jurisdiction to ensure that it has claims over transnational corporations doing business in Canada, so that where Canada has provided for causes of action that include extraterritorial actions, Canadian courts can adjudicate the claims.

transnational business, but also so that there becomes a true transnational personal jurisdiction over TNCs.

Although this book proposes that Congress provide for general jurisdiction only for federal claims in the United States, it might be feasible to require such consent in cases in federal court involving diversity jurisdiction whenever a cause of action exists for extraterritorial conduct, even if provided for by the states. This would also address some of the limitations in specific personal jurisdiction set forth in *Nicastro*. However, to the degree that the Fifth Amendment applies to federal courts' assertions of personal jurisdiction when the claim involves a federal cause of action rather than the Fourteenth Amendment, personal jurisdiction only for federal claims may best withstand scrutiny.[121]

It remains undecided whether individual states can constitutionally require corporations doing business within it to consent to general personal jurisdiction through registering their business in a state and appointing an agent.[122] Before *Daimler*, several courts found that registration to do business and appointment of an agent constituted consent for *specific* personal jurisdiction.[123] But numerous courts also found that consent to *general* personal jurisdiction by way of registration and appointment of an agent for service was constitutional,[124] with the circuit

---

[121] *See, e.g.*, Aaron Simowitz, *Legislating Transnational Jurisdiction*, 57 Va. Int'l L. (2017) (noting arguments that Fifth Amendment applies to federal courts' assertion of general personal jurisdiction, which is arguably less restrictive). However, given that Fed. R. Civ. P. (4)(k) bases even federal courts' jurisdiction on whether the state court would have jurisdiction, it may well be, however, that the Fourteenth Amendment applies regardless.

[122] *See e.g.*, Tanya J. Monestier, *Registration Statutes, General Jurisdiction, and the Fallacy of Consent*, 36 Cardozo L. Rev. 1343 (2015) (questioning the constitutionality of state registration statutes as implied consent to general personal jurisdiction in light of *Goodyear* and *Daimler*); *see also* Robertson & Rhodes, *supra* note 119 at 649, 673 (also questioning whether states provide for general personal jurisdiction). *See* Brown v. Lockheed Martin Corp., No. 14-4083, 2016 WL 641392, at *15 (2d Cir. Feb. 18, 2016) ("[T]he analysis that now governs general jurisdiction over foreign corporations ... suggests that federal due process rights likely constrain an interpretation that transforms a run-of-the-mill registration and appointment statute into a corporate 'consent' – perhaps unwitting – to the exercise of general jurisdiction by state courts"). *But see* Acorda Therapeutics Inc. v. Mylan Pharm. Inc., No. 2015-1456, 2016 WL 1077048, at *11 (Fed. Cir. Mar. 18, 2016) (noting that "*International Shoe* and *Daimler* did not overrule th[e] historic and oft-affirmed line of binding precedent" that "the appointment of an agent by a foreign corporation for service of process could subject it to general personal jurisdiction") (O'Malley, J., concurring).

[123] *See* Monestier, *supra* note 122, at 1369, citing Holloway v. Wright & Morrissey, Inc., 739 F.2d 695, 696–99 (1st Cir. 1984); Grey Line Tours v. Reynolds Elec. & Eng'g Co., 238 Cal. Rptr. 419, 421–22 (Cal. Ct. App. 1987); Staley-Wynne Oil Corp. v. Loring Oil Co., 162 So. 756, 757–59 (La. 1935); Springle v. Cottrell Eng'g Corp., 391 A.2d 456, 459–69 (Md. Ct. Spec. App. 1978); Mittelstadt v. Rouzer, 328 N.W.2d 467, 469–70 (Neb. 1982); Osage Oil & Ref. Co. v. Interstate Pipe Co., 253 P. 66, 69 (Okla. 1926); Eure v. Morgan Jones & Co., 79 S.E.2d 862, 863–68 (Va. 1954).

[124] *See* Monestier, *supra* note 122 at 1359, 1369, *citing* Bane v. Netlink, Inc., 925 F.2d 637, 640–41 (3d Cir. 1991); Knowlton v. Allied Van Lines, Inc., 900 F.2d 1196, 1199-2000 (8th Cir. 1990); Bohreer v. Erie Ins. Exch., 165 P.3d 186, 191–94 (Ariz. Ct. App. 2007); Sternberg v. O'Neil, 550

courts split on the issue.[125] Moreover, several courts found that registering to do business and appointing an agent did not create a separate jurisdictional basis, but is only a procedural mechanism for ensuring service of process.[126] At least one jurisdiction, the District of Columbia, has a statute that explicitly states that the

---

A.2d 1105, 1109–16 (Del. 1988); Confederation of Can. Life Ins. Co. v. Vega y Arminan, 144 So. 2d 805, 808–10 (Fla. 1962); Allstate Ins. Co. v. Klein, 422 S.E.2d 863, 864–65 (Ga. 1992); Merriman v. Crompton Corp., 146 P.3d 162,170–77 (Kan. 2006); Rykoff-Sexton, Inc. v. American Appraisal Associates, 469 N.W.2d 88, 89–91 (Minn. 1991); Read v. Sonat Offshore Drilling, Inc., 515 So. 2d 1229, 1230–31 (Miss. 1987); Allied-Signal Inc. v. Purex Indus., Inc., 576 A.2d 942, 943–45 (N.J. Super. Ct. App. Div. 1990); Werner v. Prins, 861 P.2d 271,272–74 (Ariz. Ct. App. 1991); Augsbury Corp. v. Petrokey Corp., 470 N.Y.S.2d 787, 789 (N.Y. App. Div. 1983); Simmers v. Am. Cyanamid Corp., 576 A.2d 376, 382 (Pa. Super. Ct. 1990); Green Mountain Coll. v. Levine, 139 A.2d 822, 824–25 (Vt. 1958). As Professor Monestier points out, "courts differ on whether it is the act of registering to do business or the act of appointing an agent for service of process that constitutes consent to personal jurisdiction," *supra* at 1359 n86, *citing* Sadler v. Hallsmith SYSCO Food Servs., Civil No. 08-4423 (RBK/JS), 2009 WL 1096309, at *2 (D.N.J. Apr. 21, 2009) ("Finally, the Court finds that even if, as Defendants maintain, Plaintiffs did not serve Hallsmith's registered agent in New Jersey, the Court would still have jurisdiction. While the language of *Allied Signal* suggests that the act of serving a corporation's registered agent confers jurisdiction on the courts of a state, the Third Circuit Court of Appeals has instead stated that the act of registering to do business constitutes consent to be sued." (citations omitted)).

[125] Before *Daimler*, circuit courts were split as to whether compliance with business registration or agent designation statutes subjected a defendant to personal jurisdiction. *See* Forest Labs., Inc. v. Amneal Pharmaceuticals L.L.C., No. 14-508–LPS, 2015 WL 880599, *9 (D.Del. Feb. 26, 2015). *See also* Kevin D. Benish, *Pennoyer's Ghost: Consent, Registration Statutes, and General Jurisdiction After Daimler Ag v. Bauman*, 90 N.Y.U. L. Rev. 1609, 1611–13 (2015) (citing the Third and Eighth Circuits holding that consent-by-registration is constitutional; citing the Second and Ninth Circuits supporting the Third and Eighth Circuits in dicta; citing the First, Fourth, Fifth, Seventh, and Eleventh Circuits holding that consent-by-registration is unconstitutional; citing that the Sixth, Tenth, D.C., and Federal Circuit Courts of Appeal have yet to take a position); "Rocky" Rhodes & Cassandra Burke Robertson, *Toward a New Equilibrium in Personal Jurisdiction*, 48 U. C. Davis L. Rev. 207, 261–62 (2014), at 229–30. *See, e.g.*, Holloway v. Wright & Morrissey, Inc., 739 F.2d 695, 697 (1st Cir. 1984); Spiegel v. Schulmann, 604 F.3d 72 (2d Cir. 2010) (dicta); Bane v. Netlink, Inc., 925 F.2d 637, 640 (3d Cir. 1991); Knowlton v. Allied Van Lines Inc., 900 F.2d 1196, 1199–200 (8th Cir. 1990); King v. Am. Family Mut. Ins. Co., 632 F.3d 570 (9th Cir. 2011) (dicta), for cases that held compliance with registration statutes could amount to valid consent to personal jurisdiction. *See* Cossaboon v. Me. Med. Ctr., 600 F.3d 25, 37 (1st Cir. 2010); Ratliff v. Cooper Labs. Inc., 444 F.2d 745, 748 (4th Cir. 1971); Siemer v. Learjet Acquisition Corp., 966 F.2d 179 (5th Cir. 1992); Wilson v. Humphreys (Cayman) Ltd., 916 F.2d 1239, 1245 (7th Cir. 1990); Consol. Dev. Corp. v. Sherritt, Inc., 216 F.3d 1286, 1293 (11th Cir. 2000), for cases that held that compliance with a state registration statute cannot be the basis for finding consent to general jurisdiction.

[126] Monestier, *supra* note 122 at 1369, *citing* Consol. Dev. Corp. v. Sherritt, Inc., 216 F.3d 1286, 1293 (11th Cir. 2000); Wenche Siemer v. Learjet Acquisition Corp., 966 F.2d 179, 180–84 (5th Cir. 1992); Leonard v. USA Petroleum Corp., 829 F. Supp. 882, 888–89 (S.D. Tex. 1993); In re Mid-Atl. Toyota Antitrust Litig., 525 F. Supp. 1265, 1277–78 (D. Md. 1981), aff'd, 704 F.2d 125 (4th Cir. 1983); Freeman v. Second Jud. Dist. Court ex rel. Cnty. of Washoe, 1 P.3d 963, 965–68 (Nev. 2000); Byham v. Nat'l Cibo House Corp., 143 S.E.2d 225, 231 (N.C. 1965); Wash. Equip. Mfg. Co., Inc. v. Concrete Placing Co., Inc., 931 P.2d 170, 172–73 (Wash. Ct. App. 1997).

registration of an agent for service does not create a mechanism for personal jurisdiction.[127]

Since *Daimler*, courts have remained split on the issue, but the only circuit court since *Daimler* to consider the issue rejected the notion of state-based consent to jurisdiction through registration and designating a registered agent.[128] In its decision,

---

[127] D.C. CODE § 29-104.14 (2011) ("The designation or maintenance in the District of a registered agent shall not by itself create the basis for personal jurisdiction over the represented entity in the District.").

[128] Brown v. Lockheed Martin Corp., 814 F.3d 619, 626 (2d Cir. 2016) ("upon our examination of the applicable Connecticut law, we conclude that by registering to transact business and appointing an agent under the Connecticut statutes—which do not speak clearly on this point—Lockheed did not consent to the state courts' exercise of general jurisdiction over it. A more sweeping interpretation would raise constitutional concerns prudently avoided absent a clearer statement by the state legislature or the Connecticut Supreme Court," but noting that a "carefully drawn state statute that expressly required consent to general jurisdiction as a condition on a foreign corporation's doing business in the state, at least in cases brought by state residents, might well be constitutional"), essentially overturning Vera v. Republic of Cuba, 91 F. Supp. 3d 561, 566–67, 571 (S.D.N.Y. 2015) (holding that the defendant corporation consented to jurisdiction for purposes of responding to subpoenas through registering to do business).

For other post-*Daimler*, cases finding that consent by registration is not valid, see, e.g., Leibovitch v. Republic of Iran, No. 08-C-1939, 2016 WL 2977273, *9 (N.D. Ill. May 19, 2016) (same, and noting that other district courts in the 7th Circuit have similarly held); Display Works, L.L.C. v. Bartley, No. 16-583, 2016 WL 1644451, *7 (D.N.J. April 25, 2016) (finding that Wisconsin corporation did not consent to general jurisdiction of New Jersey by registering to do business and appointing an agent, both because the statute did not expressly state the company was subjecting itself to jurisdiction, and because more recent, contact-based jurisprudence has called into question the consent by registration theory); Lanham v. Pilot Travel Centers, No. 03:14-CV-01923-HZ, 2015 WL 5167268, *11 (D. Or. Sept. 2, 2015) (finding that registration pursuant to Oregon's foreign business registration statute did not provide a basis for consent to jurisdiction, given that the statute did not mention jurisdiction); Keeley v. Pfizer, Inc., No. 415-CV-00583 ERW, 2015 WL 3999488, *4 (E.D. Mo. July 1, 2015) (rejecting consent to jurisdiction simply because a company was registered with Missouri and required to appoint an agent for service of process); AstraZeneca AB v. Mylan Pharm., Inc., 72 F. Supp. 3d 549, 556 (D.Del. 2014) ("In light of the holding in *Daimler*, the court finds that Mylan's compliance with Delaware's registration statutes—mandatory for *doing business* within the state—cannot constitute consent to jurisdiction, and the Delaware Supreme Court's decision in Sternberg v. O'Neil, 550 A.2d 1105, 1116 (Del. 1988) [which held that compliance with registration statutes creates] can no longer be said to comport with federal due process"), *aff'd* on different grounds (court also found specific jurisdiction); Fiduciary Network, L.L.C. v. Buehler, No. 3:15-CV-0808, 2015 WL 2165953 (N.D. Tex. May 8, 2015).

For cases finding registration constitutes consent, see, e.g., Mitchell v. Eli Lilly and Company, 159 F. Supp. 3d 967, 977-79 (E.D. Mo. 2016) (finding Missouri's business registration statute and requirement of agent for service of process equated to consent for general personal jurisdiction, stating that neither Daimler nor Goodyear addressed consent as a separate basis); Acorda Therapeutics, Inc. v. Mylan Pharmaceuticals Inc., 78 F. Supp. 3d 572, 588 (D.Del. 2015) ("*Daimler* does not eliminate consent as a basis for a state to establish general jurisdiction over a corporation which has appointed an agent for service of process in that state, as is required as part of registering to do business in that state, noting that Daimler did not address consent"), *aff'd* on different grounds, 817 F.3d 755 (Fed. Cir. 2016) (district court also found specific jurisdiction, and appellate court affirmed on that basis); Otsuka Pharmaceutical

however, the Second Circuit held open the possibility that "a carefully drawn state statute that expressly required consent to general jurisdiction in exchange for a foreign corporation's doing business in the state, at least in cases brought by state residents, might well be constitutional."[129] In fact, Pennsylvania has a statute – and it appears to be the only state with such a statute – that specifically provides for general personal jurisdiction over a foreign corporation that has "qualified as a foreign corporation" under the state registration statute.[130] The courts in Pennsylvania have applied the statute according to its language.[131] Although it has not been interpreted since *Daimler*, it might fit into the type of statute contemplated in *Brown*.

In addition to the fact that it may be most efficient for Congress to enact such a statute rather than individual states, a federal statute might also survive constitutional challenges that state legislation might not, especially where the foreign corporations are domiciled outside of the United States.[132] For example, some might argue that allowing states to legislate and potentially impede commerce with corporations domiciled abroad might be unconstitutional under the Dormant Commerce Clause.[133] As noted earlier, the Supreme Court in 1910 found that it was a violation

---

Co., Ltd. v. Mylan Inc., 106 F. Supp. 3d 456, 468 (D.N.J. 2015) (finding registration under New Jersey business statute constituted consent to be sued, even in light of *Daimler*, noting that *Daimler* suggests consent is a separate basis of jurisdiction); Forest Labs., 2015 WL 880599, at *10 (finding *Daimler* did not affect the rule that registering to do business constituted consent to personal jurisdiction, and that the Delaware Supreme Court decision in Sternberg v. O'Neil, *supra*, is still good law).

[129] See Brown, *supra* note 122. Similarly, another federal case suggests that a state could theoretically have a corporation consent to jurisdiction if due process was satisfied, but also finding that simply registering and naming an agent does not satisfy due process. See Keeley v. Pfizer, *supra* note 128 at *4.

[130] 42 PA. CONS. STAT. § 5301(a)(2)(i)–(ii) (West 2013).

[131] Eagle Traffic Control, Inc. v. James Julian, Inc., 933 F. Supp. 1251, 1256 (E.D. Pa. 1996) ("[Plaintiff] bases general personal jurisdiction over [the defendant] on the ground that it is qualified to do business within this state as a foreign corporation. Pennsylvania's personal jurisdiction statute expressly grants jurisdiction in such an instance ... The bottom line is that Pennsylvania's long arm statute provides for personal jurisdiction when a foreign corporation takes the particular action of becoming authorized to do business in Pennsylvania.").

[132] I take no personal view on whether states can constitutionally enact their own consent statutes for TNCs doing business in the states, and a full analysis of the constitutionality of such state action is outside the scope of this chapter. The point I am trying to make is that a federal statute would not be as vulnerable to constitutional challenges.

[133] The Dormant Commerce Clause does not expressly exist in the text of the United States Constitution. It is, rather, a doctrine deduced by the U.S. Supreme Court and lower courts from the actual Commerce Clause of the Constitution, which provides Congress with the authority to regulate commerce with foreign nations and the several states. U.S. CONST. art. I, § 8, cl. 3. See also Or. Waste Sys., Inc. v. Dep't of Envtl. Quality, 511 U.S. 93, 98 (1994) ("[T]he Clause has long been understood to have a 'negative' aspect that denies the States the power unjustifiably to discriminate against or burden the interstate flow of articles of commerce" (citing Wyoming v. Oklahoma, 502 U.S. 437, 454 (1992) and Welton v. Missouri, 91 U.S. 275 (1875))). Some scholars question whether it actually exists as a prohibition on State Actions.

of the Commerce Clause for a state to impose limitations on a foreign corporation doing business within the state, and that only Congress could do so.[134]

Even if such is not prohibited under the Dormant Commerce Clause, some might challenge state laws requiring consent due to other federal-related concerns. One example is implied federal preemption.[135] Although states primarily regulate business, whether domestic or foreign, Congress has increasingly "occupied the field"[136] when it comes to interstate and foreign commerce.[137] Moreover, some courts might strike down state consent statutes under the foreign affairs doctrine,[138] with courts ultimately finding that only Congress can impose conditions requiring a non-US-based corporation to consent to general personal jurisdiction in exchange for doing business.

Regardless of whether or not individual states might be able to constitutionally require such consent as a condition for doing business due to the Commerce Clause or foreign preemption, there is no constitutional rule that prevents the United States from requiring such consent.[139] In fact, the Commerce Clause expressly allows this. The Commerce Clause clearly gives Congress the power to "Regulate Commerce with foreign Nations."[140] Having Congress enact such a statute would also satisfy

---

See, e.g., Tim A. Lemper, *The Promise and Perils of "Privileges or Immunities": Saenz v. Roe* 119 S. Ct. 1518 (1999), 23 HARV. J. L. & PUB. POL'Y 295, 309 (1999) (noting Supreme Court Justices' critiques of the Dormant Commerce Clause as an "over-broad and illegitimate constraint on state power"); S. Mohsin Reza, *Daimlerchrysler v. Cuno: An Escape from the Dormant Commerce Clause Quagmire?* 40 U. RICH. L. REV. 1229, 1251 (2006) (discussing Justice Thomas and Justice Scalia's criticisms of the Dormant Commerce Clause); Norman R. Williams, *Why Congress May Not "Overrule" the Dormant Commerce Clause*, 53 UCLA L. REV. 153, 163 (2005).

[134] *See* International Textbook Co. v. Pigg, 217 U.S. 91, 108–09 (1910). Interestingly, none of the cases discussed above cite that case. It is unclear why.

[135] Preemption is the principle (derived from the Supremacy Clause) that a federal law can supersede or supplant any inconsistent state law or regulation. *Preemption*, BLACK'S LAW DICTIONARY (10th ed. 2014), Westlaw (database updated 2016). Implied preemption is determined by "inquiring whether Congress has occupied a particular field with the intent to supplant state law or whether state law actually conflicts with federal law." Cipollone v. Liggett Grp., Inc., 505 U.S. 504, 532 (1992).

[136] Field preemption is a form of implied preemption where the federal government indicates it intends to occupy a specific regulatory field, and thus any conflicting state law could be struck down. Pennsylvania v. Nelson, 350 U.S. 497 (1956). *See also* Gade v. Nat'l Solid Wastes Mgmt. Ass'n, 505 U.S. 88, 108 (1992) ("[U]nder the Supremacy Clause, from which our pre-emption doctrine is derived, any state law, however clearly within a State's acknowledged power, which interferes with or is contrary to federal law, must yield" (internal quotation marks omitted)).

[137] *See, e.g.*, Sherman Antitrust Act, 15 U.S.C. §§ 1–7 (2012); Wickard v. Filburn, 317 U.S. 111, 124 (1942) (holding that Congress can regulate any commercial activity that has an effect on interstate trade); Taft-Hartley Act, 29 U.S.C. §§ 141–531 (2012) (labor); Copyright Act of 1976, 17 U.S.C. §§ 101–810 (2012).

[138] Under the foreign affairs doctrine, state laws that could affect foreign affairs, a power the federal government assigns to the federal government, are invalid. Zschernig v. Miller, 389 U.S. 429, 432 (1968).

[139] *See generally* Benish, *supra* note 125.

[140] U.S. CONST. art. I, § 8, cl. 3.

issues related to federal preemption and the foreign affairs doctrine. Moreover, limiting general jurisdiction to federal causes of action would allow courts to rest more assured that Congress and the executive branch have considered foreign policy implications.

A federal statute could simply state that all businesses domiciled abroad that are "doing business" in the United States need to register with each state where it does business and provide an agent for service (which they typically already have to do),[141] and explicitly provide that by doing so, the foreign corporation is consenting to general personal jurisdiction for any federal statutory claims that provide for extraterritorial application.[142] Such explicit language would provide fair notice to foreign corporations that are subject to the general jurisdiction to US courts where a cause of action exists, alleviating due process concerns.

A federal statute has the additional benefit of satisfying Fed. R. Civ. P. 4(k)(1)(C), which provides that the service of summons establishes personal jurisdiction over the defendant when "authorized by a federal statute." The statute should also indicate that for a claim arising under federal law, Fed. R. Civ. P. 4(k)(2) applies if the foreign corporation is doing business equally throughout the United States, allowing any federal court to assert jurisdiction over any corporation domiciled abroad in such circumstances. It is important to note although the Supreme Court has not decided the issue, lower circuit courts have held that it is constitutional to aggregate contacts for purposes of personal jurisdiction against a foreign defendant pursuant to the Fifth Amendment.[143] Thus, if the Fifth Amendment's Due Process

---

[141] All businesses, foreign or not, and incorporated or not, already typically have to register with each state in which they do business (even if they are not incorporated there), and establish a registered agent. *See* Caron Beesley, *Selling into the U.S. as a Foreign Business: Should You Incorporate Your Business Here?* U.S. SMALL BUSINESS ADMINISTRATION, https://lavernesbdc.org/news/selling-into-the-u-s-as-a-foreign-business-should-you-incorporate-your-business-here/, last visited February 24, 2020). It seems the only exception to this is if a foreign business does its selling only online or through a US wholesaler. *Id.*

[142] Alternatively, Congress could enact a statute allowing states to enact their own statutes requiring consent to general personal jurisdiction for foreign corporations that do business within the state. For example, Congress has authorized state actions that might otherwise have been deemed preempted before. *See e.g.,* Sudan Accountability and Divestment Act of December 31, 2007 ("SADA"), Pub. L. No. 110-74, 21 Stat. 2516 (2007) (authorizing states to divest from companies that conduct business operations in Sudan). For a discussion of the constitutionality of the SADA and similar legislation, see Perry S. Buchky, *Darfur, Divestment, and Dialogue,* 30 U. PA. J. INT'L L. 823 (2009). For the reasons discussed herein, however, I believe a federal statute is more efficient, more consistent, and more likely to satisfy due process and other Constitutional concerns.

[143] *See, e.g.,* Securities Investor Protection Corporation v. Vigman, 764 F.2d 1309, 1315 (9th Cir. 1985) (where a federal court has federal question jurisdiction over case (as opposed to diversity jurisdiction), the court's personal jurisdiction over a defendant is not limited to the forum states' personal jurisdiction over the defendant; rather, the Fifth Amendment allows for nationwide personal jurisdiction over a defendant who has sufficient nationwide contacts), *citing* Johnson Creative Arts & Wool v. Masters, Inc. 743 F. 2d 947, 950 (1st Cir. 1984) ("'[M]inimum contacts' with a particular district or state for purposes of personal jurisdiction

Clause applies to foreign defendants in federal causes of action rather than the Fourteenth's Due Process Clause, asserting jurisdiction only for federal claims may best withstand scrutiny.[144]

There is no specific definition for what constitutes "doing business," and courts typically determine it on a case-by-case basis.[145] Congress could continue to allow individual states or courts to determine what this term means, but that might raise due process concerns. Alternatively, Congress could provide a definition for purposes of the statute in a myriad of ways, setting forth a minimum monetary amount for transactions, trade, or sales, or the establishment of one or more offices, whether directly or through a subsidiary. But Congress should certainly include that doing business means conducting such business through a subsidiary or similar entity.

As mentioned previously, such expanded jurisdiction is not quite as expansive as it sounds because there are a limited number of claims that include extraterritorial conduct.[146] Moreover, a court would also still have the doctrine of *forum non conveniens*[147] available to it.

7.6.2 A Statutory Enactment Would Provide for an Even Playing Field for US Corporations

Allowing for personal jurisdiction over foreign corporations that conduct substantial and continuous business in the United States could actually be good for US corporations, because it would create an even playing field. Under current personal jurisdiction rules, and the ruling in *Jesner*, only those corporations incorporated or headquartered in the United States can be sued under the ATS. Yet, TNCs that also conduct business in the United States and gain enormous benefit from operating in the United States – some perhaps that do more business than US-based corporations – now no longer have to worry about being sued under these same statutes because US courts cannot assert personal jurisdiction over them for the same violations. This means that foreign corporations not only have less exposure from lawsuits, but will have to expend less and invest less money in human rights compliance than US corporations. This puts those foreign corporations that otherwise do business in the United States at a competitive edge.

---

is not a limitation imposed on the federal courts in a federal question case by due process concerns. The Constitution does not require the federal districts to follow state boundaries."). See also Daetwyler Corp. v. R. Meyer, 762 F.2d 290, 293–95 (3d Cir. 1985).

[144] See, e.g., Simowitz, *supra* note 121 (noting arguments that Fifth Amendment applies to federal court's assertion of general personal jurisdiction, which is arguably less restrictive).

[145] Specific "Doing Business Activities" that Affect the Foreign Qualification Requirement, WOLTERSKLUWER (Nov. 2012), https://ct.wolterskluwer.com/sites/default/files/CT_Corporation_What_Constitutes_DBA_Foreign-Qualification_WhitePaper_0.pdf (last visited January 1, 2020).

[146] See Chapter 4 discussing subject matter jurisdiction.

[147] This doctrine allows courts to dismiss a case, even where it can assert jurisdiction, on the basis that another jurisdiction is ostensibly more "convenient" for the parties and witnesses. Gulf Oil Corp. v. Gilbert, 330 U.S. 501 (1947).

Finally, Justice Ginsburg argued for narrow jurisdiction partly because it would provide certainty and clarity, which she felt was important out of fairness to foreign corporations.[148] Providing for broad general personal jurisdiction where a TNC does business provides the same level of certainty and clarity.

7.6.3 Comity and Foreign Relations Are Not Substantial Impediments

Justice Ginsburg, in her *Daimler* opinion, argues that broad personal jurisdiction poses comity and foreign relations concerns as one justification for limiting general personal jurisdiction.[149] There should be little question that it would be best for the United States, Canada, and Europe to move toward equally broad general personal jurisdiction over TNCs in order to ensure remedies for individual victims, for consistency in the enforcement of judgments, and in allying US lawmakers' and judges' concerns of comity and foreign relations. However, even if the United States took this approach on its own, concerns of comity and foreign relations, although important, should not be substantial impediments. This is especially the case because the expansive personal jurisdiction this book advocates would only apply in those situations where Congress has provided for causes of action, ostensibly after taking foreign relations into consideration.

First, it is important to address the Restatement (Third) of The Foreign Relations Law of the United States' (Restatement) view on what this chapter has deemed "personal jurisdiction" but what the Restatement calls "adjudicative jurisdiction,"[150] given its recognition as an informative legal treatise on international law. Arguably, the Restatement's authoritative view on the subject should provide assurance to Congress and policymakers that what this chapter is proposing is within the bounds of what the Restatement recognizes as authoritative international law on the subject, and ease comity and foreign relations concerns to a large extent.

The Restatement allows assertions of adjudicative (personal) jurisdiction and considers such reasonable both where, inter alia, the defendant consents to such jurisdiction and where the defendant "regularly carries on business."[151] The greater restrictions, from a comity perspective, arguably involve causes of action for extraterritorial conduct, or what the Restatement terms "jurisdiction to prescribe."[152] However, the Restatement allows lawmakers to enact causes of action for extraterritorial conduct where actions are directed against the nation's security[153] or that are in the interests of its citizens.[154] Importantly, the Restatement allows for prescriptive

---

[148] Daimler AG v. Bauman 34 S. Ct. 746 (2014) at 760.
[149] *Id.* at 763.
[150] Restatement (Third) of the Foreign Relations Law of the United States § 421 (1987).
[151] *Id.* at § 421 (2)(g) (consent), and (2)(h) ("regularly carries on business").
[152] *Id.* at § 402–04.
[153] *Id.* at § 402(3).
[154] *Id.* at § 402(2) and (3). However, such has to be reasonable. *Id.* at § 403. Although "reasonableness" takes into consideration a variety of factors including whether another nation has an

jurisdiction for those offenses that are recognized as of universal concern, such as violations of CIL.[155] Moreover, such prescriptions are not limited to criminal law, but allow for civil actions that provide a remedy or restitution for these offenses.[156] Thus, providing for general personal jurisdiction over those TNCs consenting to general personal jurisdiction for the privilege of doing business in the United States for claims of extraterritorial violations of international law – such as international human rights violations, terrorism, and human trafficking (among potential others) – does not violate international law and is seen as a proper exercise of authority. Moreover, given that Congress has provided for claims involving extraterritorial conduct, one can argue that Congress (and the executive, through signing of such bills) has taken potential conflicts with other nations into account before enacting such legislation.

Second, as discussed above, EU countries protect their own corporations from expansive jurisdiction by other EU countries, but do not protect corporations that are domiciled outside an EU country (such as in the United States) from expansive jurisdiction.[157] Thus, TNCs domiciled in the United States are actually subject to fairly broad jurisdiction in numerous European countries.[158] They are similarly exposed to broader jurisdictional rules in Canada.[159] Thus, US courts' assertion of jurisdiction over EU-domiciled TNCs should not pose comity problems with nations in Europe or Canada.

Third, the United States has allowed foreign corporations without headquarters in the United States to be sued in US courts for decades without serious foreign policy repercussions. Moreover, if comity was a major concern, one would think that Congress would have limited general personal jurisdiction by statute, but it never did.

Finally, as discussed above, by limiting general personal jurisdiction to federal causes of action, courts can be more assured that comity implications of subjecting foreign corporations to general jurisdiction of US courts have been considered and weighed by Congress and the executive branch.

7.6.4 *The EU and European Countries Should Similarly Expand Jurisdiction over TNCs*

The EU should similarly amend the Brussels Regulation, recast so that transnational enterprises doing business in the EU would be subjected to general personal

---

interest in regulating the conduct and the likelihood of conflict with another nation. *Id.* at § 403 (2). It also allows lawmakers to take into consideration the legal and economic order, and the degree to which the desirability of such recognition is generally accepted. *Id.* at § 403 (2)(c) and (e).

[155] *Id.* at § 404.
[156] *Id.* at comment (b).
[157] *See* Chapter 6 discussing personal jurisdiction.
[158] *Id.*
[159] *Id.*

jurisdiction where the Member State has decided to provide for causes of action for extraterritorial conduct. As mentioned above, there are EU Member State laws that already allow for victims in host countries to bring claims against corporations domiciled in the member country for certain law violations, although none explicitly provide for violations of international human rights norms.

For countries in the EU, the Brussels Regulation, recast should be amended to broaden general jurisdiction with regard to claims involving violation of international law, to allow EU Member States to assert jurisdiction over TNCs that conduct business in the member country, regardless of its domicile, and to ensure that all Member States will enforce the judgments of a sister Member State. This could be accomplished by specifically stating that the EU Member States will hear claims of international law violations against companies that conduct a certain threshold of economic activity within the EU. This could also include expanding the Regulation to set forth that one way in which such substantial business can be established is where the transnational company has a "branch, agency, or other establishment" domiciled within its jurisdiction, similar to allowing jurisdiction over such companies as it now does in the areas of insurance (where the claim arises out of the operation of that branch),[160] or in employment (where the claim arises out the employment).[161] Granted, the current regulations allow for assertions over parent companies in these situations only where the claim is related to the operations of the branch, agency, or other establishment, and thus only where there is some sort of nexus, or connection. However, by allowing jurisdiction over a separate legal entity in such cases, the EU has already demonstrated that separate legal personality should not matter.

Expanding such jurisdiction throughout the EU would accomplish two of the purposes which the Brussels Regulation claims to be concerned about: access to justice, and consistency and fairness to defendants. Regarding the first, the EU notes one of the primary reasons for the jurisdictional rules set forth in Brussels is to enhance "access to justice."[162] Moreover, being a multilateral institution made up of individual states, the EU should implement the UNGPs, which in seeking to ensure that victims can obtain a remedy, allow for such jurisdiction, at least where victims cannot otherwise obtain a remedy.

With regard to the latter, the EU's jurisdictional rules are not governed by constitutional limits on assertions of jurisdiction to hear a case against a particular defendant in the way the United States' *in personam* jurisdictional rules are. However, the EU Regulation articulates concerns similar to due process concerns articulated in US courts. For example, the Regulation notes that requiring a close

---

[160] Regulation 1215/2012 of the European Parliament and of the Council of 12 December 2012 on Jurisdiction and the Recognition and Enforcement of Judgments in Civil and Commercial Matters, 2012 O.J. (L 351), art. 11.
[161] *Id.* at art. 20.
[162] *Id.* at Preamble (1) and (3).

connection between the action and the court ensures "legal certainty," and avoids "the possibility of the defendant being sued in a court of a Member State which he could not have reasonably foreseen."[163] Providing for jurisdiction to hear a human rights claim over a defendant business, where that business conducts business in the Member State, would provide for legal certainty and would allow such defendants to foresee such jurisdiction.

Moreover, having consistent EU rules apply to *in personam* jurisdiction over non-EU-domiciled defendants, at least for violations of international law, should not be too controversial, given that several European countries already allow for such expansive jurisdiction over such defendants. Having a consistent, broader jurisdiction would also allow for consistency for such defendants, and thus would provide more consistent and fair notice.

---

[163] *Id.* at Preamble (16).

8

Overcoming Other Barriers to Remedy

In addition to the main doctrinal barriers listed in previous chapters, there are other substantive legal barriers victims face when trying to obtain a judicial remedy for TNC-related extraterritorial human rights abuses. For example, there remains the unsettled questions under international and domestic law of whether a corporation can violate international law, and thus whether it can be sued for violations of international law, and the unsettled law regarding the legal standard for corporate vicarious liability for human rights violations.

Other barriers include doctrines such as *forum non conveniens* and the "choice of law" doctrine, unnecessarily short statutes of limitations, limits on collective actions, costs of litigation, and restrictive discovery rules that make it difficult to obtain the information which plaintiffs need when pursuing a legal case against a corporation. This chapter discusses each of these additional barriers in less detail than the primary legal barriers discussed in prior chapters, and offers some recommended solutions to overcome them.

8.1 UNSETTLED LEGAL STANDARDS FOR CORPORATE LIABILITY

In attempting to hold corporations – which are considered legal persons – liable, and thus accountable, for violations of international law, significant barriers that exist are the unsettled questions of whether, and the proper analysis of how, a corporation can be liable for international human rights violations.[1] And also, the legal standard for proving a business's liability when that liability is indirect, or vicarious, such as aiding and abetting. This is a critical issue since most cases against corporations for violations of international law do not allege that the corporation

---

[1] Some would argue this is now a settled question in the United States. It probably is, but the Supreme Court still has not directly held that corporations can be liable for violations of international law, and the law in the US Court of Appeals for the Second Circuit is that they are not.

directly violated the victims' rights, but that it did so through aiding and abetting either another entity, government, or its security forces.

8.1.1 *Corporate Liability for CIL Violations is Unsettled*

Whether businesses (as opposed to individuals) can be liable for violations of CIL is still not completely settled. The vast majority of US courts have held that corporations can be sued under the ATS for violations of CIL.[2] The outlier is the US Court of Appeals for the Second Circuit.[3] In Jesner v. Arab Bank, the majority did not address this question. Only a three-judge plurality[4] looked to international law and

---

[2] *See* Kiobel v. Royal Dutch Petroleum, 133 S. Ct. 1659, 1663 (2013); *see also* Abelesz v. Magyar Nemzeti Bank, 692 F.3d 661 (7th Cir. 2012) (agreeing with concurrence in *Kiobel* that "there is a sufficient legal basis to hold corporations liable under the ATS for genocide"); Sarei v. Rio Tinto, PLC, 671 F.3d 736, 747 (9th Cir. 2011) (declining to follow the Second Circuit and finding corporations can be liable under the ATS), *vacated on other grounds*, 133 S. Ct. 1995 (2013); Flomo v. Firestone Nat. Rubber Co., LLC, 643 F.3d 1013, 1017 (7th Cir. 2011) ("The factual premise of the majority opinion in the *Kiobel* case is incorrect."); Doe v. Exxon Mobil Corp., 654 F.3d 11, 41 (D.C. Cir. 2011) (rejecting the Second Circuit's analysis that corporations cannot be liable under the ATS), *vacated on other grounds*, 527 F. Appx. 7 (D.C. Cir. 2013); Sinaltrainal v. Coca-Cola Co., 578 F.3d 1252, 1263 (11th Cir. 2009) ("In addition to private individual liability, we have also recognized corporate defendants are subject to liability under the ATS and may be liable for violations of the law of nations."); Romero v. Drummond Co., 552 F.3d 1303, 1315 (11th Cir. 2008) ("The text of the Alien Tort Statute provides no express exception for corporations, and the law of this Circuit is that [the ATS] grants jurisdiction from complaints of torture against corporate defendants."); Holocaust Victims of Bank Theft v. Bank, 807 F. Supp. 2d 689, 694 (N.D. Ill. 2011), *vacated and remanded sub nom.*, Abelesz v. Magyar Nemzeti Bank, 692 F.3d 661 (7th Cir. 2012); Wissam Abdullateff Sa'eed Al-Quraishi v. Adel Nakhla, 728 F. Supp. 2d 702, 753 (D. Md. 2010) ("There is no basis for differentiating between private individuals and corporations [under the ATS]"); In re Xe Servs. Alien Tort Litig., 665 F. Supp. 2d 569, 588 (E.D. Va. 2009) ("Nothing in the ATS or *Sosa* may plausibly be read to distinguish between private individuals and corporations; indeed, *Sosa* simply refers to both individuals and entities as 'private actors' ... [T]here is no identifiable principle of civil liability which would distinguish between individual and corporate defendants in these circumstances.") (internal citations omitted); In re S. African Apartheid Litig., 617 F. Supp. 2d 228, 254–55 (S.D.N.Y. 2009) (rejecting argument that corporate liability cannot be imposed under the ATS); Presbyterian Church of Sudan v. Talisman Energy, Inc., 374 F. Supp. 2d 331, 335 (S.D.N.Y. 2005) ("Talisman's argument that corporate liability under international law is not ... sufficiently accepted in international law to support an ATS claim is misguided."); In re Agent Orange Prod. Liab. Litig., 373 F. Supp. 2d 7, 58 (E.D.N.Y. 2005) ("A corporation is not immune from civil legal action based on international law."); Presbyterian Church of Sudan v. Talisman Energy, Inc., 244 F. Supp. 2d 289, 319 (S.D.N.Y. 2003) ("A private corporation is a juridical person and has no *per se* immunity under U.S. domestic or international law ... [W]here plaintiffs allege *jus cogens* violations, corporate liability may follow."); *but cf.* In re S. African Apartheid Litig., Nos. 02 MDL 1499 (SAS); 02 Civ. 4712 (SAS); 02 Civ. 6218 (SAS); 03 Civ. 1024 (SAS); 03 Civ. 4524 (SAS); 2009 WL 5177981, at *2 (S.D.N.Y. Dec. 31, 2009) (denying defendants' motion for certification of interlocutory appeal, because there were not "substantial grounds for disagreement on the issue of whether the ATS extends liability to corporations").

[3] Royal Dutch Petroleum Co., 621 F.3d 111 (2d Cir. 2010).

[4] 138 S. Ct. 1386 (2018), Justices Kennedy, Roberts, Thomas.

(mistakenly) found that "The international community's conscious decision to limit the authority of these international tribunals to natural persons counsels against a broad holding that there is a specific, universal, and obligatory norm of corporate liability under currently prevailing international law."[5] Four justices dissented in an opinion that noted that corporate liability was not even a question to be determined by looking to international law; instead, international law determines what substantive conduct violates the law of nations and leaves the specific rules of how to enforce international norms and remedies to states.[6]

No international criminal tribunal has directly ruled on the issue,[7] nor does the statute of the International Criminal Court (ICC) provide that corporations can be liable.[8] In September 2016 the Office of the Prosecutor (OTP) updated its case selection process to include crimes that resulted in "the destruction of the environment, the illegal exploitation of natural resources or the illegal dispossession of land."[9] Although the Paper does not say it directly, these crimes often involve – and may implicate – the executives or employees of multinational corporations, particularly those in the mining and agribusiness sectors.[10] In a separate development, a recent petition requests the ICC to investigate violations alleged against Chiquita corporate officials.[11] Outside the ICC, case law shows that corporate actors can be held civilly liable for international human rights crimes, but no criminal law cases regarding international crimes have been brought against corporations themselves.[12]

Despite the dearth of corporate prosecutions, individual corporate liability for international crimes has been accepted since the International Military Tribunal of Nuremberg (IMT).[13] Although prosecutors declined to try corporate actors at the IMT,[14] some were convicted during subsequent trials in the Allied sectors of

---

[5] *Id.*, Slip Op at 15.
[6] *Id.*, Slip Op at 14–15.
[7] The International Tribunal for Rwanda tried and convicted media executives responsible for broadcasts intended to inflame the public to commit acts of genocide in the cases of Ferdinand Nahimana, Jean-Bosco Barayagwiza, and Hassan Ngeze.
[8] Nadia Bernaz, *An Analysis of the ICC Office of the Prosecutor's Policy Paper on Case Selection and Prioritization from the Perspective of Business and Human Rights*, 15 J. OF INT'L CRIMINAL JUSTICE 527 (2017). The decision to exclude corporations was grounded in the goal of creating an institution that would tackle impunity while securing the maximum number of signatures; i.e. it was about the statute and not about corporate liability under international law. *Id.*
[9] *Id.* at 1–2.
[10] *Id.* For example, industrial accidents often cause environmental destruction, and financial aims often motivate exploitation of natural resources or land grabbing. *Id.* at 7.
[11] International Human Rights Clinic at Harvard Law School, *The contribution of Chiquita corporate officials to crimes against humanity in Colombia*, Article 15 Communication to the International Criminal Court (2017).
[12] Wolfgang Kaleck & Mirian Saage-Maaß, *Corporate Accountability for Human Rights Violations Amounting to International Crimes: The Status Quo and its Challenges*, 8 JOURNAL OF INTERNATIONAL CRIMINAL JUSTICE 699, 700 (2010).
[13] *Id.*, at 701.
[14] Possibly due to their larger goal not to destroy Germany's economic elite as the country transitioned. *See* Kaleck and Saage-Maas, *supra* note 12 at 718.

Germany.[15] Corporations were dismantled and subjected to other penalties under international law, but not criminally prosecuted.[16] The International Tribunal for Rwanda tried and convicted media executives for their role in the Rwandan genocide.[17] More recently, the Special Tribunal for Lebanon held corporations accountable, though it was only for offenses "against the administration of justice."[18]

In recent years, courts in the Netherlands have established jurisdiction over TNCs accused of foreign human rights abuses.[19] In doing so, they have overcome an obstacle to corporate liability for international crimes by exercising jurisdiction over extraterritorial cases based on the principles of nationality, territoriality, or universality.[20] Public international law generally recognizes these principles, which suggests that the primary barriers to corporate accountability elsewhere – in Europe, in Canada, or in the US – are of a political, not doctrinal, nature.[21]

French courts, meanwhile, appear poised to hear the first case regarding criminal allegations that a parent company aided and abetted in crimes against humanity.[22] In 2011, as Syria's civil war commenced and other multinationals pulled out of the country, Lafarge made a calculated decision to stay put.[23] Over the next four years, it paid millions of Euros to militant groups, including the so-called Islamic State, in order to keep its operations running.[24] Lafarge has said it will try to have the charges dropped, claiming that the company as a whole should not be punished for the actions of its Syrian subsidiary.[25] In the past, other companies have faced charges of complicity in crimes against humanity, though the cases are usually dropped.[26]

---

[15] Bernaz, *supra* note 8 at 4–5. In the British sector, for example, prosecutors convicted two businessmen for aiding and abetting murder by supplying concentration camps with Zyklon B, which the Nazis then used to lethal end in their gas chambers. See Kaleck & Saage-Maas, *supra* note 12 at 701.

[16] Michael Bazyler & Jennifer Green, *Nuremberg-Era Jurisprudence Redux: The Supreme Court in Kiobel v. Royal Dutch Petroleum Co. and the Legacy of Nuremberg*, 7 CHARLESTON L. REV. 23 (2012).

[17] *Supra* note 7.

[18] Bernaz, *supra* note 8 at 5.

[19] Cedric Ryngaert, *Accountability for Corporate Human Rights Abuses: Lessons from the Possible Exercise of Dutch National Criminal Jurisdiction Over Multinational Corporations*, 29 CRIMINAL LAW FORUM 1, 5–6 (2018).

[20] *Id.* at 5, 12, 17.

[21] *Id.* at 7–8.

[22] *See* Agence France-Presse, *Lafarge Charged with Complicity in Syria Crimes Against Humanity*, THE GUARDIAN (June 28, 2018), https://www.theguardian.com/world/2018/jun/28/lafarge-charged-with-complicity-in-syria-crimes-against-humanity (last visited January 1, 2020).

[23] *See id.*

[24] Estimates range between $5 million and €13 million (approximately $15.2 million). *See id.*; *see also* Liz Alderman, *French Cement Giant Lafarge Indicted on Terror Financing Charge in Syria*, N.Y. TIMES (June 28, 2018), https://www.nytimes.com/2018/06/28/business/lafarge-holcim-syria-terrorist-financing.html (last visited January 1, 2020).

[25] *See* THE GUARDIAN, *supra* note 22.

[26] *See id.*

Regardless of the outcome, the investigation signals that courts may be open to recognizing liability beyond that of the subsidiary.[27]

There is no question that corporations can engage in international crimes. They cooperate with military regimes and dictatorships, and profit from the violence,[28] facilitate the regime's human rights violations,[29] or directly support the repression. They involve themselves in civil war or conflict, providing goods and illicit funds,[30] financing paramilitaries,[31] or providing military and intelligence services.[32] Dutch and French courts may be on the frontlines of corporate criminal prosecution, but a successful conviction of a company for violating CIL still seems some way off.

8.1.2 *Unsettled Legal Standard for Vicarious Liability*

In addition to the unsettled question of whether a corporation can be held liable under international law, the legal standard for vicarious liability for corporations who are alleged to commit human rights violations is also in flux. The recent international jurisprudence on this subject includes inconsistent standards set forth by two international criminal tribunals' appeals chambers. In the 2013 case of *Prosecutor v. Perišić*, the ICTY Appeals Chamber set a very high standard for aiding and abetting. It held that for a defendant to be liable under an aiding and abetting theory, the prosecution had to establish that the defendant's assistance was "specifically directed" at aiding the commission of the offense.[33] More recently, the Special Court of Sierra Leone Appeals Chamber, in the case of *Prosecutor v. Taylor*,

---

[27] *See id.* ("That the courts are finally recognizing the scope and seriousness of these allegations is absolutely historic.").

[28] *See* Kaleck & Saage-Maas, *supra* note 12 at 703–04 (first citing Doe I v. Unocal, 395 F.3d 932, 939, 947 (9th Cir. 2002); then citing Wiwa v. Royal Dutch Petroleum; then citing Wiwa v. Anderson; and then citing Wiwa v. Shell Petroleum Development Company (a synopsis of the three cases can be found at Wiwa et al. v. Royal Dutch Petroleum et al., CENTER FOR CONSTITUTIONAL RIGHTS, https://ccrjustice.org/home/what-we-do/our-cases/wiwa-et-al-v-royal-dutch-petroleum-et-al (last visited June 13, 2018)).

[29] *See* Kaleck & Saage-Maas, *supra* note 12 at 705–06 (first citing In re South African Apartheid Litigation, 633 F. Supp. 2d 117 (S.D.N.Y. 2009); and then citing Frans van Anraat (a synopsis of his case can be found at *Frans van Anraat*, TRIAL INTERNATIONAL, https://trialinternational.org/latest-post/frans-van-anraat/ (last modified June 7, 2016).

[30] *See* Kaleck & Saage-Maas, *supra* note 12 at 708 (citing the 2017 conviction of Guus Kouwenhoven by a Dutch court for aiding and abetting war crimes and illegally trading arms to Liberia).

[31] *See e.g.*, Kaleck & Saage-Maas, *supra* note 12 at 708–09 (describing a case brought against Chiquita Brands International alleging that it had made payments to the United Self-Defense Forces of Colombia, a paramilitary organization designated as a terrorist group by the United States; Chiquita agreed to pay a $25 million fine in 2007).

[32] *See* Kaleck & Saage-Maas, *supra* note 12 at 709 (citing Saleh v. Titan (a synopsis of this case can be found at *Saleh, et al. v. Titan, et al.*, CENTER FOR CONSTITUTIONAL RIGHTS, https://ccrjustice.org/home/what-we-do/our-cases/saleh-et-al-v-titan-et-al (last visited June 13, 2018))).

[33] Prosecutor v. Perišić, Case No. IT-04-81-A (Int'l Crim. Trib. for the Former Yugoslavia Feb. 28, 2013).

confirmed that the *mens rea* standard for aiding and abetting was knowledge.[34] Although it should be noted that in both these cases the international courts were considering the standard in relation to a criminal claim and not a civil claim, US courts typically look to international tribunals' decisions when determining the substantive international law to apply in civil claims before them.[35]

In the United States, the Supreme Court has made it clear that under the ATS, CIL norms provide the applicable law for the underlying claims.[36] Additionally, as litigation under state law becomes more prevalent, practitioners will likely argue that state common law incorporates CIL, just as federal common law does under the ATS.[37] For those cases, CIL should also apply to the underlying claim.

Judges, however, differ on whether international law or domestic law provide the applicable law for the other aspects of ATS claims, such as whether and under what circumstances there is vicarious liability – i.e., whether aiding and abetting is a cognizable claim, and the standards for aiding and abetting liability.[38] With regard to aiding and abetting liability under the ATS, it is unsettled whether a plaintiff must establish: (1) that the business had knowledge and gave substantial assistance with such knowledge; or (2) that the business acted with intent or purpose to violate the law. Some courts and individual judges have opined that courts should look to international law to determine the standard for such vicarious liability, with differing views on what international law requires.[39] In 2009, the Second Circuit looked to international law and found that businesses could be held liable for aiding and abetting, but only where they provide substantial assistance with the purpose of aiding the unlawful conduct.[40] In 2011, the D.C. Circuit agreed with the Second Circuit that international law should apply to the question of vicarious liability,

---

[34] Prosecutor v. Taylor, No. SCSL-03-01-A, 10766, 10949-50 (Special Ct. for Sierra Leone Sept. 26, 2013).

[35] See Andrei Mamolea, Note, *The Future of Corporate Aiding and Abetting Liability Under the Alien Tort Statute: A Roadmap*, 51 SANTA CLARA L. REV. 79 (2011).

[36] See Sosa v. Alvarez-Machain, 542 U.S. 692, 729 (2004) ("Whereas Justice Scalia sees these developments as sufficient to close the door to further independent judicial recognition of actionable international norms ... the door is still ajar subject to vigilant doorkeeping, and thus open to a narrow class of international norms today.").

[37] *Symposium Issue: Human Rights Litigation in State Courts and Under State Law*, 3 U.C. IRVINE L. REV. (2013) (discussing whether CIL was part of the general common law and thus state law).

[38] See discussion *infra*.

[39] *Compare* Khulumani v. Barclay Nat. Bank, 504 F.3d 254, 268–69, 277 (2d Cir. 2007) (Katzmann, C.J., concurring) (looking to international law and finding that liability exists for aiding and abetting, and also finding that it requires practical assistance which has a "substantial effect" on the perpetration of the crime), *with id.* at 336–37 (Korman, J., concurring in part, dissenting in part) (looking to international law to determine norm, and finding that the determination of whether aiding and abetting liability exists is to be determined on a case-by-case basis and that, where it does exist, it requires substantial assistance with knowledge of the common purpose).

[40] Presbyterian Church of Sudan v. Talisman Energy, Inc., 582 F.3d 244, 259 (2d Cir. 2009) (noting that majority of courts follow a purposeful standard under international law).

concluding that aiding and abetting liability exists under international law and thus can be the subject of an ATS suit.[41] It also agreed that international law should govern the standard for aiding and abetting.[42] However, it found that knowledge with substantial assistance was the appropriate standard under international law, disagreeing with the purposeful standard the Second Circuit applied.[43] Another judge opined that while the underlying claims (i.e., torture, extrajudicial killing) should be determined by international law, the standard for liability under the ATS, including aiding and abetting, should be governed by domestic law, which he found requires only knowledge and substantial assistance.[44] Thus, there remains disagreement concerning the standards for aiding and abetting liability in the international litigation context under the ATS.[45]

By contrast, under domestic tort law, aiding and abetting liability is fairly well settled, with the leading case applying the knowledge and substantial assistance test.[46] Similarly, the Restatement (Second) of Torts characterizes the domestic test

---

[41] Doe v. Exxon Mobil Corp., 654 F.3d 11, 32 (D.C. Cir. 2011), *vacated on other grounds*, 527 F.App'x 7 (D.C. Cir. 2013).
[42] Doe v. Exxon Mobil Corp., *id.* at 32.
[43] *Id.* at 33–35, 39.
[44] Khulumani, *supra* note 39 at 284, 288–89 (Hall, J., concurring).
[45] Several cases discuss the disagreement among the courts about what law should apply and what the standard should be. *See* Sarei v. Rio Tinto, PLC, 671 F.3d 736, 765–66 (9th Cir. 2011) (recognizing that there are differing standards in international law of the required *mens rea* for aiding and abetting war crimes), *cert. granted, vacated*, 133 S. Ct. 1995 (2013); Aziz v. Alcolac, Inc., 658 F.3d 388, 396–98 (4th Cir. 2011) (assessing various standards for aiding and abetting liability); Doe v. Exxon Mobil Corp., *supra* note 41 at 32–39 (discussing the different standards for aiding and abetting liability); Presbyterian Church of Sudan, *supra* note 40 at 259 (noting that majority of courts follow a purposeful standard under international law with only a few, like Khulumani, going toward a knowledge standard); Khulumani, *supra* note 39 at 284 (Hall, J., concurring) (courts must turn to international law to divine standards for primary liability, but must turn to federal common law to divine standards for accessorial liability); Doe v. Nestle, S.A., 748 F. Supp. 2d 1057, 1082–88 (C.D. Cal. 2010) (discussing the *mens rea* standards applied for aiding and abetting), *vacated sub nom.* Doe v. Nestle USA, Inc., 738 F.3d 1048 (9th Cir. 2013); Abecassis v. Wyatt, 704 F. Supp. 2d 623, 654–55 (S.D. Tex. 2010) (noting the disagreement on whether the knowingly or purposefully standard of aiding and abetting should be applied); In re Chiquita Brands Int'l, Inc. [Alien Tort Statute & S'holder Derivative Litig.], 690 F. Supp. 2d 1296, 1309–11 (S.D. Fla. 2010) (examining the aiding and abetting under domestic law standards); In re S. African Apartheid Litig., 624 F. Supp. 2d 336, 342–43 (S.D.N.Y. 2009) (discussing the split in the Khulumani case on what the proper standard should be for aiding and abetting liability).
[46] Halberstam v. Welch, 705 F.2d 472 (D.C. Cir. 1983) (finding that liability depends on "whether a defendant knowingly gave 'substantial assistance' to someone who performed wrongful conduct, not ... whether the defendant agreed to join the wrongful conduct"). Hundreds of lower court cases have relied on the test set forth in *Halberstam* (Westlaw search performed by author), including the following circuit courts: Khulumani, *supra* note 39 at 329 (adopting *Halberstam* test in the Second Circuit); Aetna Cas. & Sur. Co. v. Leahey Const. Co., 219 F.3d 519, 534 (6th Cir. 2000); In re Temporomandibular Joint (TMJ) Implants Prods. Liab. Litig. Eyeglasses, 113 F.3d 1484, 1495 (8th Cir. 1995); Fassett v. Delta Kappa Epsilon (New York), 807 F.2d 1150, 1163 (3d Cir. 1986).

as follows: a person is liable if he "knows that the other's conduct constitutes a breach of duty and gives substantial assistance or encouragement to the other."[47] It is not necessary for the defendant to know exactly what illegal conduct the perpetrator is involved in; thus, it is not necessary for the defendant to share the same intent to commit the crime.

The standard for aiding and abetting is unresolved and could have great implications for lawsuits against transnational businesses committing human rights violations abroad. Requiring a plaintiff to prove that a business had the specific intent to purposefully violate a specific human rights norm, rather than giving substantial assistance with mere knowledge of the violation, is a much higher standard to meet, and thus a much more difficult case to make.[48]

English law imposes civil liability where assistance to a tort is given as part of a common design, described as "joint torts" or "joint tortfeasance," but does not stretch to civil liability for knowingly aiding and abetting a tort.[49] Likewise in Canada, there is no tort of "aiding and abetting" another person to commit a tort, even knowingly. As in the UK, the closest relevant law is that of joint tortfeasorship and joint liability for a tort.[50]

8.1.3 Overcoming the Barrier of Unsettled Legal Standards for Corporate Liability

The simple solution to overcome the barriers created by unsettled areas of the law is to codify the law to allow for clarity. Where it is not otherwise clear in any domestic system that corporations can violate and thus be civilly liable for international law violations, policymakers should enact legislation, or amend existing legislation, to state that corporations, as legal persons, are capable of violating international law. Similarly, policymakers should codify the law to ensure that the "knowledge with substantial assistance" standard is the governing standard for aiding and abetting legislation, and not the "intent standard." The intent standard is nearly impossible to prove. Although there might exist viable arguments as to why the intent standard should be applied to criminal liability, there are no strong arguments as to why the intent standard should be required for civil liability purposes.

Creating legislative clarity would entail enacting a statute that states that where a business provides another entity or person with "substantial assistance" that allows

---

[47] Restatement (Second) of Torts § 876(b) (1979).
[48] It is possible that some courts will find that knowledge with substantial assistance is evidence of purposeful intent even if they adopt the purpose standard.
[49] See Fish & Fish Ltd v. Sea Shepherd UK [2015] UKSC 10 and Corporate War Crimes, *Slipping Through the Net? Joint Tortious Liability in English Law* (May 24, 2015), https://corporatewarcrimes.com/2015/05/24/slipping-through-the-net-joint-tortious-liability-in-english-law/ (last visited January 1, 2020).
[50] Lee v. Transamerica Life Canada [2017] BCSC 843 ¶ 74.

that entity or legal person to violate international human rights law, and the business does so knowing that its assistance will in fact provide such substantial assistance to the other entity or person in committing a human rights violations, the business should be liable, at least civilly, for the violation. It should then be seen as being jointly and severally liable to the victims, and thus responsible for ensuring that the victims receive the full remedy for their harm.

Similarly, in order to ensure that victims are compensated for their harm, policy-makers should ensure that where a business benefits financially from what it knows, or should have known, to be a violation of international human rights law, it should be forced to disgorge such profits. There is already legislation in the United States that provides for civil liability to any person or entity that knowingly benefits from one type of international human rights violation – trafficking. The Trafficking Victims Protection Act allows for civil claims against a person who knowingly benefits financially from trafficking.[51] Model legislation could be enacted that is similar but covers other human rights violations.

8.2 DISMISSALS BASED ON *FORUM NON CONVENIENS*

One legal barrier in the United States and Canada is the doctrine of *forum non conveniens*. This doctrine allows a court to dismiss a case, even where it can assert jurisdiction, on the basis that another forum – usually in the host country – is more appropriate and convenient because the parties, witnesses, and evidence reside there.[52] *Forum non conveniens* is not a barrier in most of Europe, given that under a EU regulation, Brussels Regulation, recast, EU national courts must accept jurisdiction over a tort claim against one of its domiciled corporations, even where the harm occurred extraterritorially.[53] In addition, the European Court of Justice has rejected the application of *forum non conveniens*.[54]

---

[51] 18 U.S.C. § 1595 (2012). The Statute reads in relevant part, "an individual who is a victim of a violation of this chapter may bring a civil action against the perpetrator (or whoever knowingly benefits, financially or by receiving anything of value from participation in a venture which that person knew or should have known has engaged in an act in violation of this chapter) in an appropriate district court of the United States and may recover damages and reasonable attorneys fees." Id.
[52] See Gulf Oil Corp. v. Gilbert, 330 U.S. 501, 508–09 (1947).
[53] See Resolution on the Commission Green Paper on Promoting a European Framework for Corporate Social Responsibility, Eur. Parl. Doc. (COM 366) 2 (2001) (noting that "the 1968 Brussels Convention ... enables jurisdiction within the courts of EU Member States for cases against companies registered or domiciled in the EU in respect of damage sustained in third countries," urging "the Commission to compile a study of the application of the extraterritoriality principle by courts in the Member States of the Union," and urging "the Member States to incorporate this extraterritoriality principle in legislation").
[54] Case C-412/98, Group Josi Reinsurance Co. SA v. Universal Gen. Ins. Co. (UGIC), 2000 E.C.R. I-05925, ¶ 34, 53 (stating that "the system of common rules on conferment of jurisdiction established in Title II of the Convention is based on the general rule, set out in the first paragraph of Article 2, that persons domiciled in a Contracting State are to be sued in the courts

In the United States, courts have held that under federal common law, dismissal of a claim based on *forum non conveniens* is appropriate where: (1) an adequate alternate forum exists which possesses jurisdiction over the whole case, including all of the parties; (2) all relevant factors of private interest favor the alternate forum, weighing in the balance a strong presumption against disturbing plaintiffs' initial forum choice; (3) if the balance of private interests is nearly equal, the court further finds that factors of public interest tip the balance in favor of trial in the alternate forum; and (4) the trial judge ensures that plaintiffs can bring their suit in the alternate forum without undue inconvenience or prejudice.[55]

When applied to cases brought against TNCs, courts dismiss the cases, expecting that they will be filed in the host countries where the violations or harm occurred.[56] This expectation is a problem because, as discussed above, the host country might not have a judicial system that is as independent, functional, or stable as the home or forum country, might not have sufficient remedies, or the government might be unwilling or unable to allow the case to proceed, sometimes due to corruption or complicity.[57] In addition, there might be safety concerns – it may be riskier for victims to file cases in the host country, either because their identity will become better known or because of the lack of a rule of law.[58] One reason that this issue is so critical is that statistics suggest "ninety-nine percent of

---

of that State, irrespective [either] of the nationality of the parties," or of "the plaintiff's domicile or seat."); *see also* Case C-281/02, Owusu v. Jackson, 2005 E.C.R. I-1383 (interpreting Council Regulation 44/2001, 2000 O.J. (L12/1)); Peter Muchlinski, *Corporations in International Litigation: Problems of Jurisdiction and the United Kingdom Asbestos Cases*, 50 INT'L & COMP. L. Q. 1, 12–13 (2001) (explaining that the Brussels Convention mandated the use of domicile as the basic principle of jurisdiction and excluded the doctrine of *forum non conveniens*).

[55] Aldana v. Del Monte Fresh Produce N.A., Inc., 578 F.3d 1283, 1290 (11th Cir. 2009). With regard to relevant factors, courts consider the relative ease of access to sources of proof; availability of compulsory process for attendance of unwilling, and the cost of obtaining attendance of willing witnesses; possibility of view of the premises, if view would be appropriate to the action; and all other practical problems that make trial of a case easy, expeditious, and inexpensive; and the enforceability of a judgment if one is obtained in the United States. The burden is on the defendant to establish that an adequate, alternate remedy is possible in the home country.

[56] *See generally* Piper Aircraft Co. v. Reyno, 454 U.S. 235 (1981) (holding that plaintiffs may not defeat a motion to dismiss on ground of *forum non conveniens* simply by showing that the substantive law to be applied in the alternative forum would be less favorable to the plaintiff than that of the chosen forum); *see also* Aguinda v. Texaco, Inc., 303 F.3d 470 (2d Cir. 2002) (holding that balancing private and public interest factors weighed strongly in favor of trial in Ecuadorian courts, which justified the conditioned dismissal of the oil company's motion to dismiss on *forum non conveniens* grounds); In re Union Carbide Corp. Gas Plant Disaster at Bhopal, India in Dec., 1984, 809 F.2d 195, 197 (2d Cir. 1987) (holding that lawsuit brought by Union of India and private plaintiffs to recover for personal injury and wrongful death actions arising out of release of gas from chemical plant in India was properly dismissed on *forum non conveniens* grounds).

[57] *See* Joel Samuels, *When is an Alternative Forum Available? Rethinking the Forum Non Conveniens Analysis*, 85 IND. L. J. 1059, 1094–97 (2010).

[58] *Id.*, at 1095–96.

cases dismissed on forum non conveniens grounds in the United States, are, for one reason or another, never refiled"[59] in the alternate forum, and the victims are therefore left without any remedy.

8.2.1 US Federal Law

Forum non conveniens has not yet become a significant barrier to accessing judicial remedies in US federal courts for human rights violations.[60] However, there have been some cases dismissed on *forum non conveniens* grounds. For example, in Aguinda v. Texaco, Inc., citizens of Peru and Ecuador brought two putative class actions alleging that the oil company polluted rainforests and rivers in those two countries, causing environmental damage and personal injuries.[61] The Second Circuit affirmed dismissal on *forum non conveniens* grounds after the oil company consented to suit in Peru and Ecuador, finding that courts in Ecuador provided an adequate alternative forum. When the plaintiffs then sued in Ecuador, Chevron challenged jurisdiction, despite the consent to suit previously given.

One of the best-known cases against a business involving human rights dismissed on *forum non conveniens* grounds is Bhopal v. Union Carbide Corporation,[62] in which the families of thousands of victims who perished from a gas leak and explosion outside Bhopal, India in 1984 and those injured in the disaster, sought damages. The dismissal on *forum non conveniens* occurred even though the Chief Justice of the Supreme Court of India indicated that the victims' only chance for a remedy would be an action in the United States, given the serious backlog of cases in India and given that Indian legal commentators simply did not think the Indian courts could handle such a complex case.[63] After the US courts dismissed the case on *forum non conveniens* grounds, the people of Bhopal and Union Carbide entered into an agreement, brokered by the Indian government, providing for a "full and final settlement" of $470 million, waiving all future claims.[64] The settlement,

---

[59] Victor Manuel Diaz, Jr., *Litigation in U.S. Courts of Product Liability Cases Arising in Latin America, Panel Talk Before the Miami Conference on Products Liability in Latin America, in* 20 ARIZ. J. INT'L & COMP. L. 47, at 93 (John F. Molloy ed. 2003) (referencing the only comprehensive study done on this subject).

[60] This is not a barrier with regard to cases pursuant to the TVPA, where Congress enacted a cause of action for violations of the TVPA in federal courts, indicating Congress' view that US courts are an appropriate forum for TVPA cases.

[61] *Aguinda, supra* note 56 at 470.

[62] In re Union Carbide Corp. Gas Plant Disaster at Bhopal, India in Dec., 1984, 809 F.2d 195 (2d Cir. 1987).

[63] *See* James B. Stewart, *Legal Liability: Why Suits for Damages Such as Bhopal Claims Are Very Rare in India*, WALL ST. J. (Jan. 23, 1985) at 1 ("'It is my opinion that these cases must be pursued in the United States,' says Y.V. Chandrachud, the Chief Justice of the supreme court of India ... Although Indian courts could attempt to set precedent in Bhopal cases, if they are tried in India, that would create even more delay in the system.").

[64] Andrew Buncombe, *The Cursed Children of Bhopal*, INDEP., Nov. 19, 2008), http://www.independent.co.uk/news/world/asia/the-cursed-children-of-bhopal-1024600.html (last visited

however, was widely criticized as providing ineffective remedies for the victims, given that the settlement resulted in recoveries of between $2,500 and $7,500 per person for deaths, and between $1,250 and $5,000 for permanent disabilities.

8.2.2 US State Law

Forum non conveniens will likely have the greatest impact in cases filed under state law, which are expected to increase in light of *Kiobel* and *Jesner*.[65] In fact, *forum non conveniens* has already been a significant barrier to victims in cases brought under state tort law for acts occurring abroad.[66]

State law *forum non conveniens* doctrine can differ from the federal *forum non conveniens* doctrine. For example, after a Texas state court ruled that Texas statutorily abolished the doctrine of *forum non conveniens*, the Texas legislature responded by enacting a statute permitting *forum non conveniens* dismissals that places a heavy burden on the plaintiff selecting the Texas forum.[67] In Florida, courts have continued to expand the state's *forum non conveniens* doctrine, going so far as to hold that "no special weight should [be] given to a foreign plaintiff's choice of forum."[68]

Further, Florida has applied its *forum non conveniens* doctrine to dismiss even those cases where a foreign country has enacted "blocking statutes" preventing the country's courts from hearing cases dismissed on the basis of *forum non conveniens* in the United States. For example, in Scotts Co. v. Hacienda Loma Linda, a Florida state court dismissed the plaintiff's claim that the defendant's product damaged its orchid crops on *forum non conveniens* grounds.[69] A Panamanian court had already refused to take jurisdiction over the lawsuit pursuant to the country's recently

---

January 1, 2020); *see also Obstacles to Justice and Redress for Victims of Corporate Human Rights Abuse* 174 OXFORD PRO BONO PUBLICO, UNIV. OF OXFORD (2008), http://www.reports-and-materials.org/Oxford-Pro-Bono-Publico-submission-to-Ruggie-3-Nov-08.pdf (last visited January 1, 2020) ("[A] settlement was arrived [at] between the UCC and the Union of India whereby UCC were supposed to pay a lump sum of U.S.$470 million towards full and final settlement of all claims, arising out of both civil and criminal liability.").

[65] Paul Hoffman & Beth Stephens, *International Human Rights Cases Under State Law and In State Courts*, 3 U.C. IRVINE L. REV. 9, 12 (2013).

[66] *See* Geoffrey P. Miller, *In Search of the Most Adequate Forum: State Court Personal Jurisdiction*, 2 STAN. J. COMPLEX LITIG. 1, 34–35 (2014); Hoffman & Stephens, *supra* note 65, at 17–20. *See also* cases discussed *infra*. For additional cases where state courts have declined jurisdiction over cases involving foreign plaintiffs where the court found that an alternative forum was available, see *Forum Non Conveniens Doctrine in State Court as Affected by Availability of Alternative Forum*, 57 A.L.R. 4th 973 § 11[b]. For those cases where state courts declined jurisdiction even where the court also found that an alternative forum was unavailable, see *id.* §12[b].

[67] Dow Chem. Co. v. Castro Alfaro, 786 S.W.2d 674 (Tex. 1990), *superseded by statute*, Tex. Civ. Prac. & Rem. Code Ann. § 71.051 (West 2009).

[68] Ciba-Geigy Ltd. v. Fish Peddler, Inc., 691 So. 2d 1111, 1118 (Fla. Dist. Ct. App. 1997).

[69] *See* Scotts Co. v. Hacienda Loma Linda, 2 So. 3d 1013, 1015 (Fla. Dist. Ct. App. 2008).

enacted blocking statute.[70] Although the Panamanian forum was therefore unavailable to the plaintiff, the Florida appellate court nevertheless reasoned that the plaintiff was not entitled to reinstatement of its claim in Florida.[71]

Another example of how *forum non conveniens* has left victims without a remedy occurred in Aldana v. Del Monte Fresh Produce N.A., Inc.[72] Brought by seven Guatemalans who alleged they were tortured for their leadership in a national labor union, a federal district court dismissed the case on *forum non conveniens* grounds.[73] The 11th Circuit affirmed the dismissal because an expert witness testified at the district court that the plaintiffs could proceed with their case in Guatemala without the need to appear during the proceedings, and thus their safety was not at issue.[74] The appellate court further noted that the *forum non conveniens* dismissals "contained an express proviso that the appellants' motions would be reconsidered if there is ever any indication that they might be required to return to Guatemala."[75] After the court dismissed the claims, the plaintiffs filed a petition in Guatemala seeking relief for the human rights violations.[76] The Guatemalan court dismissed the case, finding that it lacked jurisdiction.[77] Under Guatemalan law, a Guatemalan court cannot hear a case if a plaintiff has already brought the case in another forum with jurisdiction – in this case, Florida.[78] Plaintiffs filed a motion for reinstatement in the federal district court, which was denied, and the denial was recently affirmed.[79] Plaintiffs are apparently left with no recourse.

8.2.3 Canada

Although some practitioners suggest that it is not as great a barrier as it once was, *forum non conveniens* still remains a potential barrier to victims seeking judicial remedy in Canada against Canadian businesses for their role in violations of human rights abroad.

---

[70] *Ciba-Geigy, supra* note 68 at 1118.
[71] *Id.* at 1017–18.
[72] *Aldana, supra* note 55.
[73] *Id.* at 1292 (finding that district court did not abuse its discretion when dismissing the case on *forum non conveniens* grounds).
[74] *Id.* at 1290.
[75] *Id.* at 1291.
[76] *See* Aldana v. Fresh Del Monte Produce, Int'l Rts. Advocates, http://www.iradvocates.org/case/latin-america-guatemala/aldana-v-fresh-del-monte-produce (last visited July 2, 2018).
[77] *Id.*
[78] *Id.*
[79] Aldana v. Fresh Del Monte Produce Inc., No. 1-3399-CIV, 2012 WL 5364241 (S.D. Fla. Oct 30, 2012), *aff'd*, 741 F.3d 1349 (11th Cir. 2014). Part of the reason for the dismissal, however, was apparently because the plaintiffs did not seek appeal in the Guatemalan courts, even though they contend they had no basis to do so. *Id.* at 1358.

Forum non conveniens has been adopted by all Canadian common law provincial courts,[80] and codified in British Columbia[81] and in the civil law jurisdiction of Quebec.[82] The issue of *forum non conveniens* has not been litigated in the context of an international human rights case against a business in any of Canada's common law jurisdictions. The issue has only been litigated in the context of a human rights case against a TNC in the civil jurisdiction of Quebec (discussed below).

The leading *forum non conveniens* common law case is Van Breda Club Resorts Ltd. v. Van Breda, decided in 2012.[83] In that case, the Supreme Court of Canada held that in order for a court to dismiss a case on *forum non conveniens* grounds, the defendant[84] must show that an alternative forum exists that is "clearly more appropriate," and that in light of the characteristics of the alternative forum, it would be fairer and more efficient to litigate the case in the alternative forum.[85] The Court explained that the factors to be taken into consideration differ from case to case, and stated that the factors

> might include the locations of parties and witnesses, the cost of transferring the case to another jurisdiction or of declining the stay, the impact of a transfer on the

---

[80] See Mikos Manolis et al., *The Doctrine of Forum Non Conveniens: Canada and the United States Compared*, 60 FED'N DEF. & CORP. COUNS. Q. 3 (2009), http://www.vermettelaw.com/uploads/tmp_files/13_151d956c246254e0e78ae164de21ceao.pdf (last visited January 1, 2020).

[81] Court Jurisdiction and Proceedings Transfer Act, S.B.C., c. 28 § 11. The statute reads:

> (1) After considering the interests of the parties to a proceeding and the ends of justice, a court may decline to exercise its territorial competence in the proceeding on the ground that a court of another state is a more appropriate forum in which to hear the proceeding. (2) A court, in deciding the question of whether it or a court outside British Columbia is the more appropriate forum in which to hear a proceeding, must consider the circumstances relevant to the proceeding, including (a) the comparative convenience and expense for the parties to the proceeding and for their witnesses, in litigating in the court or in any alternative forum, (b) the law to be applied to issues in the proceeding, (c) the desirability of avoiding multiplicity of legal proceedings, (d) the desirability of avoiding conflicting decisions in different courts, (e) the enforcement of an eventual judgment, and (f) the fair and efficient working of the Canadian legal system as a whole.

> This statute was intended to codify the common law test. See Teck Cominco Metals Ltd. v. Lloyd's Underwriters [2009] 1 S.C.R. 321, para. 22 (Can.). In addition, the Uniform Law Conference of Canada proposed a uniform Act to govern issues related to jurisdiction and to the doctrine of *forum non conveniens* that reads substantially the same. See Court Jurisdiction and Proceedings Transfer Act, S.B.C., c. 28; Club Resorts Ltd. v. Van Breda, [2012] 1 S.C.R. 572, paras. 40–41 (Can.).

[82] Quebec civil law provides that a Court can decline jurisdiction if it considers that a foreign court is better situated to hear the dispute. That statute reads: "Even though a Quebec authority has jurisdiction to hear a dispute, it may, exceptionally and on an application by a party, decline jurisdiction if it considers that the authorities of another State are in a better position to decide the dispute." Civil Code of Québec, S.Q. 1991 c. 1, s. 3135 (Can.).

[83] *Club Resorts* [2012] 1 S.C.R. 572 at paras. 101–12.

[84] Prior to this case, the provinces were divided as to whether defendants or plaintiffs had the burden on this issue. Manolis, *supra* note 80, at 9, 33.

[85] *Club Resorts*, *supra* note 83 at para. 109.

conduct of the litigation or on related or parallel proceedings, the possibility of conflicting judgments, problems related to the recognition and enforcement of judgments, and the relative strengths of the connections of the two parties.[86]

The first apparent lawsuit in Canada brought under provincial tort law against a Canada-based business for extraterritorial human rights and environmental abuses, Recherches Internationales Quebéc v. Cambior, Inc.,[87] was brought in Quebec and dismissed on *forum non conveniens* grounds. In 1995, the tailings dam at Cambior's Omai gold mine in Guyana failed, releasing over three billion liters of toxic waste into the Essequibo River and contaminating the water supply of thousands of indigenous people, many of whom sued Cambior in Quebec. The judge dismissed the case, finding that Guyana was the appropriate forum and that the plaintiffs did not have a right to a forum in Quebec.[88] Another Canadian case, Bil'in (Vill. Council) v. Green Park Int'l, was also dismissed on *forum non conveniens* grounds.[89] In July 2008, the Village Council of Bil'in (Palestine) filed suit in the Superior Court of Quebec against Green Park International Ltd., claiming that the business and its director were participating in war crimes by helping build settler villages on Palestinian land.[90] In September 2009, the court dismissed the case on *forum non conveniens* grounds, positing that there was little connection between Quebec and the events that took place in Palestine and that the case was more appropriately heard in Israel's High Court of Justice.[91]

Notwithstanding these cases, practitioners report that in the case of Choc v. Hudbay Minerals, Inc.,[92] the defendant withdrew its motion to dismiss the case based on *forum non conveniens* in February 2013, just before the Ontario court was to make a ruling.[93] Canadian practitioners suspected that Hudbay withdrew the motion because it knew it might well lose after closely reviewing the law in *Van Breda* and the facts associated with the *forum non conveniens* factors.[94] Those representing victims of corporate human rights abuses viewed this as a major victory.[95]

Choc notwithstanding, a review of Canada's statutory and common law reveals that whether a plaintiff can defeat a *forum non conveniens* motion by arguing that it

---

[86] *Id.* at para. 110.
[87] Recherches Internationales Quebéc v. Cambior, Inc., 1998 CarswellQue 4511 (Can. R.J.Q.) (WL).
[88] *Id.*
[89] Bil'in (Vill. Council) v. Green Park Int'l, 2009 QCSC 4151, paras. 175–76 (Can. Que. Sup. Ct.).
[90] Motion Introducing a Suit, Bil'in (Village Council) & Ahmed Issa Yassin v. Green Park Int'l, Inc, No. 500-17-044030-081 (Superior Court, Province of Quebec, District of Montreal July 7, 2008).
[91] *Bil'in, supra* note 89 at para. 335.
[92] Choc v. Hudbay Minerals, Inc., 2013 ONSC 1414 (Can. Ont.).
[93] *See Choc v. HudBay Minerals Inc. & Caal v. HudBay Minerals Inc.*, http://www.chocversushudbay.com/ (last updated Sept. 15, 2017).
[94] Canadian Consultation. Notes and emails on file with author.
[95] *Id.*

would be difficult to obtain an adequate remedy in the host country is still unsettled in both the common and civil law. In fact, the notions of adequate remedy and futility do not appear to be a part of Canada's common law test.[96] Therefore, *forum non conveniens* is still a hurdle in Canadian human rights litigation.

8.2.4 Overcoming the Barrier of Forum Non Conveniens

The United States and Canada should consider enacting a similar requirement as the Brussels Regulation, recast, requiring that the respective country's courts must recognize extraterritorial civil claims brought under any statute against a corporation domiciled in the respective country. Such a statute would indicate to courts that the respective lawmakers felt it appropriate that each country's courts hear tort matters that occur extraterritorially. In addition, this would provide each country's businesses with certainty.

Alternatively, lawmakers should codify the doctrine of *forum non conveniens* so that the factors for *forum non conveniens* dismissals are clear, and correctly and consistently applied to prevent improper dismissals. This could include drafting a model *forum non conveniens* statute for adoption.

8.2.4.1 United States

In the United States, such a statute could simply provide for a presumption, which a defendant could overcome, that a foreign forum is not adequate where a foreign plaintiff sues in US federal or state courts for acts that occur abroad. This is because a plaintiff's willingness to incur litigation costs implies a need for access to the US forum, given the significant costs (in terms of time, effort, and money) in bringing a case outside of one's own country. To overcome the presumption, the burden should be on the defendants to establish that:

- the foreign forum is a better and more convenient alternative for the witnesses and the parties;
- the public policy of the United States can be achieved through filing in the foreign forum;
- an adequate remedy, similar to what the plaintiff could achieve in courts in the United States, is available and would be provided as promptly as in US courts;
- the State's judiciary is stable;
- the defendant would agree to personal and subject matter jurisdiction in the foreign forum;
- there are no rules which would prevent the plaintiff from obtaining a remedy; and

---

[96] Adequate forum and futility are not listed as common law factors codified in British Columbia.

- that the State does not have "blocking statutes" that would prohibit the plaintiff from refiling in the foreign forum. Any such statute should also allow courts to set conditions for dismissals on *forum non conveniens* grounds.

Such statutes should also provide that any case dismissed on *forum non conveniens* grounds be dismissed "without prejudice," meaning that the case can be refiled in US courts if one of the conditions is not met. Alternatively, the court could keep jurisdiction over the matter pending the resolution of litigation in the host forum.

8.2.4.2 Canada

It appears that the notion that plaintiffs must have an adequate available remedy abroad is not yet firmly rooted in the *forum non conveniens* law in Canada, and this requirement is not contained in either British Columbia's statute, which is meant to codify common law, or in the Uniform Court Jurisdiction and Proceedings Transfer Act (CJPTA) drafted by the Uniform Law Conference of Canada. It is also not contained in Quebec's law. To rectify this, the Uniform Law Conference of Canada and lawmakers, especially at the provincial level where human rights litigation occurs, should amend their model law and statutes to require that courts find that there is an adequate remedy in the foreign forum before dismissing the case on *forum non conveniens* ground. The Uniform Law Conference should also consider drafting a model statute setting forth the factors for "forum by necessity" to similarly provide jurisdiction to Canadian courts over victims' claims of harm by acts of Canadian corporations, where they would otherwise not be able to access an adequate remedy in the host state.

8.3 BARRIERS PRESENTED BY "CHOICE OF LAW" DOCTRINE

8.3.1 United States

In the United States, after *Kiobel*, *Jesner*, and the likely consequence of more human rights litigation in state courts (or in federal courts under diversity jurisdiction applying state common law), choice of law analysis will take on added importance.[97] The types of state tort claims that plaintiffs have brought in the past

---

[97] Several scholars have written on the conflict of laws and the impact it has on human rights litigation. See, e.g., Roger P. Alford, *The Future of Human Rights Litigation After Kiobel*, 89 NOTRE DAME L. REV. 1749, 1770–72 (2014) ("If international law is incorporated into the national laws of all relevant jurisdictions ... this may result in ... a 'false conflict,' allowing the forum court to apply domestic law where ... identical to foreign law ... [I]f the competing laws are the same, there is no need to choose between them."); Patrick J. Borchers, *Conflict-of-Laws Considerations in State Court Human Rights Actions*, 3 U.C. IRVINE L. REV. 45, 60 (2013) (noting that state courts may not be better forums for human rights cases because many state courts' choice of law analysis will apply the law of foreign nations, resulting in significantly

and will likely bring in the future that arise out of violations of international human rights include: wrongful death, assault and battery, negligence, nuisance, false imprisonment, intentional and negligent infliction of emotional distress, and even unlawful business practices, as was claimed in the *Unocal* case filed in California state court.[98]

Each state in the United States employs its own choice of law analysis.[99] A federal district court that has jurisdiction over claims of state law due to diversity jurisdiction applies the choice of law principles of the forum state (the state in which the federal court resides) in order to establish the applicable substantive law for a plaintiff's claims.[100] In a choice of law analysis, the court will typically first determine if an actual conflict exists between domestic law – the law of the forum state – and foreign law. If not, the court will apply the law of the forum state.[101] If there is a difference in the law – or a conflict – the court will then decide which law to apply.[102] Typically, the court will apply the substantive law of the state or country where the injury occurred (typically the host state), unless the forum state has a greater interest in determining a particular issue or has a more significant relationship to what occurred and to the parties.[103]

---

lower damage remedies); Donald Earl Childress III, *The Alien Tort Statute, Federalism, and the Next Wave of Transnational Litigation*, 100 GEO. L. J. 709, 744–49 (2012) (discussing the differing conflict of law rules among the states, the constitutional limits on choice of law analysis, and the impact choice of law will have on available remedies); William S. Dodge, *Alien Tort Statute: The Road Not Taken*, 89 NOTRE DAME L. REV. 1577, 1578–87 (2014) (discussing the implications of choice of law analysis under the ATS); Jeffrey A. Meyer, *Extraterritorial Common Law: Does the Common Law Apply Abroad?* 102 GEO. L. J. 301, 314–18 (2014) (describing the various state choice of law tests and the differing impact each could have on human rights litigation); see generally Anthony J. Colangelo & Kristina A. Kiik, *Spatial Legality, Due Process, and Choice of Law in Human Rights Litigation Under U.S. State Law*, 3 U.C. IRVINE L. REV. 63 (2013) (discussing how the Constitution might limit certain choice of law analyses).

[98] Doe v. Unocal, Nos. BC 237 980, BC 237 679, 2002 WL 33944504, at *2, 14 (Cal. App. Dep't Super. Ct. June 7, 2002) (granting summary judgment for defendants in part).

[99] See Meyer, *supra* note 97.

[100] Klaxon Co. v. Stentor Electric Mfg. Co., 313 U.S. 487 (1941).

[101] See, e.g., DP Aviation v. Smiths Indus. Aerospace and Def. Sys. Ltd., 268 F.3d 829, 845 (9th Cir. 2001) ("Washington [State]'s principles governing conflict of laws require the application of Washington substantive law unless a conflict of law is presented to the court.").

[102] In making a choice of law decision in personal injury cases, a court should consider: (a) the needs of the interstate and international systems; (b) the relevant policies of the forum; (c) the relevant policies of other interested states and the relative interests of those states in the determination of the particular issue; (d) the protection of justified expectations; (e) the basic policies underlying the particular field of law; (f) certainty, predictability, and uniformity of result; and (g) ease in determination and application of the law to be applied. Restatement (Second) of Conflict of Laws § 6 (1971).

[103] Many, if not most, courts apply the "most significant relationships test" to determine which law to apply. In determining which state has the most significant relationship to the occurrence and parties, the contacts that are to be taken into account in applying these principles are: (a) the place where the injury occurred; (b) the place where the conduct causing the injury occurred; (c) the domicile, residence, nationality, place of incorporation, and place of business of the

Applying the law of the host state can present significant barriers to litigation, such as when the chosen law affects statutes of limitations, does not recognize or limits vicarious or secondary liability, has elements for its torts that are more difficult to prove, or provides for immunity that might not apply under the forum state's common law. In determining choice of law questions, there should be an interest in ensuring that the plaintiff has a remedy – especially when the defendant's conduct is considered to be in violation of the law of nations.[104]

8.3.2 Europe

In the European Union, the Rome II Regulation[105] applies to tort liability claims presented to the national courts of the EU Member States.[106] This Regulation in principle designates the law of the state in which the harm occurred (the *lex loci delicti*) as the applicable law. Civil liability claims shall be decided on the basis of the rules in force in the host state, where the damage occurred.[107] While this is the general rule, and the one most likely to apply in most instances, there are a number of exceptions,[108] including three that are of particular interest where claims are based on the allegation of human rights violations. First, provisions of the law of the forum may apply, "in a situation where they are mandatory irrespective of the law otherwise applicable to the non-contractual obligation."[109] Thus, it is possible to argue that, where the law of the state where the harm occurred is not sufficiently protective of the human rights of the person harmed (including where core labor rights as recognized in the International Labour Organization (ILO) conventions as confirmed in the UNGPs), the law of the forum state will apply. For instance, courts in Germany have recognized that the right to maternity leave or to sick pay are both mandatory in that sense,[110] and also possibly the right to form unions and the prohibition on discrimination.[111]

---

parties; and (d) the place where the relationship, if any, between the parties is centered. *Id.* at § 145.
[104] *See* Alvarez-Machain v. United States, 331 F.3d 604, 635 (9th Cir. 2003), *rev'd on other grounds sub nom.* Sosa v. Alvarez-Machain, 542 U.S. 692 (2004).
[105] Council Regulation 864/2007 2007 O.J. (L 199) 40 (EC) [hereinafter Rome II Regulation].
[106] 2007 O.J. (L 199) 40.
[107] Rome II Regulation, *supra* note 105 at art. 4(1).
[108] For example, there are exceptions where the harm is manifestly more closely connected with another state and where the claimant and the corporation share a common "habitual residence." *See id.* at arts. 4(3), 4(2).
[109] *Id.* at art. 16.
[110] Miriam Saage-Maaß, LABOR CONDITIONS IN THE GLOBAL SUPPLY CHAIN: WHAT IS THE EXTENT AND IMPLICATIONS OF GERMAN CORPORATE RESPONSIBILITY? 7 FRIEDRICH EBERT STIFTUNG (2011), citing Bundesarbeitsgerichts [BAG] [Federal Labor Court] Dec. 12, 2001, Entscheidungen des Bundesarbeitsgerichts [BAGE] 100, 130 to § 14 I MuSchG and § 3 EFZG.
[111] For other examples, see Robert Grabosch, *Rechtsschutz vor deutschen Zivilgerichten gegen Beeinträchtigungen von Menschenrechten durch transnationale Unternehmen, in* TRANSNATIONALE UNTERNEHMEN UND NICHTREGIERUNGSORGANISATIONEN IM VÖLKERRECHT 69, 84–86 (Ralph Nikol, Thomas Bernhard, & Nina Schniederjan, eds. 2013).

Second, "[i]n assessing the conduct of the person claimed to be liable, account shall be taken, as a matter of fact and in so far as is appropriate, of the rules of safety and conduct which were in force at the place and time of the event giving rise to the liability."[112] This provision can apply where there are global supply chains, because it implies that where harm occurs in a host state as a result of the conduct of a business domiciled in the forum state, the definition of the conduct that may be considered reasonable shall be defined in accordance with the law of the forum state. Therefore, in an EU Member State where a law provides that a failure to act with due diligence may engage liability, companies domiciled in that Member State could be found liable on that basis. This is true even if the harm occurs in a third state, and even though the law applicable to the claim for damages filed before national courts in the European Union would in principle be the state where the harm occurred. This is consistent with Guiding Principle 2 of the UNGPs, which clarifies that "States should set out clearly the expectation that all business enterprises domiciled in their territory and/or jurisdiction respect human rights throughout their operations."[113] Specifically, to the extent that the duty to act with due diligence is imposed on companies operating from within the European Union, these companies should be made aware that, as a result of the Rome II Regulation (and Article 17 in particular), this standard of conduct shall apply also to assess whether they are liable for human rights violations that occur outside the European Union, which they would have been able to prevent.

Third, the law of the state where the harm occurred may not apply "if such application is manifestly incompatible with the public policy (ordre public) of the forum."[114] This exception might be applied when the laws of the state where the harm occurred are considered to be contrary to the protection of human rights.[115]

Lastly, European law mandates that for injuries occurring after January 11, 2009, damages are to be calculated under the law of the country where the injury occurred.[116] The economies of host countries are typically less developed and their currency weaker.[117] This will almost always mean that the damages will be much lower if the forum country's laws are applied.

---

[112] Rome II Regulation, *supra* note 105 at art. 17.
[113] John Ruggie, *Guiding Principles on Business and Human Rights: Implementing the United Nations "Protect, Respect, and Remedy" Framework*, U.N. Doc A/HRC/17/L.17/31 (June 16, 2011), at princ. 2.
[114] Rome II Regulation, *supra* note 105 at art. 26.
[115] Kuwait Airways Corp. v. Iraq Airways Co. [2002] 2 A.C. 883 ¶ 18 (Eng.).
[116] Rome II Regulation, *supra* note 105.
[117] *See generally Purchasing Power Parities (PPPs), Data and Methodology*, Organisation for Economic Co-operation and Development (OECD), http://www.oecd.org/std/purchasingpowerparitiespppsdata.htm (last visited July 2, 2018) (providing data on purchasing power parities for OECD countries).

8.3.3 *Canada*

In Ontario, the choice of law question does not arise unless one of the parties specifically raises the issue.[118] If neither party raises the issue, then domestic law is presumptively applied.[119] However, if one party does raise the issue, then the court begins a rules-based analysis to determine which law – domestic or foreign – it should apply.[120] Generally, domestic law will govern all procedural issues, and all matters relating to the substantive rights of the parties may be governed by foreign law.[121] The first step involves "characterizing the dispute" – contract, property, matrimonial, etc.[122] The next step is to examine various "connecting factors" to determine which law to apply to the dispute.[123] Connecting factors include the parties' place of residence, their place of domicile, where their claim is actionable, or where the harm took place (*lex loci delicti commissi* or *lex loci*).[124] Based on this analysis, the court will decide whether to apply the law of domestic court or the law of the foreign jurisdiction.[125] In Tolofson v. Jensen, the Supreme Court of Canada held that a court may exercise "a limited discretion" in cases where the application of foreign law "could give rise to injustice."[126]

In Das v. George Weston Limited, four Bangladeshi citizens sued a Canadian retailer, Loblaws, for its connection to a manufacturer with a factory in Rana Plaza.[127] In 2013, the Rana Plaza factory collapse led to 1,130 deaths, 2,520 serious injuries, and global outcry for supply chain transparency and accountability.[128] In Ontario, the parties raised the choice of law issue and the court began its analysis by characterizing the claims as a tort case and a breach of fiduciary duty case.[129] Plaintiffs argued that their claims should be covered by Ontario law because Loblaws, a Canadian company, conducted an international business knowing that employees deep in the supply chain were exposed to dangerous working conditions.[130] Defendants, a retail company, argued that Bangladesh law was more appropriate.[131] Under Bangladesh law, the plaintiffs' claims would be statutorily

---

[118] Das v. George Weston Limited, [2017] ONSC 4129 at para. 215 (citing Pettkus v. Becker [1980] 2 S.C.R. 834, 853–54).
[119] *Das, supra* note 118.
[120] *Id.* at para 223.
[121] *Id.* at para 213 (citing Somers v. Fournier (2002), 60 O.R. (3d) 225 (C.A.)).
[122] *Das, supra* note 118 at para. 224.
[123] *Id.* at para 223.
[124] *Id.*
[125] *Id.*
[126] *Id.* at para 278.
[127] *Id.* at para 1.
[128] *Id.*
[129] *Id.* at para 227.
[130] *Id.* at para 235.
[131] *Id.* at para 207.

barred because they were filed more than a year after the events at Rana Plaza.[132] In determining which law to apply, the court looked first for a connecting factor. Plaintiffs presented as connecting factors "such activities as gaining knowledge about the history of Bangladesh factory disasters in Ontario ... and arranging visits to Bangladesh from Ontario.'"[133] In rejecting this argument, the court described this as a "very thin connecting factor"[134] given the fact that the injuries and death caused by the collapse of Rana Plaza occurred in Bangladesh.[135] The court held that the law of Bangladesh governed both the tort and breach of fiduciary duty claims.[136]

8.3.4 Overcoming the Barrier of Choice of Law Statutes

8.3.4.1 United States

As mentioned above, under choice of law analysis, whether governed by statute or common law, courts typically apply the law of the country where the harm occurred unless the forum state has a greater interest in determining a particular issue, or if it has a more significant relationship to what occurred and to the parties. States should either amend existing choice of law statutes or enact new choice of law statutes to clarify that where TNCs over which the court has personal jurisdiction have engaged in illegal conduct abroad, the law of the forum state applies where the plaintiffs would not receive an adequate remedy if the law of the country where the harm occurred applies. This could be accomplished by enacting this language, or through legislation clarifying that courts should take such considerations into account when determining whether the forum state has a "greater interest" in a particular issue.

8.3.4.2 Europe

The European Commission or a European Parliament resolution should enact an interpretative communication to clarify that, consistent with Article 16 of the Rome II Regulation, the law of the forum should be applied instead of the law of the place of harm where the latter law is not sufficiently protective of the human rights of victims. This may be the case, for example, when the law of the state where the harm occurred does not recognize certain human rights, such as core labor rights, or where it severely restricts the ability of victims to bring claims. The European Union Agency for Fundamental Rights (FRA) made this recommendation in 2017: in a report on access to remedy, it suggested that the EU should analyze the

---

[132] *Id.* at para 208.
[133] *Id.* at para 237.
[134] *Id.*
[135] *Id.* at para 240.
[136] *Id.* at para 266.

consequences of a revision to the Rome II Regulation, which would allow exceptions on choice of law, in cases of business-related human rights abuse.[137]

8.4 BARRIERS PRESENTED BY STATUTES OF LIMITATIONS

Statutes of limitations are common in all jurisdictions. Such statutes pose particular hurdles for claims involving human rights abuses committed abroad, given the difficulty in investigating such claims and gathering evidence.

8.4.1 US Federal Law

The ATS does not contain a statute of limitations.[138] Courts that have applied a statute of limitations under the ATS have adopted the TVPA's ten-year statute of limitations rather than the statute of limitations of a similar state tort.[139] Adopting the TVPA's statute of limitations typically results in a greater limitations period for plaintiffs than if the court had adopted that of the state. In addition, extraordinary circumstances typically lead courts to apply principles of equitable tolling.[140] Thus, even where statutes of limitations have been imposed under the ATS, they have not posed much of a hurdle at the federal level. This has been positive for victims, given that in most other countries, where claims for human rights abuses are typically brought under local tort law and not international law, the statute of limitations for torts is much shorter – typically between two and five years.[141]

8.4.2 US State Law

Statutes of limitations are often barriers to cases brought under state law. State statutes of limitations are often fairly short, with many states imposing a one-year limit for intentional tort claims.[142] As more human rights litigation moves to state

---

[137] *Improving Access to Remedy in the Area of Business and Human Rights at the EU Level*, EUROPEAN UNION AGENCY FOR FUNDAMENTAL RIGHTS 10–11 (Apr. 10, 2017). Such an exception already exists for environmental damages, meaning that the law of the country where the cause of the damage originated, rather than where the damage occurred, can be applied. *Id.*

[138] 28 U.S.C. § 1350 (2012).

[139] Chavez v. Carranza, 559 F.3d 486, 492 (6th Cir. 2009); Jean v. Dorelien, 431 F.3d 776, 778 (11th Cir. 2005); Van Tu v. Koster, 364 F.3d 1196, 1199 (10th Cir. 2004); Papa v. United States, 281 F.3d 1004, 1012–13 (9th Cir. 2002).

[140] *See, e.g., Chavez, supra* note 139 ("The TVPA 'calls for consideration of all equitable tolling principles in calculating this [statute of limitations] period with a view towards giving justice to plaintiff's rights.'" (quoting S. Rep. No. 02-249, at 10-11)); *Jean, supra* note 139 at 778 ("However, this statute of limitations is subject to the doctrine of equitable tolling.").

[141] *Limitation Periods*, PRACTICAL LAW (Jan. 1, 2018), http://us.practicallaw.com/1-518-8770?q=& qp=&qo=&qe= (last visited January 1, 2020).

[142] *See, e.g.,* Cal. Civ. Proc. Code § 355.1 (West 2013) (imposing a one-year statute of limitations); N.Y. C.P.L.R. 215 (McKinney 2014) (imposing a one-year statute of limitations).

courts, this will pose a challenge. There will also be uncertainty as to the particular statute of limitations that applies.[143] Whether the forum state or foreign country's statute of limitations applies will depend on the choice of law analysis each state employs, and that varies widely from state to state. Under some states' choice of law analysis, foreign law will supply the applicable statute of limitations. If the host country has a short statute of limitations, that could be a problem for victims. Of course, it could be beneficial if the host country has a relatively long statute of limitations, but as discussed above, that is not common. If the country incorporates international human rights law norms directly into domestic law, this might include the longer statutes of limitations associated with international violations because many countries now recognize that genocide, crimes against humanity, and war crimes are not subject to any statutory limitations.[144] That might mean a longer period in which to file a claim, just as with the ATS. Consistent with this approach, as discussed below, the American Bar Association's Section of International Law recommended that the statute of limitations for these offenses be removed.[145] While more generous statutes of limitations do not pose a serious barrier to a remedy, shorter statutes of limitations, as well as lingering uncertainty regarding the proper time limit, pose significant barriers to victims.

8.4.3 Europe

In Europe, the Rome II Regulation controls the statute of limitations.[146] It provides that the statute of limitations of the law of the country found to apply under a choice of law analysis will govern the limitations period.[147] The Regulation specifically notes that the first choice in the choice of law analysis should be the law of the

---

[143] See, e.g., Richard Herz, *The Future of Alien Tort Litigation: Kiobel and Beyond*, 106 AM. SOC'Y INT'L L. PROC. 493, 493–94 (2013) (discussing the fact that states have different conflict of law analyses and differing statutes of limitations, which could cause the period for bringing a claim to run out well before a victim is able to come forward); Hoffman & Stephens, *supra* note 65, at 19 (noting that the statutes of limitations at the state court level are much shorter than the ten-year limit generally applied to ATS claims through the TVPA statute of limitations); Anthony Blackburn, *Striking a Balance to Reform the Alien Tort Statute: A Recommendation for Congress*, 53 SANTA CLARA L. REV. 1051, 1063–64 (2013) (discussing the varying results that will occur through the choice of law rules of forum which states use due to lack of statute of limitations for the ATS); Patrick J. Borchers, *supra* note 97 at 49–55 (discussing the difficulties which plaintiffs encounter under state choice of law rules).

[144] See Convention on the Non-Applicability of Statutory Limitations to War Crimes and Crimes Against Humanity, Nov. 26, 1968, 754 U.N.T.S. 73; Rome Statute of the International Criminal Court, *opened for signature* July 17, 1998, art. 29, 37 I.L.M. 999, 1018, 2187 U.N.T.S. 90, 107 (entered into force July 1, 2002).

[145] BARTON LEGUM, *Resolution 107A: Report to the House of Delegates*, A.B.A. SEC. INT'L L. REP. (Aug. 2013), https://www.americanbar.org/content/dam/aba/uncategorized/international_law/2013_hod_annual_meeting_107A.authcheckdam.pdf (last visited January 1, 2020).

[146] Rome II Regulation, *supra* note 105 at art. 4.

[147] *Id.*

country where the harm occurred.[148] As discussed above, this will often mean a shorter statute of limitations given that local torts typically have shorter statutes of limitations.[149] Even where the law of the forum applies, there will be shorter statutes of limitations given that the claims there are rarely brought as international claims, but rather as tort claims.[150] In other situations, the statute of limitations in a host country may not be easy to determine, and may require further expertise and research, posing additional barriers.

8.4.4 Overcoming Barriers Created by Statutes of Limitations

State legislatures should be encouraged to amend their statutes of limitations, which limit the time in which victims may bring cases, by lengthening the statute of limitations for human rights claims that occur abroad. In addition, both state and federal lawmakers should be encouraged to amend any statutes to ensure that there is no statute of limitations for certain claims, such as genocide, war crimes, and crimes against humanity. As mentioned above, the American Bar Association, in August 2013, passed a resolution taking this position with regard to these human rights crimes.[151] Expanding the statute of limitations takes into consideration the complexities associated with both international human rights litigation and working with communities located abroad for which there may be language and cultural complexities. Alternatively, because it could be argued that expanding statutes of limitations could prejudice defendants in some circumstances, lawmakers should at a minimum allow more liberal tolling of statutes of limitations in certain situations, such as where security and costs are an issue, or where the case is especially complex.

8.5 BARRIERS CREATED BY RESTRICTIVE DISCOVERY RULES

Plaintiffs face numerous practical barriers in investigating and proving transnational businesses' involvement in human rights violations. One of the largest barriers to human rights litigation for corporate abuses is obtaining the necessary information and evidence for communities and victims to pursue the litigation, especially in a court abroad. This barrier is often more pronounced than in other human rights cases, given that businesses' involvement can be vicarious. The complexities of the

---

[148] *Id.*
[149] *See* Klaxon, *supra* note 100.
[150] *See* John Terry & Sarah Shody, *Could Canada Become a New Forum for Cases Involving Human Rights Violations Committed Abroad?* 1 COM. LITIG. & ARB. REV. 63, 64 (2012) (discussing human rights tort claims filed in Canada); Jodie A. Kirshner, *A Call for the EU to Assume Jurisdiction over Extraterritorial Corporate Human Rights Abuses*, 13 NW. J. INT'L HUM. RTS. 1, 25 (2015) (discussing human rights claims filed as tort actions in European countries); Robert McCorquodale, *Waiving Not Drowning: Kiobel Outside the United States*, 107 AM. J. INT'L L. 846, 850 (2013).
[151] BARTON LEGUM, *supra* note 145.

corporate structure have implications for the gathering of evidence and providing discovery in transnational human rights litigation as well. For example, parent companies over which the courts have jurisdiction may deny any involvement in subsidiaries' actions, yet often will not produce information regarding the subsidiaries, including information regarding their relationships to the subsidiaries. Unless a plaintiff can establish that the parent company has information only it knows, show that the plaintiff cannot easily obtain the information through public records, and articulate specifically what they are looking for, a court will typically refuse any discovery order.

In addition, the difficult task of pursuing, preserving, and gathering evidence and providing testimony in the face of security risks and harm for human rights violations is a barrier to bringing claims. Such risks increase, or at least were believed by victims to increase, when corporate interests are involved. Even if victims or witnesses are willing to provide testimony, securing such testimony by deposition or in court is difficult. The taking of depositions abroad is quite costly, and there are often complications involving travel and security in the host state. In one case, a judge reportedly asked the plaintiff's lawyers to prove that they could actually take a deposition in order to continue the case.[152]

Discovery is normally not done through interstate judicial cooperation or through various mechanisms of the Hague Convention, given the complications and the length of time it takes to secure such cooperation and support. Discovery is usually secured through procedures under the domestic rules of civil procedure, with duties inherent under the rules on both sides of the litigation, and intervention by the court when needed.

8.5.1 *United States*

In the United States, an additional hurdle is getting a victim or witness to the United States for a trial. A victim or witness will have to obtain a visa, and doing so is very difficult. For example, a person coming to the United States temporarily will need to establish strong ties to the host country in order to convince the State Department that they will return to the host country.[153] If during the application process they

---

[152] See Gwynne Skinner, *Beyond Kiobel: Providing Access to Judicial Remedies for Corporate Accountability for Violations of International Human Rights Norms by Transnational Corporations in a New (Post-Kiobel) World*, 46 COLUM. HUM. RTS. L. REV. 158, 244 n393 (2014).

[153] *Attorney General Guidelines for Victim & Witness Assistance*, U.S. DEP'T OF JUST. 12 (May 2012), http://www.justice.gov/olp/pdf/ag_guidelines2012.pdf (last visited January 1, 2020). *See also Visitor Visas: Business and Pleasure*, U.S. DEP'T OF ST. – BUREAU OF CONSULAR AFF., https://travel.state.gov/content/dam/visas/PDF-other/VisaFlyer_B1B2_March_2015.pdf (last visited July 3, 2018) (explaining the process and requirements for applying for a visitor visa); § 1101(a)(15)(F)(i) ("an alien having a residence in a foreign country which he has no intention of abandoning"); § 1101(a)(15)(H) (must have no intention of abandoning foreign residence and only coming temporarily to the United States for specific work or training); § 1101(a)(15)(J) ("an alien having a

express fear of returning because of their involvement in the case, the State Department may believe they will in fact not return and deny them the visa. Unfortunately, individuals cannot apply for asylum at a US embassy; they must be in the United States to apply for asylum.[154] In other situations, the victim or witness might not have appropriate documents in order to secure a passport or a visa. Where victims or witnesses have obtained visas, it has typically required the active involvement of the court.

8.5.2 Canada

Canada has discovery rules that are somewhat similar to the United States, but, like the United Kingdom discussed below, the discovery process is more restrictive.[155] For example, only one representative of a corporate party can be deposed, and questions asked during discovery must be directly relevant to the issue and not simply be able to lead to discoverable evidence.[156] In addition, obtaining discovery abroad can be difficult for those who file in Canada because Canada is not a party to the Hague Convention on Taking Evidence Abroad.[157] The courts are willing to issue Letters of Request (which request evidence), but the requirements are stringent.[158]

8.5.3 Europe

Unlike the United States, most of Europe generally lacks discovery and disclosure rules requiring the opposing party to provide information in its possession.[159] In many European countries, courts often refuse plaintiffs' discovery requests unless they can articulate specifically what they are looking for – often a daunting task.

The majority of EU states are based on the civil law tradition, and so there are no party-based discovery procedures.[160] The gathering of evidence is "strictly a judicial function" driven by the presiding judge.[161] Even in the common law system of the

---

residence in a foreign country which he has no intention of abandoning"); § 1101(a)(15)(M) (same); § 1101(a)(15)(O)(ii)(IV) (same); § 1101(a)(15)(P) (same); § 1101(a)(15)(Q) (same).

[154] *See, e.g., Politica Asylum and Refugees,* U.S. EMBASSY & CONSULATE IN POLAND, https://pl.usembassy.gov/visas/politica-asylum-and-refugees/ (last visited July 3, 2018). Those who fear persecution can apply for refugee resettlement, but this is available only at sites in Athens, Frankfurt, Hong Kong, Madrid, Manila, Mexico City, New Delhi, Rome, and Vienna. *Id.*

[155] Helen Bergman Moure, Brett Harrison, David A. Marquez-Lechuga, & Gavin Foggo, *E-Discovery Around the World,* 21 PRAC. LITIGATOR 41, 52–56 (2010).

[156] *Id.* at 52.

[157] *Id.* at 55.

[158] *Id.* at 55–56.

[159] *See* Manning Gilbert Warren III, *The U.S. Securities Fraud Class Action: An Unlikely Export to the European Union,* 37 BROOK. J. INT'L L. 1075, 1086 (2012).

[160] *Id.*

[161] *Id.*

United Kingdom, where the opposing party has a duty to turn over documents, discovery requests are more restrictive.[162] Where a human rights violation would also constitute a criminal offense, which might lead to civil damages, then in some countries such as Belgium, France, and Germany, the prosecutor might be able to gather evidence. But that depends on the prosecutor deciding to prosecute which, as discussed above, rarely happens in human rights cases involving transnational businesses.

In the Netherlands, the Code of Civil Procedure requires that where a plaintiff seeks corporate documents for a case, the plaintiff needs to demonstrate a legitimate interest and – more problematic – they need to specify the documents requested.[163] While these requirements are meant to prevent "fishing for evidence," they have proven to be a major obstacle to acquire evidence.

Switzerland is perhaps the country (of those reviewed) with the greatest barriers to accessing evidence. Switzerland does not have any procedure for the disclosure of documents during litigation between parties, although a court can order a party to produce certain documents or other evidence.[164] However, in January 2011, a new obstacle came into existence with changes in the Swiss Civil Code.[165] The Code allows a defending party in a civil suit to invoke confidentiality and refuse to provide discovery.[166] A party can support a refusal to cooperate by setting forth plausible reasons why preserving confidentiality is more important than turning over the information.[167]

These discovery barriers have a significant impact on victims' ability to successfully litigate human rights cases.

8.5.4 Overcoming Barriers Created by Discovery Rules

To enhance transparency and accountability, businesses should be required to report publicly on significant human rights risks and impacts – including providing specific human rights impact assessments – in relation to their core business activities, and monitor their compliance with mandatory reporting requirements. In line with the human rights due diligence concept, this includes reporting on their subsidiaries, wherever incorporated and operating, and their business relationships. The requirement to disclose this information should be subject to an assessment of the severity of the impacts on the individuals and communities concerned, not to a

---

[162] *Id.*
[163] Wetboek van Burgerlijke Rechtsvordering [Rv] [Code of Civil Procedure] art. 843(a) (Neth.).
[164] European Consultation, May 15, 2013. Notes on file with author.
[165] *Id.*
[166] The Swiss Code of Civil Procedure entered into effect in 2011. Some of these provisions include the justified refusal to cooperate (Article 162), the right to refuse [to cooperate] (Article 163), and the unjustified refusal (Article 164). Schweizerische Zivilprozessordnung [ZPO], [Swiss Code of Civil Procedure], Dec. 19, 2008, SR 272, arts. 162–64 (Switz.).
[167] ZPO art. 163(2) (Switz.).

consideration of their materiality to the financial interests of the company or its shareholders.

This could be supported by ensuring that data disclosure and whistle-blowing regulations require information about corporate human rights violations to be provided, and support the ability of those who have information to give it without legal consequences or personal security difficulties. This would also be enhanced by requiring corporations to provide these reports and assessments as a compulsory condition to have access to export credits, to be awarded public contracts, or to other financial benefits provided by the state.

8.5.5 Reform Access to Evidence

The ability of victims to access evidence is crucial because plaintiffs have to provide proof that the defendant business managed, failed to manage, or was otherwise involved in the harmful operation carried out by its subsidiary or other business partner. Such information is however rarely publicly available; in most situations it is in the possession of the defendant. Therefore, there should be legislative reform to increase the access to evidence and broaden the disclosure rules in the type of cases under consideration here. This reform should be coupled with legislative proposals on collective action, as described below.

In addition, given the difficulty some witnesses and victims have in coming to the forum country to prosecute their otherwise valid case, lawmakers should also consider creating special litigant visas for victims and witnesses, and involve the courts in the process for applying for and approving such visas. With regard to depositions, alternative options such as depositions by video should be explored. This would not eliminate all procedural hurdles, but it would be a good start.

8.6 BARRIERS CREATED BY COSTS OF LITIGATION

Like most transnational litigation, litigating claims for violations of human rights by TNCs is very expensive for a variety of reasons: the complexity of the corporate structure; gathering evidence abroad and often from witnesses who are fearful of retaliation; the need to retain experts if a choice of law analysis is required and for determining substantive law; and international flights in order to engage in depositions and trial.

The cost of litigation is an even greater barrier in much of Europe and Canada, given the loser pays rules that exist there.[168] In addition, recent legal developments

---

[168] *See generally* Gilbert Warren III, *supra* note 159 at 1085–86 (2012) (explaining that every EU member besides Luxembourg has adopted the loser pays system, requiring the losing party to pay the costs of the winning party); Samuel Issacharoff & Geoffrey P. Miller, *Will Aggregate Litigation Come to Europe?*, 62 VAND. L. REV. 179, 203 (2009) (discussing loser pays systems in Europe); Johan Ysewyn, *Private Enforcement of Competition Law in the EU: Trials and*

in the United Kingdom regarding how legal fees are awarded have made judicial remedies even more financially inaccessible there.[169] For human rights victims, who often lack financial resources, the cost of litigation can completely preclude access to a judicial remedy. There is also the risk that a defendant will bring unwarranted counterclaims or retaliatory claims against litigants or the attorneys who represent them as a tactic meant to intimidate the plaintiffs and those who represent them. These claims are often referred to as Strategic Lawsuits Against Public Participation (SLAPP suits),[170] and are discussed below.

8.6.1 United States

In the United States, unlike Canada and much of Europe (discussed *infra*), the general rule is that each side in the litigation pays its own lawyers' fees.[171] There are exceptions to this general rule; most notably, if a judge determines that a party acted in bad faith, the judge can order that the party pay its opponent's costs, including lawyers' fees.[172] Such an award, however, is within the court's discretion. Most plaintiffs in human rights litigation have very few, if any, financial resources, and thus, courts usually do not award such costs against them, nor does it appear that defendants typically seek such costs. In one important human rights case, however, the defendant submitted a bill of costs.[173] The court agreed it should award costs,

---

Tribulations, 19 SPG INT'L L. PRACTICUM 14, 17 (2006) (discussing loser pays systems in Europe); Beth Stephens, *Translating Filartiga: A Comparative and International Law Analysis of Domestic Remedies for International Human Rights Violations*, 27 YALE J. INT'L L. 1, 29, 33 (2002) (discussing the loser pays systems in Europe and Canada); Caroline Davidson, *Tort Au Canadien: A Proposal For Canadian Tort Legislation on Gross Violations of International Human Rights and Humanitarian Law*, 38 VAND. J. TRANSNAT'L L. 1403, 1441 (2005) (discussing the loser pays system in Canada, but also noting that it has been relaxed in recent years); Philip J. Havers, *Take the Money and Run: Inherent Ethical Problems of the Contingency Fee and Loser Pays Systems*, 14 NOTRE DAME J. L. ETHICS & PUB. POL'Y 621, 632–39 (2000) (discussing the loser pays system in England).

[169] Legal Aid, Sentencing and Punishment of Offenders Act, 2012, c. 10 (Eng.) [hereinafter LASPO].

[170] The goals of a SLAPP suit are typically to intimidate and silence critics. *See* Carson Hilary Barylak, *Reducing Uncertainty in Anti-SLAPP Protection*, 71 OHIO ST. L. J. 845, 846 (2010). A SLAPP suit is one that "(1) involve[s] communications made to influence a government action or outcome, (2) which result[s] in civil lawsuits (complaints, counterclaims, or cross-claims) (3) filed against non-governmental individuals or groups (4) on a substantive issue of some public interest or social significance." *Id.* (internal citations omitted). Typically SLAPP suits involve defamation claims, but may also allege fraud or malicious prosecution. *Id.*

[171] Jarno Vanto, *Attorneys' Fees as Damages in International Commercial Litigation*, 15 PACE INT'L L. REV. 203, 204 (2003).

[172] Fed. R. Civ. P. 54(d); *see also* Fed. R. Civ. P. 11 (stating that "a sanction ... may include part or all of the reasonable attorney's fees and other expenses directly resulting from the violation").

[173] Al Shimari v. CACI Int'l, Inc., 951 F. Supp. 2d 857, 871 (E.D. Va. 2013), *vacated and remanded on other grounds*, 840 F.3d 147 (4th Cir. 2016).

ordering the four Iraqi plaintiffs, who had few resources, to pay $14,000 to the business.[174]

Many statutes in the United States allow prevailing plaintiffs to recover their fees and costs,[175] but the ATS, TVPA, and state common law do not. Federal and state courts and state bar association rules allow lawyers to be compensated on a contingency basis,[176] which means that plaintiffs do not have to pay lawyers' fees. Rather, lawyers will recover a certain percentage of any settlement or award of fees. This has resulted in a few lawyers taking ATS human rights cases, but overall, these cases are seen as so risky and unlikely to result in any award of fees or costs that it is difficult to persuade lawyers to take them. Most human rights cases in the United States are taken pro bono, either by NGOs, pro bono lawyers, or legal clinics, which typically do not charge the client legal fees. However, given the lack of fee recovery, the high costs, and that cases can often take years to litigate, finding representation in these cases is typically a significant barrier to accessing effective remedies.

8.6.2 Canada

Like the United States, Canada allows contingency fees.[177] However, each province has a loser pays system where the loser in litigation typically has to pay the prevailing party's costs, including lawyers' fees, although often on a partial scale. This system allows plaintiffs to recover their costs and fees if they prevail. However, a losing plaintiff may well have to pay fees and costs incurred by the defendant. The financial risk borne by plaintiffs is much greater because they typically have fewer resources than a defendant corporation. Thus, the risk of losing – even if it is small – can have

---

[174] Bill of Costs, *Al Shimari v. CACI Int'l, Inc.*, 951 F. Supp. 2d 857 (E.D. Va. Aug. 20, 2013) (No. 1:08-CV-827), *rev'd*, 758 F.3d 516 (4th Cir. 2014).

[175] Among many others, these include most civil rights statutes. *See, e.g.*, 42 U.S.C. § 1988(b) (giving the court discretion in civil rights cases to allow the prevailing party to include attorney's fees in its costs). According to two authors, more than 150 federal and state civil statutes currently provide statutory fees to prevailing plaintiffs. Catherine R. Albiston & Laura Beth Nielsen, *The Procedural Attack On Civil Rights: The Empirical Reality Of Buckhannon For The Private Attorney General*, 54 UCLA L. REV. 1087, 1089 (2007) (citing *Ruckelshaus v. Sierra Club*, 463 U.S. 680, 684 (1983); *Marek v. Chesny*, 473 U.S. 1, 43–51 (1984) (Brennan, J., dissenting) (listing federal statutory fee-shifting provisions); *Coulter v. Tennessee*, 805 F.2d 146, 152–55 (6th Cir. 1986) (listing federal statutes authorizing the award of attorney's fees)).

[176] *See* Model Rules of Prof'l Conduct, R. 1.5(c) (1983). According to the American Bar Association, California is the only state that has not adopted the model rules. *See Jurisdictions that have Adopted the ABA Model Rules of Professional Conduct* (previously the Model Code of Professional Responsibility), http://www.americanbar.org/groups/professional_responsibility/publications/model_rules_of_professional_conduct/alpha_list_state_adopting_model_rules.html (last visited July 2, 2018).

[177] Davidson, *supra* note 168 at 1443 (citing *McIntyre Estate v. Ontario (Attorney General)* (2002), 218 D.L.R. 4th 193 (Can. Ont. C.A.) (holding that contingency fees were permissible in civil cases in Ontario as long as they are reasonable and fair, and noting that "every Canadian province and territory other than Ontario ha[d] enacted legislation or rules of course to permit and regulate the use of contingency fees")).

serious financial implications. In addition, the loser pays concept applies throughout the case, so that if a party brings a motion and loses, it has to pay costs. If the losing party does not pay the costs, the case can be dismissed. In Canada, there is no restriction on lawyers or NGOs paying costs (although, like in the United States, clients remain ultimately responsible), so if a lawyer or NGO wants a case to go forward, they can pay the costs. But similarly, one must have a law firm or NGO that has the money to pay the costs of litigation in the event of a loss. Moreover, foreign plaintiffs can be required to post a "security for costs" that will go toward defendants' costs if the defendants prevail. However, in determining the security amount, the court can take into account the financial resources of the plaintiff.

In recent years, Canadian courts have relaxed the loser pays rules, minimizing its impact on losing plaintiffs, especially where matters of constitutional law or public interest are at issue.[178] It should be noted that in public interest litigation in British Columbia, plaintiffs can apply for a no-costs ruling, where the court will refrain from imposing costs on the losing party, and it appears that this practice might be increasing in other parts of Canada.[179] Yet, even though the loser pays system in Canada has been relaxed, many of those involved in Canadian litigation report that the system still poses barriers to human rights lawsuits for the reasons described above – the risk of costs and fees being imposed is enough to give plaintiffs (and often attorneys) pause. Although a court might choose not to impose costs because of a plaintiff's financial situation, the threat of such costs might still be enough to dissuade plaintiffs from bringing suit. Due to the loser pays scheme, one law firm chose not to appeal a case that it had lost because it simply could not absorb the financial risk if it were to lose on appeal.[180]

8.6.3 Europe

Most EU Member States also have loser pays statutes wherein the party that loses has to pay the costs of the other party.[181] According to practitioners and NGOs, this

---

[178] See Skinner, *supra* note 152 at 236 (citing Davidson, *supra* note 168 at 1441–42; Chris Tollefson, *Costs on Public Interest Litigation Revisited*, 39 ADVOC. Q. 197, 200 (2012)).

[179] For a recent discussion on public interest litigation and costs, *see* Tollefson, *id.* (noting that "[t]he 15 or so years since [the author] first wrote on the topic have seen some major legal developments in the realm of public interest costs law in Canada and the Commonwealth with likely more to come"). In addition, class action litigation in Quebec allows some class actions to apply for and receive funding to prosecute the class action. *See An Act Respecting the Class Action*, R.S.Q., c. R-2.1 (Can. Que.) (discussing class action funding, required procedures, and rights of qualifying applicants).

[180] Canadian Consultation. Notes and emails on file with author.

[181] See the articles described *supra* note 168, that discuss the loser pays system in Europe. *See also* Wetboek van Burgerlijke Rechtsvordering [Rv] [Code of Civil Procedure] art. 237 (Neth.); Zivilprozessordnung [ZPO] [Code of Civil Procedure], Dec. 5, 2005, BGBL. Il at 83, as amended, § 91 (Ger.); Code de procédure civile [C.P.C.] [Code of Civil Procedure] art. 700 (Fr.).

rule discourages many victims of human rights abuses from bringing civil claims in European countries' courts. This is true even though plaintiffs can also recover if they win, because, like in Canada, the risk is still too great for most victims given their often precarious economic situation. Just the threat of having to pay fees, even if the attorneys argue that a judge is not likely to award costs against them, is enough to discourage many potential plaintiffs, especially those who are not sophisticated in how the courts work. Their fear is often legitimate. For example, in 2013, NGOs representing Palestinians brought a case in France against the businesses Alstom and Veolia, alleging that they were complicit with Israel in violating international humanitarian law in the Occupied Palestinian Territories by constructing light rail through Jerusalem.[182] After the plaintiffs lost, the court ruled that they had to pay €90,000 even though the French civil code allowed the court to take into account the specific financial situation of the plaintiffs in deciding what, if any, costs to order.[183]

In EU Member States, if the plaintiff wins and thus the defendant has to pay damages as well as fees and costs, the Rome II Regulation requires that damages be assessed under the law and procedure of the country where the harm occurred.[184] This is problematic because it will typically mean both a lower damage award and a lower award of costs and fees given that host countries' economies are often on a smaller scale. Moreover, attorney fee rates and costs are much lower in the typical host country. In Switzerland (which is not part of the EU), foreigners can access legal aid in some situations, but plaintiffs must show that they have a fair chance of winning at the outset,[185] and even then, legal aid is not available for all costs associated with the litigation.[186]

In the United Kingdom, the problems associated with costs and fees have become greater since the passage of the Legal Aid, Sentencing and Punishment of Offenders Act 2012 (LASPO).[187] Under LASPO, any legal fees awarded to a successful plaintiff now have to be paid out of the damages awarded and cannot exceed 25 percent of the damages.[188] In reality, legal fees might exceed damages, especially given the

---

[182] Cour d'appel [CA] [regional court of appeal] Versailles, 3ème ch., Mar. 22, 2013, 11/05331 (Fr.), http://www.volokh.com/wp-content/uploads/2013/04/French-Ct-decision.pdf (last visited January 1, 2020). See also, *Veolia & Alstom Lawsuit (re Jerusalem Rail Project)*, BUSINESS & HUMAN RIGHTS RESOURCE CENTRE, http://business-humanrights.org/en/veolia-alstom-lawsuit-re-jerusalem-rail-project#c86290 (last visited July 2, 2018).

[183] *Id.*

[184] Rome II Regulation, *supra* note 105 at arts. 4, 15.

[185] *See* LDIP, art. 11c, *revised by* Zivilprozessordnung [ZPO], Code de procédure civil [CPC], Codice di procedura civile [CPC], Dec. 19, 2008, SR 272, RS 210, annex 1, ch. II(18) (Switz.) ("L'assistance judiciaire est accordée aux personnes domiciliées à l'étranger aux mêmes conditions qu'aux personnes domiciliées en Suisse." [Legal assistance is provided to persons living abroad under the same conditions as those living in Switzerland.]).

[186] *Id.*

[187] LASPO, *supra* note 169.

[188] *Id.* at § 44 (discussing conditional free agreements).

Rome II Regulation. Thus, finding an attorney to take the case given this situation can be difficult. Special Representative John Ruggie commented on the barriers created by LASPO in a letter to the UK Justice Minister, noting that, particularly in cases involving large multinational enterprises, LASPO creates a "significant barrier to legitimate business-related human rights claims being brought before UK courts in situations where alternative sources of remedy are unavailable."[189]

In addition, although legal aid funded some of the earliest cases filed against UK businesses for human rights violations committed abroad, such aid is now significantly limited, making it very difficult to obtain aid for human rights cases against UK businesses for conduct that occurred abroad.[190]

8.6.4 Overcoming Barriers of Costs of Litigation

As discussed above, business and human rights litigation in the transnational context is highly expensive. This situation is further exacerbated by the inequality of the parties – while the plaintiffs usually belong to the most marginalized groups, the defendants are usually very well resourced. The United States, Canada and Europe could significantly improve the situation by reforming legal aid and addressing the costs of legal proceedings so that these claims can be economically feasible for the parties and their lawyers. In Europe, policymakers should enact legislation to improve the legal aid system. What such reforms would entail depends somewhat on the legal traditions in each country.

8.6.4.1 United States

In order for human rights cases to be more economically viable, lawmakers should enact legislation providing that prevailing plaintiffs in human rights cases be awarded attorney fees. Enforcement of international human rights law is good public policy, and allowing the recoupment of fees gives lawyers an incentive to engage in "private" enforcement in this important area of law. This also provides the benefit of having such costs borne by the defendants and not directly by the public.[191] There is significant precedent for such attorney fee provisions, especially for statutes in the areas of civil rights, discrimination, and environmental abuses.[192] As the Congressional Research Service notes:

---

[189] Owen Bowcott, *Legal Aid Cuts Will Stop Cases Like Trafigura, UN Official Warns*, THE GUARDIAN (June 16, 2011), http://www.theguardian.com/law/2011/jun/16/united-nations-legal-aid-cuts-trafigura (citing Letter from John Ruggie, Special Representative of the Secretary-Gen. for Bus. and Hum. Rts, to Jonathon Djanogly, UK Just. Minister (May 16, 2011)).
[190] *See* Skinner, *supra* note 152 at 240 n367.
[191] *See* Albiston & Nielsen, *supra* note 175 at 1090.
[192] *Id.* at 1089.

There are also roughly two hundred statut[es] ... which were generally enacted to encourage private litigation to implement public policy. Awards of attorneys' fees are often designed to help to equalize contests between private individual plaintiffs and corporate or governmental defendants. Thus, attorneys' fees provisions are most often found in civil rights, environmental protection, and consumer protection statutes.[193]

Congress has recognized the value of prevailing plaintiff attorney fee awards in many contexts, and human rights violations seem to be consistent with the types of violations for which Congress has enacted attorney fees – civil rights claims and environmental claims, for example. There will be those who argue that incentivizing such claims will result in numerous frivolous lawsuits. However, to be sure, even if such fee awards were enacted, attorneys would be cautious in bringing such claims given the complexities of these cases and the costs associated with them (which will need to be paid or absorbed if they do not prevail). It is unlikely that the prospect of such fee awards will cause the flood gates of lawsuits to open; yet, it would go a long way in incentivizing attorneys to consider taking these cases and act as private enforcers of human rights norms.

8.6.4.2 Canada

In Canada, the loser pays doctrine significantly inhibits victims from accessing judicial remedies in Canada. Canadian lawmakers should consider codifying certain rules allowing plaintiffs in public interest litigation to seek a "no cost ruling," and clarify that such public interest litigation can take place against businesses for human rights abuses abroad. Businesses should anticipate risks of litigation when operating in foreign states and should be expected to understand that litigation is a cost of doing business abroad. The equities in this equation should be on the side of victims, especially victims who presumably do not have the financial means to engage in such lawsuits, and their advocates, public interest law groups. Lawmakers could still allow courts to award damages for lawsuits they find to be frivolous, if there is concern that this will encourage vexatious litigants.

8.6.4.3 Europe

EU Member States, the EU Commission, and Switzerland should examine the possibilities for providing financial support to victims of alleged human rights violations, to enable them to bring cases in the EU and in Switzerland respectively. At the EU level, one option could include extending Council Directive 2002/8/EC of 27 January 2003, which already provides framework for legal aid in cross-border disputes within the EU. This could be extended to cover all cases where claims are

---

[193] *Awards of Attorneys' Fees by Federal Courts and Federal Agencies*, CONGR. RES. SRV. (June 20, 2008), http://www.fas.org/sgp/crs/misc/94-970.pdf (last visited January 1, 2020).

filed on the basis of a jurisdiction attributed by the Brussels Regulation, recast. Extending this framework to extraterritorial disputes concerning third states can be justified on the basis of Article 81(2)(e) of the Treaty on the Functioning of the European Union (TFEU), which allows for the adoption of legislative measures "when necessary for the proper functioning of the internal market, aimed at ensuring ... effective access to justice." FRA made a similar recommendation in 2017 when it suggested that Member States set minimum standards for needs-based legal aid for plaintiffs seeking judicial remedy for business-related human rights abuses, even if they do not reside within the European Union.[194] In the same report, FRA affirmed the 2016 advice of the UN High Commissioner for Human Rights ("2016 UN Guidance"), which highlighted the need for advice on litigation funding options for plaintiffs.[195] The 2016 UN Guidance called on the EU to "more forcefully encourage the availability of litigation funds," which can include support from public, private, or crowd-funding options.[196] It also called on the EU to establish "an online overview of available litigation funding" for potential claimants.[197]

8.7 BARRIERS CREATED BY COLLECTIVE REDRESS AND CLASS ACTION MECHANISMS

Collective redress and class actions can be efficient mechanisms in seeking remedies for numerous victims. Proceeding as a class action – where an entire class of victims is represented by a representative or representatives – in a human rights case has some advantages, notably that a positive outcome in the case can result in a remedy for numerous victims without the need for their involvement in the case and in a relatively efficient manner. Another advantage is that, unlike other types of litigation where clients are typically responsible to pay the expenses, repayment of expenses can be contingent on the outcome of litigation.[198] In such cases, the law firm remains responsible for the costs. This can allow a group of victims to pursue a case without the need to worry about costs. Litigating a suit as a class can also help protect individual plaintiffs from intimidation and threats.

8.7.1 *United States*

The United States allows for class actions, but proceeding as a class has become increasingly difficult. A few ATS cases have been certified as class actions,[199] but

---

[194] *Improving Access to Remedy, supra* note 137.
[195] *Id.*
[196] *Id.*
[197] *Id.*
[198] *See, e.g.,* Wash. Ct. R. Prof. Conduct 1.8(e)(2) (allowing contingency fees contingent on outcome of litigation in some situations).
[199] *See* In re S. African Apartheid Litig., 617 F. Supp. 2d 228 (S.D.N.Y. 2009); Sarei *v.* Rio Tinto PLC, 221 F. Supp. 2d 1116 (C.D. Cal. 2002), *aff'd*, 456 F.3d 1069 (9th Cir. 2006), *and withdrawn and superseded in part on reh'g* 487 F.3d 1193 (9th Cir. 2007), *and aff'd in part, rev'd in part,*

given the complexity of class action litigation generally, including the difficulty associated with the required notification of potential class members,[200] not many have. Class action litigation in the United States became more difficult after the 2011 Supreme Court decision in Wal-Mart v. Dukes.[201] The case involved 1.5 million women suing Wal-Mart for gender discrimination, relying primarily on statistical information rather than on proof of a general policy of discrimination.[202] Class certification is complex; it requires common questions of law or fact, and a showing that claims of the representatives are typical of the claims of the entire class.[203] In Wal-Mart, the court found that for each putative class member, a different reason might exist as to why they were terminated, even if the reasons were discriminatory.[204] Because of the potential variability in each plaintiff's situation, the plaintiffs did not have enough in common to constitute a class.[205] The court held that the only way to establish commonality was to prove the existence of a general policy treating a group of people the same way, and that where there *may* be differences in the way individuals are treated, a class action cannot survive.[206] The court appeared to require a higher bar for establishing commonality than had historically been required. In the context of many cases, including human rights abuses where circumstances among victims can differ, this poses significant challenges.

Many practitioners are not even considering class actions anymore, under the belief that it is not possible or feasible after *Wal-Mart*. Although cases involving multiple plaintiffs can still proceed, limiting class actions will affect the ability of large numbers of victims to obtain a remedy in a manner that class actions can make more efficient.

8.7.2 Canada and Europe

Canada also allows class actions, although there are certainly limitations to proceeding as a class.[207] Europe, however, does not recognize class

---

vacated in part, and remanded on reh'g en banc, 550 F.3d 822 (9th Cir. 2008), *and aff'd in part, rev'd in part sub nom.* 671 F.3d 736 (9th Cir. 2011), *cert. granted, vacated and remanded*, 133 S. Ct. 1995 (2013) (mem.).

[200] *See generally*, Fed. R. Civ. P. 23 (requiring that the class members provide notice detailing the action, the class defined, the claims, and the exclusionary effect of the action to all members of the class identified after reasonable effort in a manner practicable under the circumstances, including individual notice).

[201] Wal-Mart Stores, Inc. v. Dukes, 131 S. Ct. 2541 (2011).

[202] *Id.* at 2459.

[203] Fed. R. Civ. P. 23.

[204] *Wal-Mart, supra* note 201 at 2552.

[205] *Id.* at 2550–57.

[206] *Id.* at 2554–57.

[207] In Canada, the requirements for class actions are more relaxed than in the United States. Louis Charette, Josée Dumoulin, Bernard Larocque, & François Praent, *Pension Plans and Class Actions: The Vivendi Case*, 81 Def. Couns. J. 288 (2014) (discussing Quebec's more liberal

actions.²⁰⁸ Some European countries have types of collective redress mechanisms, but they have not been very effective. France allows a consumer organization to proceed on behalf of at least two individual consumers in certain situations, although such organizations have no right to conduct outreach.²⁰⁹ In the Netherlands, NGOs can litigate on behalf of public interests, but Dutch law generally does not allow class actions, even for human rights and environmental claims that might affect numerous victims.²¹⁰ In Germany, a single party may transfer their claim to another party, but there are significant restrictions.²¹¹ In the United Kingdom, a court can consolidate several cases that present common issues; "lead cases" are then chosen and litigants in the other cases can "opt in," but these are not class actions.²¹²

> treatment of class actions in Quebec compared with that of Canada's other provinces). In 2010, a trio of cases in Canada solidified a trend where the courts typically will more liberally allow certification of a class where there is a "common issue," meaning that success for one member of the class must bring with it a benefit for all other members. *Id.* at 292. Classes can be maintained if there are common questions, even if the answers may be nuanced for individual claims, unlike in *Wal-Mart. Id.* The rules for authorizing class actions are more liberal in Quebec than other provinces. *Id. See also* Steven F. Rosenhek & Vaso Maric, *Canadian Price-Fixing Class Actions: The Supreme Court of Canada Gives the Green Light to Indirect Purchaser Claims*, 81 DEF. COUNS. J. 302 (2014) (discussing the situation of class action suits in Canada following a recent Canadian Supreme Court case allowing class certification); Tanya J. Monestier, *Is Canada the New Shangri-La of Global Securities Class Actions?* 32 NW. J. INT'L L. & BUS. 305 (2012) (looking at the conflict of law, recognition of judgments, jurisdiction, and other issues that are raised within Canada by the certification of global classes); and Michael A. Eizenga, Dany H. Assaf, & Emrys Davis, *Antitrust Class Actions: A Tale of Two Countries*, 25-SPG ANTITRUST 83 (2011) (comparing the US and Canadian class action environments). *See also* Davidson, *supra* note 168 at 1442–43 (discussing class actions in Canada).
> ²⁰⁸ *See, e.g., Consumer Class Actions in the EU: The Status of the Debate within the Consumer Products and Retail Sector* (April 2009), https://www.lexology.com/library/detail.aspx?g=8c51cb73-f7b1-49bc-86d6-722f00580104 (last visited February 24, 2020) ("The Commission has been keen to stress that US-style class actions will not be imported into Europe.").
> ²⁰⁹ Loi 92-60 du 18 janvier 1992 [Law 92-60 of Jan. 4, 1992], *Journal Officiel de la République Française* [J.O.] [*Official Gazette of France*], Jan. 21, 1992, p. 968; C. Cons. art. L-422 (Fr.).
> ²¹⁰ Nicola Jägers, K.D. Jesse, & Jonathan Verschuure, *The Future of Corporate Liability for Extraterritorial Human Rights Abuses: The Dutch Case Against Shell*, AM. J. INT'L L. UNBOUND e-36, e-41 (2014), available at https://pure.uvt.nl/portal/files/1577353/Jagers_et_al_AJIL_Unbound_2014.pdf. It does appear that Dutch law provides that once a settlement has been reached in a case, it can be declared binding on others unless they "opt out," but it is new and largely untested. Burgerlijk Wetboek [BW] [Civil Code] arts. 7.907–7.910 (Neth.); Wetboek van Burgerlijke Rechtsvordering [Rv] [Code of Civil Procedure] arts. 1013–18 (Neth.); Act on the Collective Settlement of Mass Damage Claims, BW arts. 90 7-910, Wetboek van Burgerlijke Rechtsvordering [Rv] [Code of Civil Procedure] art. 1013 (Neth.); *see also* Nicola M.C.P. Jägers & Marie-José van der Heijden, *Corporate Human Rights Violations: The Feasibility of Civil Recourse in the Netherlands*, 33 BROOK J. INT'L L. 833, 849 (2008) ("Under current Dutch law, an NGO can bring a case where harm occurs to the general interest it is promoting as its objective, according to its articles of association.").
> ²¹¹ *See Prozessstandschaft,* RECHTSWÖRTERBUCH, http://www.rechtswoerterbuch.de/recht/p/prozessstandschaft/ (Ger.) (last visited January 1, 2020).
> ²¹² *See* Arroyo v. BP Exploration Co. (Colo.) [2010] EWHC (QB) 1643; *see also, Civil Practice Direction, 19B – Group Litigation,* MINISTRY OF JUSTICE, https://www.justice.gov.uk/courts/

8.7.3 Overcoming Barriers Presented by Limits on Collective Actions

Human rights violations frequently involve a large number of victims. Collective violations are unlikely to be remedied adequately through individual complaints.

8.7.3.1 United States

In the United States, the twin decisions of Wal-Mart v. Dukes and AT&T v. Concepcion effectively prevented employees from bringing suit as a class against their employers. Whereas *Wal-Mart* established a higher bar for proving commonality, the *Concepcion* court affirmed that companies can include waivers of the right to bring suit as a class in arbitration agreements.[213] Together, these decisions reflect the Supreme Court's belief "that companies must be protected from litigation that is large simply because companies are large."[214]

Yet, US courts have historically treated ATS class actions more leniently than they do mass tort class actions.[215] As a result, their hostility to class action lawsuits in mass tort litigation is not reflected in their behavior toward class actions brought under the ATS, often "the only viable way for cases to come to court."[216] As in Europe, there is a pressing need to reform the law, ensuring that courts do not hold class actions under the ATS to the same high standards as traditional tort classes.

8.7.3.2 Europe

Though most European countries have not adopted the class action mechanism, some analogous collective redress mechanisms have emerged in recent years. However, the effectiveness of these mechanisms is usually limited by restrictive conditions. The most effective collective redress mechanism is provided in the United Kingdom, where procedural rules enable courts to allow collective actions

---

procedure-rules/civil/rules/part19/pd_part19b (last visited July 3, 2018). *See also, Group Litigation Orders*, HM Cts & Tribunals Serv., http://www.justice.gov.uk/courts/rcj-rolls-building/queens-bench/group-litigation-orders (last updated Dec. 6, 2019). In addition, the United Kingdom recognizes a procedure called a representative action, where a representative can represent a party or parties not before the court, but again, that is not a class action: the parties must be actively in litigation. Civil Procedure Rules, 1998, § 19.6 (U.K.).

[213] Catherine Fisk & Erwin Chemerinsky, *The Failing Faith in Class Actions: Wal-Mart v. Dukes and AT&T Mobility v. Concepcion*, 7 Duke J. of Const. Law & Pub. Pol'y 73, 73 (2011).
[214] *Id.* at 74.
[215] *See e.g.*, Doe v. Karadzic, 176 F.R.D. 458, 461 (S.D.N.Y. 1997) (holding that claims of "rape, murder, or otherwise abuse" all arise from the same "ethnic cleansing campaign" and so satisfy the commonality requirement) (see also Hilao v. Marcos, 103 F.3d 767, 774 (9th Cir. 1996) (holding that the representatives' injuries were "virtually identical" to those of other class members regardless of whether they were tortured, disappeared, or executed)).
[216] Margaret G. Perl, *Not Just Another Mass Tort: Using Class Actions to Redress International Human Rights*, 88 Geo. L. J. 773, 797 (1999).

on an opt-in basis. While this mechanism has enabled some groups to bring what amounts to collective claims, considerable negotiation is required between each party's lawyers for the process to be effective, and it remains at the discretion of the court to allow it.

There is a need to reform EU Member States' laws, as well as the law of Switzerland, to enable collective actions (in various forms, including class actions and public interest litigation filed by NGOs) to be brought against businesses domiciled in Europe. FRA made this recommendation in 2017, noting that "in this way, victims can join forces to overcome obstacles, or organizations may act on behalf of victims."[217] These reforms should include enabling claims to be brought, based expressly on human rights terminology and by reference to the human rights included in the UNGPs and in European human rights treaties, including the European Convention on Human Rights, the European Social Charter and the Charter of Fundamental Rights.

8.8 RETALIATORY LAWSUITS

Retaliatory lawsuits by businesses or their executives against those who bring human rights claims – called SLAPP[218] suits – is a troubling trend that is developing across the globe. For example, in *Chevron*, discussed above, which involved Texaco's extraction efforts in Ecuador, Chevron sued the plaintiffs for fraud and sued their lawyer under the Racketeer Influenced Corrupt Organizations (RICO) Act for conspiracy in US federal court in February 2011.[219] The lawsuit alleges that the plaintiffs' lawyers and representatives conspired to extort up to $113 billion from Chevron through the Ecuadorian legal proceedings. The allegations involve the lawyer's influence over an expert in the case. Whether or not the claims about the lawyer are true, the suit against the plaintiffs appears retaliatory.

Chevron also sued another of the plaintiffs' lawyers in federal court in California for malicious prosecution.[220] The US District Court in San Francisco applied California's anti-SLAPP statute, which allows a court to dismiss these retaliatory lawsuits.[221] Though Chevron's malicious prosecution claim was ultimately denied, it had successfully forced the lawyer, a solo practitioner, to expend a great amount of time and expense for his defense.[222]

---

[217] *Improving Access to Remedy, supra* note 137.
[218] See Barylak, *supra* note 170.
[219] Chevron v. Donziger, 296 F.R.D. 168, 168 (S.D.N.Y. 2013).
[220] Chevron v. Bonifaz, No. 09-05371 CW, 2010 WL 1948681, at *1 (N.D. Cal. May 12, 2010).
[221] *Id.*
[222] See Skinner, *supra* note 152 at 235 n331 (2014). For the latest developments in this case, *see*, *In Federal Appeal, Donziger Seeks Reversal of Chevron's Latest Subpoena "Assault" on Indigenous Peoples*, CSR WIRE (Dec. 18, 2018) https://www.csrwire.com/press_releases/41624-In-Federal-Appeal-Donziger-Seeks-Reversal-of-Chevron-s-Latest-Subpoena-Assault-on-Indigenous-Peoples (last visited January 1, 2020).

In yet another case, a corporate defendant in two long-standing human rights lawsuits involving allegations that the corporation paid the paramilitary group United Self-Defense Forces of Colombia (known by its Spanish acronym AUC) to kill labor leaders,[223] sued the plaintiff's lawyer for defamation.[224] The state in which he is being sued, Alabama, does not have an anti-SLAPP statute. The case is currently being litigated.

Like California, many states have anti-SLAPP statutes, allowing the party or lawyer being sued to request the court to dismiss the case promptly in order to avoid the burden and costs of litigation and to recover fees.[225] However, there is currently no federal anti-SLAPP statute. Federal courts are divided as to whether state anti-SLAPP statutes apply to state claims being litigated in a federal court sitting in diversity. The three federal appellate courts that have considered the issue have found they must enforce state anti-SLAPP statutes in federal court diversity cases, overturning their respective district courts.[226] However, a federal district court in the District of Columbia has cast doubt on whether the D.C. anti-SLAPP statute applies in federal diversity cases, implicitly holding that it does not.[227] Similarly, a federal district court in Illinois held in 2013 that a Washington state anti-SLAPP statute would not be applicable in its diversity case because it conflicted with the Federal Rules of Civil Procedure.[228] A Massachusetts federal district judge recently made the same finding.[229] Thus, there is no guarantee that state anti-SLAPP statutes will provide safety to plaintiffs and plaintiffs' lawyers in human rights cases.

---

[223] Baloco ex rel. Tapia v. Drummond Co., 640 F.3d 1338 (11th Cir. 2011); Giraldo v. Drummond Co., No. 2:09-CV-1041-RDP, 2013 WL 3873960, at *1 (N.D. Ala. July 25, 2013) (dismissing plaintiff's claims pursuant to *Kiobel*).

[224] See Drummond Co. v. Collingsworth, No. 2:11-CV-3695-RDP (N.D. Ala. filed Oct. 21, 2011). The defendant has also sent him burdensome discovery requests. See Mike Scarcella, *Human Rights Lawyer Fights Drummond Over Subpoena*, THE BLT: THE BLOG OF LEGAL TIMES (Aug. 19, 2013), http://legaltimes.typepad.com/blt/2013/08/human-rights-lawyer-fights-drummond-over-subpoenas.html (last visited January 1, 2020).

[225] Approximately twenty-nine states, as well as the District of Columbia and Guam, have enacted anti-SLAPP statutes. Sandrine Fontaine, Simon Savry-Cattan & Cécile Villettelle, *Les poursuites stratégiques alterant le debat public: Quelle regulation face au phenomene des poursuites-bailllons en France?* 13 (Jan. 28, 2018), https://www.business-humanrights.org/en/france-report-examines-concept-of-strategic-lawsuits-against-public-participation-slapps (last visited January 1, 2020) (follow "Download the full document here" hyperlink) (citing *State Anti-SLAPP Reference Chart*, PUBLIC PARTICIPATION PROJECT, https://anti-slapp.org/your-states-free-speech-protection#scorecard (last accessed July 12, 2018)). See also, https://www.protecttheprotest.org/category/resource-categories/our-cases/ (last visited January 1, 2020).

[226] Godin v. Schencks, 629 F.3d 79 (1st Cir. 2010) (overturning district court); Henry v. Lake Charles Am. Press, LLC, 566 F.3d 164 (5th Cir. 2009) (overturning district court and enforcing anti-SLAPP statute); United States ex rel. Newsham v. Lockheed Missiles & Space Co., 190 F.3d 963 (9th Cir. 1999) (overturning district court and holding, as matter of first impression, that California's anti-SLAPP statute may be applied in federal diversity suits).

[227] 3M Co. v. Boulter, 842 F. Supp. 2d 85 (D.D.C. 2012).

[228] Intercon Solutions, Inc. v. Basel Action Network, 969 F. Supp. 2d 1026, 1026 (N.D. Ill. 2013).

[229] S. Middlesex Opportunity Council, Inc. v. Town of Framingham, Civil Action No. 07-12018-DPW, 2008 WL 4595369, at *1 (D. Mass. Sept. 30, 2008).

8.8.1 Addressing Retaliatory Lawsuits

In order to address the growing problem of retaliatory lawsuits, each state should enact anti-SLAPP statutes to deter lawsuits that are meant simply to chill victims and their lawyers from bringing legitimate cases. Similarly, Congress should enact a federal anti-SLAPP statute given the uncertainty as to whether a state's anti-SLAPP statute applies in federal court. Such statutes are needed given the rising number of SLAPP suits.

Outside the United States, few anti-SLAPP regulations even exist. This is due, in part, to the fact that the very definition varies across jurisdictions.[230] It is also because anti-SLAPP legislation must be flexible enough to allow both victims and businesses their day in court.[231] Nevertheless, UN working bodies have started to address the issue. In August 2017, the UN Committee on Economic, Social and Cultural Rights declared that states have an obligation to protect individuals within their jurisdiction from retaliatory lawsuits by corporations.[232] In early 2018, a group of six Members of the European Parliament (MEPs) proposed anti-SLAPP legislation across the bloc. They suggested that businesses could face financial fines if they pursued "vexatious lawsuits" against journalists. The MEPs also suggested that journalists be allowed to "expediently" dismiss such lawsuits, and receive access to a fund to support such lawsuits if they go forward. In their letter, the MEPs highlighted a handful of lawsuits they labeled as SLAPP claims, including a suit against the *Guardian* newspaper and the BBC by Appleby for the Paradise Papers investigations.[233]

8.9 LACK OF CRIMINAL PROSECUTIONS AND RESTITUTION

Outside of civil claims, criminal prosecutions can provide an important vehicle for holding corporations legally accountable for human rights abuses. In some jurisdictions, victims can bring a criminal complaint to a public prosecutor or use a criminal proceeding to assist with subsequent potential civil recovery. Some countries, such as the United States and Switzerland, allow criminal jurisdiction over certain extraterritorial human rights abuses. Others, such as the United Kingdom, have no specific statute prosecutors to rely on with respect to criminal liability for

---

[230] Sandrine Fontaine, Simon Savry-Cattan, & Cécile Villetelle, *Les poursuites stratégiques altérant le débat public: quelle régulation face au phénomène des poursuites-bâillons en France?* [*Strategic Lawsuits against Public Participation: How to Regulate Those Legal Actions in France?*] 8 (2018), https://www.sciencespo.fr/ecole-de-droit/sites/sciencespo.fr.ecole-de-droit/files/rapport-final-slapp.pdf (Fr.) (last visited January 1, 2020).

[231] Stephanie Kirchgaessner, *MEPs Call for Power to Tackle "Vexatious Lawsuits" Targeting Journalists*, THE GUARDIAN (Feb. 22, 2018), https://www.theguardian.com/world/2018/feb/22/meps-call-for-power-to-tackle-vexatious-lawsuits-targeting-journalists (last visited January 1, 2020).

[232] Committee on Econ., Social and Cultural Rights, *General comment No. 24 (2017) on State obligations under the International Covenant on Economic, Social and Cultural Rights in the context of business activities*, U.N. Doc. E/C.12/GC/24 ¶44 (2017).

[233] See Kirchgaessner, *supra* note 231.

extraterritorial human rights crimes. Even where such prosecutions are possible, however, there are very few such prosecutions, and many local prosecutors are reluctant to bring such prosecutions for a variety of reasons.

8.9.1 United States

The United States has federal criminal statutes in the area of human rights that apply extraterritorially and which could be invoked against businesses, namely those regarding genocide,[234] war crimes,[235] torture,[236] and forced recruitment of child soldiers.[237] Under each of these statutes, persons (a term which ostensibly includes businesses[238]) can also be prosecuted for conspiring to engage in these crimes. In addition, under general federal criminal law, those who aid or abet crimes can be prosecuted as principals.[239] The aiding and abetting law ostensibly reaches extraterritorial conduct, as it does not provide that the conduct at issue occur within the United States.

The United States Department of Justice Human Rights and Special Prosecutions Section (HRSP), established in March 2010, is charged with prosecuting these crimes. However, like in other countries, US prosecutions against businesses for these human rights crimes remain rare. Moreover, federal criminal prosecutions of these crimes do not generally result in restitution to victims. Although a court can order that property be returned to victims or order other equitable relief, these criminal statutes do not provide civil remedies for victims of such abuses. The Department of Justice houses the Office for Victims of Crime, which has a victims' compensation fund, but that fund does not provide direct compensation to victims. Thus, federal criminal prosecutions in the United States have had little impact on the awarding of damages to victims. Civil liability, which can occur through a showing that a business was "more likely than not" involved in abuse rather than a showing "beyond a reasonable doubt," has been more useful in compensating victims.

Human rights advocates have highlighted that they have tried to persuade HRSP to investigate companies for their participation in human rights abuses, but as of yet, no business has been prosecuted under these statutes.[240] As mentioned above, Chiquita was prosecuted for making payments to the AUC paramilitary

---

[234] 18 U.S.C. § 1091 (2012).
[235] 18 U.S.C. § 2441 (2012).
[236] 18 U.S.C. § 2340A (2012).
[237] 18 U.S.C. § 2442 (2012).
[238] 1 U.S.C. § 1 (2012).
[239] 18 U.S.C. § 2 (2012). As of yet, none of the human rights statutes or other general criminal statutes allow for liability under a "command responsibility" theory, wherein upper level officers may be held responsible for the abuses of those they supervise, where they know about such abuses and fail to stop them. See Amy J. Sepinwall, *Failures to Punish: Command Responsibility in Domestic and International Law*, 30 MICH. J. INT'L L. 251, 261 (2009).
[240] Consultation, in Washington, D.C. (June 24, 2013).

organization, which had been designated a Foreign Terrorist Organization by the US government, but this was a violation of a different US statute. Chiquita pled guilty in 2007, and paid a $25 million fine to the United States.[241]

8.9.2 Europe

In some European jurisdictions, contingent criminal claims arise from civil claims relating to transnational human rights abuse associated with businesses. In many European countries, the prosecution of criminal offenses is the exclusive prerogative of the public prosecutor, acting in the name of society.[242] However, most legal systems allow the victim who has been aggrieved by the conduct that is allegedly criminal to play an active role. The victim in general may file a complaint alleging that a criminal offense has been committed, and if the public prosecutor refuses to investigate or concludes that there is no reason for the prosecution to be launched, the victim will have the possibility to challenge that decision.

In Germany, this appeal against the prosecutor's decision is referred to as *Klageerzwingung*, and it leads to a judicial review of the prosecutor's decision.[243] The same possibility is stated, for instance, in Article 12 of the Dutch Code of Criminal Procedure.[244] Moreover, during the criminal trial, witnesses, such as the individual affected, can and should be heard by the court directly. This allows the victim to rely on the public prosecution for the collection of evidence. Finally, the victim generally will be allowed to claim damages for the prejudice suffered as a result of the criminal conduct, such damages being awarded directly by the criminal court (this is the institution called *Adhäsionsverfahren* in German criminal procedure).[245] In practice, this option remains in the realm of theory, because for a number of objective and subjective reasons, including complexity of these cases, lack of resources and know-how, as well as lack of mandate, public prosecutors do not pursue these types of cases.[246]

---

[241] *See Chiquita Brands International Pleads Guilty to Making Payments to a Designated Terrorist Organization And Agrees to Pay $25 Million Fine*, Press Release, DEPARTMENT OF JUSTICE (Mar. 19, 2007), http://www.justice.gov/opa/pr/2007/March/07_nsd_161.html (last visited January 1, 2020).

[242] *See* C.H. Brants-Langeraar, *Consensual Criminal Procedures: Plea and Confession Bargaining and Abbreviated Procedures to Simplify Criminal Procedure*, 11.1 ELECTRONIC J. COMP. L. (2007) *1, *9, http://www.ejcl.org/111/art111-6.pdf (last visited January 1, 2020); COUNCIL OF EUROPE, *Bordeaux Declaration – Judges and Prosecutors in a Democratic Society* (2009), https://wcd.coe.int/ViewDoc.jsp?id=1560897&site=CM#P30_883 (last visited January 1, 2020).

[243] John H. Langbien, *Controlling Prosecutorial Discretion in Germany*, 41(3) U. CHI. L. REV. 439, 463 (1974).

[244] Brants-Langeraar, *supra* note 242, at *10.

[245] Kerstin Braun, *Giving Victims a Voice: On the Problems of Introducing Victim Impact Statements in German Criminal Procedure*, 14(9) GERMAN L. J. 1889, 1891 (2013).

[246] For examples of prosecutors declining to pursue these types of cases, see the DLH and Amesys case studies.

In France, victims of criminal offenses may file a claim for compensation by joining the criminal procedure. Damages may then be awarded by the criminal court. Moreover, the victim having filed the claim for damages is recognized certain prerogatives in the criminal procedure.[247] In October 2011, the *Fédération Internationale des Ligues des Droits de l'Homme* (FIDH) and the *Ligue des Droits de l'Homme* (LDH), both NGOs, filed a criminal complaint in France against Amesys, alleging that the business was complicit in grave violations of human rights, including torture, committed by members of the Gaddafi regime in Libya.[248] The Paris prosecutor's office announced in April 2012 that it would not open an investigation into this case, stating that the alleged acts did not qualify as criminal.[249] After the investigating judge stepped in and ordered an investigation into whether Amesys and its management could be held criminally liable,[250] the Paris *Tribunal de Grande Instance* opened a judicial investigation in May 2012.[251] The Paris prosecutor then appealed this decision, but, in January 2013, the Court of Appeal rejected this appeal.[252] FIDH publicly stated that there have been "road blocks erected by the Paris [p]rosecutor's office" throughout the case and suggested that the prosecutor was "reluctant to allow an impartial and independent inquiry into this matter."[253] The newly formed Paris Court section specializing in crimes against humanity, genocide, and war crimes now manages the case.[254]

There exists in Switzerland a similar system: victims of criminal offenses may join their claim for compensation to the criminal prosecution, and be awarded damages

---

[247] *See* Gwynne Skinner, Robert McCorquodale, Olivier de Schutter, & Andie Lambe, THE THIRD PILLAR: ACCESS TO JUDICIAL REMEDIES FOR HUMAN RIGHTS VIOLATIONS BY TRANSNATIONAL BUSINESS 33 n201 (2013) (citing *France*, EUROPEAN JUSTICE, https://e-justice.europa.eu/content_rights_of_victims_of_crime_in_criminal_proceedings-171-FR-maximizeMS-fr.do?clang=fr&idSubpage=1&member=1 (last visited June 4, 2019) (Fr.)).

[248] *FIDH and LDH File a Complaint Concerning the Responsibility of the Company AMESYS in Relation to Acts of Torture*, INTERNATIONAL FEDERATION FOR HUMAN RIGHTS (FIDH) (Oct. 19, 2011), https://www.fidh.org/en/region/north-africa-middle-east/libya/FIDH-and-LDH-file-a-complaint (last visited June 4, 2019).

[249] *Amesys Case: The Investigation Chamber Green Lights the Investigative Proceedings on the Sale of Surveillance Equipment by Amesys to the Khadafi Regime*, INTERNATIONAL FEDERATION FOR HUMAN RIGHTS (FIDH) (Jan. 15, 2013), https://www.fidh.org/en/region/north-africa-middle-east/libya/Amesys-Case-The-Investigation-12752# (last visited June 4, 2019) [hereinafter FIDH Amesys].

[250] *See, A Giant Leap Backwards: Corporations Divesting Toxic Surveillance Companies*, PRIVACY INT'L (Oct. 25, 2013), https://privacyinternational.org/blog/1561/giant-leap-backwards-corporations-divesting-toxic-surveillance-companies (last visited June 4, 2019).

[251] Paul Sonne & David-Gauthier-Villars, *Tech Firm Amesys Faces French Judicial Probe*, WALL ST. J., (May 22, 2012), https://www.wsj.com/articles/SB10001424052702304791704577420392081640000 (last visited June 4, 2019).

[252] FIDH Amesys, *supra* note 249.

[253] *Id.*

[254] *Opening of a Judicial Inquiry Targeting Amesys for Complicity in Acts of Torture in Libya*, FÉDÉRATION INTERNATIONALE DES LIGUES DES DROITS DE L'HOMME (FIDH), http://www.fidh.org/en/north-africa-middle-east/libya/Opening-of-a-judicial-inquiry (last updated July 11, 2013).

in the course of the criminal conviction.[255] Further, in Switzerland, legal persons, including businesses, may be criminally liable since October 1, 2003 under a new provision of the Criminal Code.[256] A business's criminal liability may be engaged if a criminal offense has been committed, and if the natural person responsible for the act cannot be identified due to the organization of the business.[257] Furthermore, even where the natural person can be identified for certain serious crimes – such as the participation in a criminal organization,[258] the financing of terrorism,[259] money laundering,[260] bribery of public officials,[261] or the provision of an advantage to a public official[262] – the business will be punished.[263] Even if the business's management was unaware of the acts being committed, the failure to take all reasonable measures required to prevent the offense will lead to liability, regardless of the individuals' criminal liability.[264] This is intended to constitute a strong incentive for the business to act with due diligence in order to avoid any such criminal act being adopted in the course of its activities.

Dutch criminal law does not make a distinction between natural and legal persons, and it would be possible on the basis of Article 51 of the Dutch Criminal Code to prosecute a legal entity for international crimes.[265] However, whether or not a person will be prosecuted is up to the public prosecutor to decide, and cases reveal that important considerations weigh against decisions to engage in proceedings.[266]

8.9.3 Overcoming Barriers Created by Criminal Prosecution

In every jurisdiction there is a potential to improve access to remedy through the mechanisms of criminal law. The detail of the recommendations for reform will differ depending on the situation in each jurisdiction. Criminal prosecution of corporations for their involvement in crimes amounting to human rights violations is possible and often appropriate. Yet currently it often remains a remote possibility. To address this, steps should be taken to clarify standards of corporate liability in the criminal and extraterritorial contexts, to define the mandate of public prosecutors to

---

[255] *See* Council of Europe, VICTIMS: SUPPORT AND ASSISTANCE 241 (2008).
[256] Strafgesetzbuch [StGB], Code penal suisse [Cp], Codice penale svizzero [Cp] [Criminal Code], Dec. 21, 1937, RS 311, art. 102 (Switz.).
[257] *Id.* § 102(1).
[258] *Id.* § 260(3).
[259] *Id.* § 260(5).
[260] *Id.* § 305(1).
[261] *Id.* § 322(3).
[262] *Id.* § 322(5).
[263] *Id.* § 102(2).
[264] Id.
[265] Sr art. 51 (Neth.).
[266] *See* Skinner, *supra* note 247 at 32 n192 (citing *What does the Public Prosecution Service Do?* OPENBAAR MINISTRIE, https://www.om.nl/algemeen/english/about-the-public/what-does-the-public/ (last visited July 10, 2018)).

pursue such cases, and to make sufficient resources available to enable them to do so. Any decision by public prosecutors not to take action should be amenable to judicial review at the request of the victims. In addition, there should be more criminal prosecutions and the enactment and enforcement of provisions for restitution to victims arising from criminal prosecutions.

8.9.3.1 United States

Federal prosecutors should more aggressively seek to prosecute businesses and individuals within businesses for their role in human rights violations that the federal government can currently prosecute, including: genocide,[267] war crimes,[268] torture,[269] and forced recruitment of child soldiers. In addition, the criminal liability statutes should be revised to allow for command responsibility liability. This one change would allow for further liability under the criminal statutes, including for business activity.

Currently, there is no specific mechanism in place that allows for victims of corporations (or their officers) which have been convicted of a human rights crime to receive compensation. Lawmakers should enact such measures ensuring restitution. There is precedent for this. For example, individuals convicted of engaging in international child pornography must pay restitution to the victims.[270] Given the difficulty those abroad have in accessing a civil remedy for criminal conduct by corporations, and given that this recommendation applies only to those corporations or their officers found guilty of a serious crime, this recommendation should not be controversial.

8.9.3.2 Europe

EU Member States and Switzerland should make it a criminal offense for corporations domiciled in their jurisdiction to contribute to human rights violations, including violations which take place outside their national territories. In addition to clarifying standards for corporate criminal liability, prosecuting authorities should be provided with the guidance and resources necessary for effective law enforcement in such cases. For example, the Serious Crimes Act (UK) and the Homicide Act (UK) could be extended to cover specifically abuses of human rights by corporations operating extraterritorially.

---

[267] 18 U.S.C. § 1801.
[268] 18 U.S.C. § 2441.
[269] 18 U.S.C. § 2340A.
[270] Mandatory restitution was part of a comprehensive federal statutory framework that also included criminalizing participation in any stage of the child pornography market. 18 U.S.C. §§ 2251–60 (2012).

Ideally, the EU Member States should also act collectively and explore opportunities to adopt an EU-wide legislative proposal in this area. EU Member States still have widely divergent approaches to the question of criminal liability of corporations for human rights violations, and therefore action at EU level would be desirable; this would also avoid a situation in which action at Member State level would be discouraged because of the fear of distorting competition. EU instruments adopted to date illustrate the potential for the EU to adopt legislation making it a criminal offense for corporations domiciled in the EU to contribute to certain human rights violations, even where such violations take place outside the EU.

Prosecutors should make their decision process more transparent by publishing guidance that explains how victims can access the judicial system. This might include: an overview of the process, a timeline of the various steps and time frames for official responses, criteria used to determine whether to pursue a complaint, and any information on reviewing that official decision.[271] In the UK, the Code for Crown Prosecutors provides transparency around prosecutors' decisions whether to pursue a case. For each claim, it describes, prosecutors apply a two-part test: "[Is] there a realistic prospect of conviction (the evidential test) and do the public interest factors against prosecution outweigh those tending in favour (the public interest test)[?]"[272] For noteworthy cases, British officials may produce public statements explaining why they have decided not to pursue a case.[273] Victims can seek a review of the decision through the Victims' Right to Review Scheme, which is accompanied by its own public guidance, or by judicial review.[274]

8.9.3.3 Training and Awareness-Raising for Public Prosecutors and Judges

In most jurisdictions where it is possible for corporations to be held criminally liable for human rights abuses committed overseas, prosecutions remain rare. For a number of reasons, linked either to the legal systems concerned or to the attitude of the prosecuting authorities, and because of the complexity of these cases, lack of resources and know-how, as well as lack of mandate, public prosecutors do not pursue cases involving corporate complicity in human rights violations that occur abroad.[275] To begin to address this, governments of the states in which such prosecutions are possible should ensure that prosecutors and judges are better

---

[271] *The Corporate Crimes Principles: Advancing Investigations and Prosecutions in Human Rights Cases*, INDEPENDENT COMMISSION OF EXPERTS 20 (Oct. 2016).
[272] *Id.* at 22.
[273] *Id.*
[274] *Id.*
[275] For instance, Amnesty International campaigned for a criminal prosecution in the UK of the company Trafigura Ltd. for its alleged conspiracy to export toxic waste to Côte D'Ivoire in 2006. The UK prosecutors decided not to prosecute however. *Too Toxic to Touch? The UK's Response to Amnesty International's Call for a Criminal Investigation into Trafigura Ltd*, AMNESTY INTERNATIONAL (2015), EUR 45/2101/ 2015.

equipped to deal with cases brought before them. This could be achieved through a range of practical measures such as providing training and sharing expertise, as well as providing public prosecutors with clear mandates and resources to enable them to pursue these cases.

Investigators and prosecutors could, for instance, be trained on the standard of evidence which is required to establish liability for corporate crimes in their jurisdiction.[276] This training could address corporate structures and decision-making procedures, effective investigation methods for cross-border offenses, and the various types of corporate crimes with a human rights perspective.[277]

---

[276] *Id.* at 30.
[277] *Id.*

Conclusion

One purpose of this book was to illustrate the power imbalance between a TNC and the communities it serves. TNCs benefit immensely through operations in developing countries that often have fragile governments and judicial systems. Nonconsenting community members, meanwhile, absorb nearly all the risk and costs – to their lives, health, and livelihoods – and are usually unable to achieve judicial remedy for harms they suffer. This paradigm is not fair, moral, or sustainable, either legally or economically.

Given the barriers victims face, a *judicial* remedy, in particular, is required. This conclusion will summarize the obstacles that prevent such victims from seeking a judicial remedy against such TNCs, and how these obstacles also work in combination to prevent victims from obtaining a remedy for their harm. It will conclude with a summary of how countries can meet their moral and legal obligations to these victims by enacting specific legislation holding such TNCs responsible for these very harmful costs to human life. The chapter will end with a challenge to countries to do so.

First, victims of business-related human rights abuses face numerous obstacles when they attempt to seek judicial remedy from a TNC from within the host state. TNCs often operate in high-risk countries whose legal systems lack causes of action, encompass an ineffective and non-independent judiciary, and fail to properly induce lawyers to take on cases about human rights violations. Additionally, these countries often fail to physically protect advocates and victims from retaliation or other forms of intimidation. Their legal codes often impose burdensome rules on victims (such as loser pays rules) that mean the case is both physically and logistically difficult to sustain. Such hurdles at the outset of a case mean that the legal system is already stacked against the victim, who usually lacks the financial resources of a TNC.

When faced with such hurdles within the host country, victims should be able to turn to another jurisdiction for remedy. But in home states, too, legal systems have failed them. TNCs are often, but not always, headquartered or do substantial business in the United States, Canada, and Europe. Hence the focus of this book. Yet, even in this alternate venue, victims usually face similar hurdles: they lack a cause of action, such that the foreign court cannot establish subject matter jurisdiction (in the US, this is framed as a restriction on the extraterritorial jurisdiction of American courts). Moreover, rules limiting shareholder liability have pushed parent companies to the fringes of responsibility. Legal doctrines such as *forum non conveniens*, and restrictive rules for example on choice of law and limitation periods, are additional hurdles that victims encounter. These are only a handful of the many burdens facing victims of human rights violations who seek judicial remedy for their injuries in foreign courts.

Non-judicial types of remedy, while theoretically an alternate source of redress, are often not as successful. Schemes at the company- or project-level, or initiatives such as the OECD's NCPs, rarely achieve success for individual victims. Moreover, because their scope is so limited, their wider impact on human rights issues is too narrow to be effective.

Together, these obstacles prevent victims from obtaining a remedy for their harm in two ways. First, they make the legal system financially and practically inaccessible to victims of business-related human rights violations. Second, for those victims who decide to pursue judicial remedy, it raises the emotional, financial, and physical costs to an overwhelming height.

Change must be implemented on a country-wide level. The United States, Canada, and EU Member States must meet their moral and legal obligations to victims of human rights violations perpetrated by companies at home in Western jurisdictions.

National legislation is a good place to start, and home countries can begin by amending the limited liability of parent companies for the illegal activities of their subsidiaries. It is my recommendation that home states legislate that parent corporations are strictly liable for any harm resulting from the extraterritorial acts of majority-owned subsidiaries and other affiliates they control which breach international human rights law, at least in those instances where the plaintiffs cannot realistically obtain a remedy from the subsidiary or affiliate in the host country. This will help clarify parent companies' responsibilities to the individuals living in the host communities.

Foreign states that may serve as forums for such claimants should also revise their legislation to ensure that they can hear victims' claims, even if they arose from extraterritorial conduct. These foreign forums must work to ensure that pursuit of these claims is economically feasible, either by clarifying and expanding legal aid standards, or by allowing for victim compensation. Home countries can also amend judicial and bar association rules to incentivize victims to bring claims, or make changes to the costly financial and discovery rules of litigation.

By their very nature, TNCs operate across borders and jurisdictions with ease. But this expansiveness also lends itself to affiliations with local suppliers, who are often allowed to act with impunity and without accountability. Local communities that bear the brunt of this relationship face legal obstacles in both national and foreign courts. It is the responsibility of host and home countries alike to implement changes that will reduce these burdens and ease access to judicial remedy.

At the beginning of this book, I said that I hope it one day becomes obsolete: that legal systems adapt and become more user-friendly, that victims' lives are not ruined because of corporate impunity, and that corporations operate more transparently. This continues to be my desire, and I challenge countries to take up the fight.

Select Bibliography

Albiston, C. & Nielsen, L.B., *The Procedural Attack On Civil Rights: The Empirical Reality Of Buckhannon For The Private Attorney General*, 54 UCLA L. REV. 1087, 1089 (2007)

Alford, R., *The Future of Human Rights Litigation After Kiobel*, 89 NOTRE DAME L. REV. 1749 (2014)

ALI, Restatement of the Law (Third) the Foreign Relations of the United States

ALI, Restatement (Second) of Conflict of Laws § 6 (1971)

Avi-Yonah, R. S., U.S. INTERNATIONAL TAXATION: CASES AND MATERIALS 192 (2002)

Bailey, W.F., THE LAW OF JURISDICTION, INCLUDING IMPEACHMENT OF JUDGMENTS, LIABILITY FOR JUDICIAL ACTS, AND SPECIAL REMEDIES (1st ed. 1899)

Barrett Ristroph, E., *How Can the United States Correct Multi-National Corporations' Environmental Abuses Committed in the Name of Trade?*, 15 IND. INT'L & COMP. L. REV. 51 (2004)

Barylak, C.H., *Reducing Uncertainty in Anti-SLAPP Protection*, 71 OHIO ST. L. J. 845 (2010)

Bazyler, M. and Green, J., *Nuremberg-Era Jurisprudence Redux: The Supreme Court in Kiobel v. Royal Dutch Petroleum Co. and the Legacy of Nuremberg*, 7 CHARLESTON L. REV. 23 (2012)

Benish, K., *Pennoyer's Ghost: Consent, Registration Statutes, and General Jurisdiction After Daimler Ag v. Bauman*, 90 N.Y.U. L. REV. 1609 (2015)

Bergman Moure, H., Harrison, B., Marquez-Lechuga, D.A. & Foggo, G., *E-Discovery Around the World*, 21 PRAC. LITIGATOR 41, 52–56 (2010)

Berle, Jr., A., *The Theory of Enterprise Entity*, 47 COLUM. L. REV. 343 (1947)

Bernaz, N., *An Analysis of the ICC Office of the Prosecutor's Policy Paper on Case Selection and Prioritization from the Perspective of Business and Human Rights*, 15 J. OF INT'L CRIMINAL JUSTICE 527 (2017)

BLACK'S LAW DICTIONARY (10th ed. 2014)

Blackburn, A., *Striking a Balance to Reform the Alien Tort Statute: A Recommendation for Congress*, 53 SANTA CLARA L. REV. 1051 (2013)

Blackstone, W., COMMENTARIES ON THE LAWS OF ENGLAND, IN FOUR BOOKS (1803)

Blumberg, P., *Limited Liability and Corporate Groups*, 11 J. CORP. L. 573 (1986)

Blumberg, P., *The Corporate Entity in an Era of Multinational Corporations*, 15 DEL. J. CORP. L. 283 (1990)

Blumberg, P., THE MULTINATIONAL CHALLENGE TO CORPORATION LAW: THE SEARCH FOR A NEW CORPORATE PERSONALITY (1993)

Blumberg, P., *The Increasing Recognition of Enterprise Liability Principles In Determining Parent and Subsidiary Corporation Liabilities*, 28 CONN. L. REV. 295 (1996)

Blumberg, P., *Asserting Human Rights Against Multinational Corporations Under United States Law: Conceptual and Procedural Problems*, 50 AM. J. COMP. L. 493 (2002)

Boggs, C., *Project Management: A Smorgasbord of International Operating Risks*, Introduction (ROCKY MOUNTAIN MINERAL LAW INST., PAPER NO. 13, 2008)

Bonacorsi, K., *Not at Home with "At-Home" Jurisdiction*, 37 FORDHAM INT'L L. J. 1821 (2014)

Borchers, P., *Conflict-of-Laws Considerations in State Court Human Rights Actions*, 3 U.C. IRVINE L. REV. 45 (2013)

Bradley, C., *Attorney General Bradford's Opinion and the Alien Tort Statute*, 106 AM. J. OF INT'L LAW 509 (2012)

Brants-Langeraar, C.H., *Consensual Criminal Procedures: Plea and Confession Bargaining and Abbreviated Procedures to Simplify Criminal Procedure*, 11.1 ELECTRONIC J. COMP. L. (2007)

Braun, K., *Giving Victims a Voice: On the Problems of Introducing Victim Impact Statements in German Criminal Procedure*, 14(9) GERMAN L. J. 1889 (2013)

Broecker, C., *Note, "Better the Devil You Know": Home State Approaches to Transnational Corporate Accountability*, 41 N.Y.U. J. INT'L L. & POL. 159 (2008)

Brownlie, I., SYSTEM OF THE LAW OF NATIONS: STATE RESPONSIBILITY (1983)

Buchky, P., *Darfur, Divestment, and Dialogue*, 30 U. PA. J. INT'L L. 823 (2009)

Burke Robertson, C. & Rhodes, C., *A Shifting Equilibrium: Personal Jurisdiction, Transnational Litigation, and the Problem of Nonparties*, 19 LEWIS & CLARK L. REV. 643 (2015)

Burley [Slaughter], A., *The Alien Tort Statute and the Judiciary Act of 1789: A Badge of Honor*, 83 AM. J. INT'L L. 461 (1989)

Casto, W., *The Federal Courts' Protective Jurisdiction Over Torts Committed in Violation of the Law of Nations*, 18 CONN. L. REV. 467 (1986)

Casto, W., THE SUPREME COURT IN THE EARLY REPUBLIC (1995)

Charette, L., Dumoulin, J., Larocque, B. & Praent, F., *Pension Plans and Class Actions: The Vivendi Case*, 81 DEF. COUNS. J. 288 (2014)

Cherif Bassiouni, M., *International Recognition of Victims' Rights*, 6 HUM. RTS. L. REV. 203 (2006)

Childress III, D., *The Alien Tort Statute, Federalism, and the Next Wave of Transnational Litigation*, 100 GEO. L. J. 709 (2012)

Chow, D., *Counterfeiting as an Externality Imposed by Multinational Companies on Developing Countries*, 51 VA. J. INT'L L. 785 (2011)

Clifton Fleming, Jr., J., *Worse Than Exemption*, 59 EMORY L. J. 79 (2009)

Clifton Fleming, Jr., J., & Peroni, R., *Reinvigorating Tax Expenditure Analysis and Its International Dimension*, 27 VA. TAX REV. 437 (2008)

Colangelo, A. & Kiik, K., *Spatial Legality, Due Process, and Choice of Law in Human Rights Litigation Under U.S. State Law*, 3 U.C. IRVINE L. REV. 63 (2013)

Cossart, S., Chaplier, J. & Beau de Lomenie, T., *The French Law on Duty of Care: A Historic Step Towards Making Globalization Work for All*, 2 BUS. HUM. RTS. J. 317–23 (2017)

Cragg, B., *Comment, Home is Where the Halt Is: Mandating Corporate Social Responsibility Through Home State Regulation and Social Disclosure*, 24 EMORY INT'L L. REV. 735 (2010)

D'Amato, A., *The Alien Tort Statute and the Founding of the Constitution*, 82 AM. J. INTL. L. 62 (1988)

Davidson, C., *Tort Au Canadien: A Proposal For Canadian Tort Legislation on Gross Violations of International Human Rights and Humanitarian Law*, 38 VAND. J. TRANSNAT'L L. 1403 (2005)

Dearborn, M., *Enterprise Liability: Reviewing and Revitalizing Liability for Corporate Groups*, 97 CAL. L. REV. 195 (2009)

de Felice, D., *Business and Human Rights Indicators to Measure the Corporate Responsibility to Respect: Challenges and Opportunities*, 37 HUM. RTS. Q. 511 (2015)

Deloitte, *Governance of Subsidiaries: A Survey of Global Companies* (Sept. 2013)

De Schutter, O., INTERNATIONAL HUMAN RIGHTS LAW: CASES, MATERIALS AND COMMENTARY (2010)

De Schutter, O., Ramasastry, A., Taylor, M., & Thompson, R., HUMAN RIGHTS DUE DILIGENCE: THE ROLE OF STATES, 7–8 (2012)

de Vattel, E., THE LAW OF NATIONS 137 (Carnegie Institute of Washington ed., Charles G. Fenwick trans. 1916) (1758)

Dhooge, L., *Due Diligence as a Defense to Corporate Liability Pursuant to the Alien Tort Statute*, 22 EMORY INT'L L. REV. 455 (2008)

Dickinson, E., *The Law of Nations as Part of the National Law of the United States–Part I*, 101 U. PA. L. REV. 26, 30–32 (1952)

Dodge, W., *The Historical Origins of the Alien Tort Statute: A Response to the "Originalists,"* 19 HASTINGS INT'L & COMP. L. REV. 221 (1996)

Dodge, W., *The Constitutionality of the Alien Tort Statute: Some Observations on Text and Context*, 42 VA. J. INT'L L. 687 (2002)

Dodge, W., *Alien Tort Statute: The Road Not Taken*, 89 NOTRE DAME L. REV. 1577 (2014)

Dodge, W., *Business and Human Rights Litigation in U.S. Courts Before and after Kiobel*, in BUSINESS AND HUMAN RIGHTS: FROM PRINCIPLES TO PRACTICE 250 (Dorothée Baumann-Pauly & Justine Nolan. eds. 2014)

Douglas, W. & Shanks, C., *Insulation from Liability Through Subsidiary Corporations*, 39 YALE L. J. 193 (1929)

Drobak, J., *Personal Jurisdiction in a Global World: The Impact of the Supreme Court's Decisions in Goodyear Dunlop Tires and Nicastro*, 90 WASH. U. L. REV. 1707 (2013)

Ehrenzweig, A., *Negligence Without Fault* (The Regents of the Univ. of Cal., 1951) (currently out of print), reprinted in 54 CAL. L. REV. 1422 (1966)

Eizenga, M., Assaf, D., & Davis, E., *Antitrust Class Actions: A Tale of Two Countries*, 25-SPG ANTITRUST 83 (2011)

Enodo Rights, *Pillar III on the Ground: An Independent Assessment of the Porgera Remedy Framework* (2016)

European Union Agency for Fundamental Rights, Improving Access to Remedy in the Area of Business and Human Rights at the EU Level (2017)

Evans, S., *The Globalization of Drug Testing: Enforcing Informed Consent Through the Alien Tort Claims Act*, 19 TEMP. INT'L & COMP. L. J. 477 (2005)

Fisk, C. & Chemerinsky, E., *The Failing Faith in Class Actions: Wal-Mart v. Dukes and AT&T Mobility v. Concepcion*, 7 DUKE J. OF CONST. LAW & PUB. POL'Y 73 (2011)

Freer, R. & Collins Perdue, W., CIVIL PROCEDURE: CASES, MATERIALS, AND QUESTIONS 32 (5th ed. 2008)

Gilbert Warren III, M., *The U.S. Securities Fraud Class Action: An Unlikely Export to the European Union*, 37 BROOK. J. INT'L L. 1075 (2012)

Goebel, Jr., J., 1 HISTORY OF THE SUPREME COURT OF THE UNITED STATES: ANTECEDENTS AND BEGINNINGS TO 1801 (Paul A. Freund ed. 1971)

Goldhaber, M., *Corporate Human Rights Litigation in Non-U.S. Courts: A Comparative Scorecard*, 3 U. C. IRVINE L. REV. 127 (2013)

Golove, D., and Hulsebosch, D., *A Civilized Nation: The Early American Constitution, the Law of Nations, and the Pursuit of International Recognition*, 85 N.Y.U. L. REV. 932 (2010)

Grabosch, R., *Rechtsschutz vor deutschen Zivilgerichten gegen Beeinträchtigungen von Menschenrechten durch transnationale Unternehmen*, in TRANSNATIONALE UNTERNEHMEN UND NICHTREGIERUNGSORGANISATIONEN IM VÖLKERRECHT 69, 84–86 (Ralph Nikol, Thomas Bernhard, & Nina Schniederjan, eds. 2013)

Graetz, M., FOUNDATIONS OF INTERNATIONAL INCOME TAX 400 (2003)

Green, J., *The Rule of Law at a Crossroad: Enforcing Corporate Responsibility in International Investment Through the Alien Tort Statute*, 35 U. PENN. J. INT'L L. 1085 (2014)

Green, L., *The Duty Problem in Negligence Cases: II*, 29 COLUM. L. REV. 255 (1929)

Hanna, C., *Corporate Tax Reform: Listening to Corporate America*, 35 J. CORP. L. 283 (2009)

Hanna, C., *The Real Value of Tax Deferral*, 61 FLA. L. REV. 203 (2009)

Hansmann, H. & Kraakman, R., *Toward Unlimited Shareholder Liability for Corporate Torts*, 100 YALE L. J. 1879 (1991)

Harper Ho, V., *Of Enterprise Principles and Corporate Groups: Does Corporate Law Reach Human Rights?* 52 COLUM. J. TRANSNAT'L L. 113, 136 (2013)

Havers, P., *Take the Money and Run: Inherent Ethical Problems of the Contingency Fee and Loser Pays Systems*, 14 NOTRE DAME J. L. ETHICS & PUB. POL'Y 621 (2000)

Henn, M., *Tax Havens and the Taxation of Transnational Corporations*, FRIEDRICH EBERT STIFTUNG (June 2013)

Herz, R., *The Future of Alien Tort Litigation: Kiobel and Beyond*, 106 AM. SOC'Y INT'L L. PROC. 493 (2013)

Hoffman, P. & Stephens, B., *International Human Rights Cases Under State Law and In State Courts*, 3 U.C. IRVINE L. REV. 9 (2013)

Independent Commission of Experts, The Corporate Crimes Principles: Advancing Investigations and Prosecutions in Human Rights Cases (Oct. 2016)

International Commission of Jurists, *Judicial Accountability: A Practitioners' Guide* (June 2016)

Int'l St. Crime Initiative, *Torture at the Río Blanco Mine—A State-Corporate Crime?*

Issacharoff, S. & Miller, G., *Will Aggregate Litigation Come to Europe?*, 62 VAND. L. REV. 179 (2009)

Jägers, N., CORPORATE HUMAN RIGHTS OBLIGATIONS: IN SEARCH OF ACCOUNTABILITY (2002)

Jägers, N. & van der Heijden, M., *Corporate Human Rights Violations: The Feasibility of Civil Recourse in the Netherlands*, 33 BROOK. J. INT'L L. 833 (2008)

Jägers, N., Jesse, K., & Verschuure, J., *The Future of Corporate Liability for Extraterritorial Human Rights Abuses: The Dutch Case Against Shell*, AM. J. INT'L L. UNBOUND e-36, e-41 (2014)

Jaworek, M. & Kuzel, M., *Transnational Corporations in the World Economy: Formation, Development and Present Position*, 4 COPERNICAN J. OF FIN. & ACCT. 55–70 (2015)

Joseph, S., *Protracted Lawfare: The Tale of Chevron Texaco in the Amazon* 3(1) JOURNAL OF HUMAN RIGHTS AND THE ENVIRONMENT (2012) 70

Kahan, D., Note, *Shareholder Liability for Corporate Torts: A Historical Perspective*, 97 GEO. L. J. 1085 (2009)

Kaleck, W. & Saage-Maaß, M., *Corporate Accountability for Human Rights Violations Amounting to International Crimes: The Status Quo and its Challenges*, 8 JOURNAL OF INTERNATIONAL CRIMINAL JUSTICE 699 (2010)

Kempin, Jr., F., *Limited Liability in Historical Perspective*, 4 AM. BUS. LAW ASSN. BULLETIN 11 (1960)

Kenney, C., *Measuring Transnational Human Rights*, 84 FORDHAM L. REV. 1053 (2015)

Khoury, S. and Whyte, D., CORPORATE HUMAN RIGHTS VIOLATIONS: GLOBAL PROSPECTS FOR LEGAL ACTION 78 (2016)

Kirshner, J., *Why is the U.S. Abdicating the Policing of Multinational Corporations to Europe?: Extraterritoriality, Sovereignty, and the Alien Tort Statute*, 30 BERKELEY J. INT'L L. 259 (2012)

Kirshner, J., *A Call for the EU to Assume Jurisdiction over Extraterritorial Corporate Human Rights Abuses*, 13 NW. J. INT'L HUM. RTS. 1 (2015)

Klemme, H., *The Enterprise Liability Theory of Torts*, 47 U. COLO. L. REV. 153 (1976)

Ku, J., *Customary International Law in State Courts*, 42 VA. J. INT'L L. 265 (Fall 2001)

Langbien, J., *Controlling Prosecutorial Discretion in Germany*, 41(3) U. CHI. L. REV. 439, 463 (1974)

Leebron, D., *Limited Liability, Tort Victims, and Creditors*, 91 COLUM. L. REV. 1565 (1991)

Lee Troutman, T., *Jurisdiction by Necessity: Examining One Proposal for Unbarring the Doors of Our Courts*, 21 VAND. J. TRANSNAT'L L. 401 (1988)

Lemper, T., *The Promise and Perils of "Privileges or Immunities": Saenz v. Roe 119 S. Ct. 1518 (1999)*, 23 HARV. J. L. & PUB. POL'Y 295 (1999)

Lowell, C., *Significance of Transfer Pricing for Multinational Enterprises*, in U.S. INT'L TAX: AGREEMENTS, CHECKLISTS AND COMMENTARY (2015)

Madison, J., JOURNAL OF THE CONSTITUTIONAL CONVENTION 60 (E. Scott ed. 1893)

Mamolea, A., Note, *The Future of Corporate Aiding and Abetting Liability Under the Alien Tort Statute: A Roadmap*, 51 SANTA CLARA L. REV. 79 (2011)

Manolis, M., Vermette, N., & Hungerford, R., *The Doctrine of Forum Non Conveniens: Canada and the United States Compared*, 60 FED'N DEF. & CORP. COUNS. Q. 3 (2009)

Manuel Diaz, Jr., V., *Litigation in U.S. Courts of Product Liability Cases Arising in Latin America, Panel Talk Before the Miami Conference on Products Liability in Latin America*, in 20 ARIZ. J. INT'L & COMP. L. 47 (John F. Molloy ed. 2003)

Mardirossian, N., *Direct Parental Negligence Liability: An Expanding Means to Hold Parent Companies Accountable for the Human Rights Impacts of Their Foreign Subsidiaries* SSRN (2015)

Mares, R., *Responsibility to Respect: Why the Core Company Should Act When Affiliates Infringe Rights*, in THE UN GUIDING PRINCIPLES ON BUSINESS AND HUMAN RIGHTS: FOUNDATION AND IMPLEMENTATION 169–92 (Radu Mares ed. 2012)

Mason Meier, B., *International Protection of Persons Undergoing Medical Experimentation: Protecting the Right of Informed Consent*, 20 BERKELEY J. INT'L L. 513 (2002)

McAllister, L., *On Environmental Enforcement and Compliance: A Reply to Professor Crawford's Review of Making Law Matter: Environmental Protection and Legal Institutions in Brazil*, 40 GEO. WASH. INT'L L. REV. 649 (2009)

McCorquodale, R., *Waiving Not Drowning: Kiobel Outside the United States*, 107 AM. J. INT'L L. 846 (2013)

Meeran, R., *Litigation of Multinational Corporations: A Critical Stage in the UK*, in LIABILITY OF MULTINATIONAL CORPORATIONS UNDER INTERNATIONAL LAW 251 (Menno T. Kamminga & Saman Zia-Zarifi eds. 2000)

Meyer, J., *Extraterritorial Common Law: Does the Common Law Apply Abroad?* 102 GEO. L. J. 301, 314–18 (2014)

Miller, G., *In Search of the Most Adequate Forum: State Court Personal Jurisdiction*, 2 STAN. J. COMPLEX LITIG. 1 (2014)

Mohsin Reza, S., *Daimlerchrysler v. Cuno: An Escape from the Dormant Commerce Clause Quagmire?* 40 U. RICH. L. REV. 1229 (2006)

Monestier, T., *Is Canada the New Shangri-La of Global Securities Class Actions?* 32 NW. J. INT'L L. & BUS. 305 (2012)

Monestier, T., *Registration Statutes, General Jurisdiction, and the Fallacy of Consent*, 36 CARDOZO L. REV. 1343 (2015)

Muchlinski, P., *Corporations in International Litigation: Problems of Jurisdiction and the United Kingdom Asbestos Cases*, 50 INT'L & COMP. L. Q. 1 (2001)

Muchlinski, P., MULTINATIONAL ENTERPRISES & THE LAW (2nd ed. 2007)

Mwaura, K., *Internalization of Costs to Corporate Groups: Part-Whole Relationships, Human Rights Norms and the Futility of the Corporate Veil*, 11 J. INT'L BUS. & L. 85 (2012)

OECD, *OECD Due Diligence Guidance for Responsible Supply Chains of Minerals from Conflict-Affected and High-Risk Areas: Third Edition* (2016)

OECD Watch, *Remedy Remains Rare* (2015)

OECD, Due Diligence Guidance for Responsible Business Conduct (2018)

Organization for International Investment, *Foreign Direct Investment in the United States 2017*

Oswald, L., *Strict Liability of Individuals Under CERCLA: A Normative Analysis*, 20 B. C. ENVT'L. AFF. L. REV. 579 (1993)

Oxford Pro Bono Publico, Univ. of Oxford, OBSTACLES TO JUSTICE AND REDRESS FOR VICTIMS OF CORPORATE HUMAN RIGHTS ABUSE (2008)

Perl, M., *Not Just Another Mass Tort: Using Class Actions to Redress International Human Rights*, 88 GEO. L. J. 773 (1999)

Randall, K., *Federal Jurisdiction Over International Law Claims: Inquiries into the Alien Tort Statute*, 18 N.Y.U. J. INT'L & POL. 1 (1985)

Rhodes, "Rocky" & Burke Robertson, C., *Toward a New Equilibrium in Personal Jurisdiction*, 48 U. C. DAVIS L. REV. 207, 261–62 (2014)

Roe, M., *Corporate Strategic Reaction to Mass Tort*, 72 VA. L. REV. 1 (1986)

Rogers, J., *The Alien Tort Statute and How Individuals "Violate" International Law*, 21 VAND. J. TRANSNAT'L L. 47 (1988)

Roin, J., *The Grand Illusion: A Neutral System for the Taxation of International Transactions*, 75 VA. L. REV. 919 (1989)

Rosenhek, S. & Maric, V., *Canadian Price-Fixing Class Actions: The Supreme Court of Canada Gives the Green Light to Indirect Purchaser Claims*, 81 DEF. COUNS. J. 302 (2014)

Ryngaert, C., *Accountability for Corporate Human Rights Abuses: Lessons from the Possible Exercise of Dutch National Criminal Jurisdiction Over Multinational Corporations*, 29 CRIMINAL LAW FORUM 1 (2018)

Saage-Maaß, M., LABOR CONDITIONS IN THE GLOBAL SUPPLY CHAIN: WHAT IS THE EXTENT AND IMPLICATIONS OF GERMAN CORPORATE RESPONSIBILITY? 7 (FRIEDRICH EBERT STIFTUNG, 2011)

Samuels, J., *When is an Alternative Forum Available? Rethinking the Forum Non Conveniens Analysis*, 85 IND. L. J. 1059 (2010)

Schrage, E., *Judging Corporate Accountability in the Global Economy*, 42 COLUM. J. INT'L L. 153 (2003)

Sepinwall, A., *Failures to Punish: Command Responsibility in Domestic and International Law*, 30 MICH. J. INT'L L. 251 (2009)

Silberman, L., *Goodyear and Nicastro: Observations from a Transnational and Comparative Perspective*, 63 S.C. L. REV. 591 (2012)

Silberman, L., *Jurisdictional Imputation in Daimler Chrysler AG v. Bauman: A Bridge Too Far*, 66 VAND. L. REV. EN BANC 123 (2013)

Simowitz, A., *Legislating Transnational Jurisdiction*, 57 VA. J. INT'L L. (2017)

Skinner, G., McCorquodale, R., De Schutter, O., & Lambe, A., THE THIRD PILLAR: ACCESS TO JUDICIAL REMEDIES FOR HUMAN RIGHTS VIOLATIONS BY TRANSNATIONAL BUSINESSES (2013)

Skinner, G., *Rethinking Limited Liability of Parent Corporations for Foreign Subsidiaries' Violations of International Human Rights Law*, 72 WASH. & LEE L. REV. 1769 (2015)

Skinner, G., *Beyond Kiobel: Providing Access to Judicial Remedies for Corporate Accountability for Violations of International Human Rights Norms by Transnational Corporations in a New (Post-Kiobel) World*, 46 COLUM. HUM. RTS. L. REV. 158 (2014)

Skinner, G., *Expanding General Personal Jurisdiction Over Transnational Corporations for Federal Causes of Action*, 121 PENN ST. L. REV. 617 (2017)

Steinhardt, R., *The Alien Tort Claims Act; Theoretical and Historical Foundations of the Alien Tort Claims Act and its Discontents: A Reality Check*, 16 ST. THOMAS L. REV. 585 (2004)

Stephens, B., *Translating Filartiga: A Comparative and International Law Analysis of Domestic Remedies for International Human Rights Violations*, 27 YALE J. INT'L L. 1, 29 (2002)

Stephens, B., *Extraterritoriality and Human Rights After Kiobel*, 28 MD. J. INT'L L. 256 (2013)

Stewart, F., *Foreign Judgments, Judicial Trailblazing and the Cost of Cross-Border Complexity: Thoughts on Chevron Corp v Yaiguaje*, 34 J. OF ENERGY & NAT. RESOURCES L. (2016)

Stone, C., *The Place of Enterprise Liability in the Control of Corporate Conduct*, 90 YALE L. J. 1, 1 (1980)

Terry, J. & Shody, S., *Could Canada Become a New Forum for Cases Involving Human Rights Violations Committed Abroad?*, 1 COM. LITIG. & ARB. REV. 63 (2012)

Thompson, R., *Unpacking Limited Liability: Direct and Vicarious Liability of Corporate Participants for Torts of the Enterprise*, 47 VAND. L. REV. 1 (1994)

Tollefson, C., *Costs on Public Interest Litigation Revisited*, 39 ADVOC. Q. 197 (2012)

Tröger, T., *Organizational Choices of Banks and the Effective Supervision of Transnational Financial Institutions*, 48 TEX. INT'L L. J. 177 (2012)

Ubertazzi, B., *Intellectual Property Rights and Exclusive (Subject Matter) Jurisdiction: Between Private and Public International Law*, 15 MARQ. INTELL. PROP. L. REV. 357 (2011)

UN Conference on Trade and Development, *World Investment Report 2014 Overview: Investing in the SDGs: An Action Plan*, U.N. Doc. UNCTAD/WIR/2014 (2014)

UN Conference on Trade and Dev., *The World's Top 100 Non-Financial MNEs, Ranked by Foreign Assets*, U.N. doc. UNCTAD/WIR/2017 (2017)

UN Organization Mission in the Democratic Republic of Congo, *Report on the Conclusions of the Special Investigation into Allegations of Summary Executions and Other Violations of Human Rights Committed by the FARDC in Kilwa (Province of Katanga) on 15 October 2004* (2005)

U.N. Working Group on the Issue of Human Rights and Transnational Corporations and other Business Enterprises, *Report*, U.N. Doc. A/72/162 (2017)

U.N. Working Group on Business and Human Rights, *Corporate Human Rights Due Diligence – Emerging Practices, Challenges and Ways Forward* (2018)

Ursin, E., *Holmes, Cardozo, and the Legal Realists: Early Incarnations of Legal Pragmatism and Enterprise Liability*, 50 SAN DIEGO L. REV. 537 (2013)

Vanto, J., *Attorneys' Fees as Damages in International Commercial Litigation*, 15 PACE INT'L L. REV. 203 (2003)

Warren, C., THE SUPREME COURT IN UNITED STATES HISTORY 1789–1835 (revised ed. 1937)

Washington, G., Fourth Annual Address, in 1 A COMPILATION OF THE MESSAGES AND PAPERS OF THE PRESIDENT 125 (James D. Richardson ed. 1911)

Williams, N., *Why Congress May Not "Overrule" the Dormant Commerce Clause*, 53 UCLA L. REV. 153 (2005)

Winslow Crosskey, W., POLITICS AND THE CONSTITUTION IN THE HISTORY OF THE UNITED STATES (1953)

Wright, C.A. & Miller, A.R., 4 FEDERAL PRACTICE AND PROCEDURE § 1066 (4th ed. 2016)

Yang, Y., *Corporate Civil Liability Under the Alien Tort Statute: The Practical Implications from Kiobel*, 40 W. ST. U. L. REV. 195 (2013)

Yilmaz-Vastardis, V. and Chambers, R., *Overcoming the Corporate Veil Challenge: Could Investment Law Inspire the Proposed Business and Human Rights Treaty?* INTERNATIONAL AND COMPARATIVE LAW QUARTERLY, 389–423 (2018)

Ysewyn, J., *Private Enforcement of Competition Law in the EU: Trials and Tribulations*, 19 SPG INT'L L. PRACTICUM 14 (2006)

Index

adjudicative jurisdiction. *See* Personal jurisdiction
Adolf Berle, Jr., 67
aided and abetted, 38, 91, 109, 112–16, 151
   intent standard, 116
   knowledge and substantial assistance, 115
Alien Tort Statute, 4, 27, 55, 90, 92
   aiding and abetting liability, 114–15
   collective redress, 144, 147
   corporate liability, 110
   Filártiga v. Peña-Irala, 37
   Jesner v. Arab Bank, 40, 71
   Kiobel v. Royal Dutch Shell, 39, 90
   origins, 23–25, 38
   personal jurisdiction, 104
   recovery of fees and costs, 139
   Sosa v. Alvarez-Machain, 38, 114
   statute of limitations, 131–32
   subject matter jurisdiction, 35–36
   Torture Victims Protection Act, 91
Alien Tort Statute, 114
alter ego, 45–46, 59
Amesys, 153
Anti-Terrorism Act, 36
authorized agent, 47

Brussels I Regulation, 57, 89, 117, 124
   expanding jurisdiction, 106–7
   financial support to victims, 144
   forum necessitatis, 92
Business and Human Rights Resource Center, 30

Chiquita, 111, 151
choice of law, 3, 59, 84, 91, 109, 137, 159
   Al Shimari v. CACI, 138
   Canada, 129
   Europe, 131–32

lex loci delicti, 127, 129
ordre public, 128
Rana Plaza factory collapse, 129
United States, 125–27, 130, 132
civil and human rights violations, 14
class actions. *See* Collective redress
Collective redress, 144
   AT&T v. Concepcion, 147
   Wal-Mart v. Dukes, 145, 147
comity, 3, 16, 60, 90, 105–6
Commerce Clause, 96, 101–2
Committee on Economic, Social and Cultural Rights, xvii, 18
Committee to End Racial Discrimination, xvii, 18
Comprehensive Environmental Response, Compensation, and Liability Act, xvii, 87–88
conflict of laws. *See* choice of law
contingency fees, 3, 30, 139
Convention Against Torture, 17
corporate citizens, 16
Corporate vicarious liability
   Prosecutor v. Perišić, 113
   Prosecutor v. Taylor, 113
Corruption in the justice sector, 32
customary international law, xvii, 89, 106
   Alien Tort Statute, 4, 16, 36–38, 41
   Araya v. Nevsun Resources Ltd., 41
   Business and Human Rights Treaty, 22
   claims of extraterritorial violations, 35–36, 91
   corporate liability, 110, 113
   limited liability, 27, 44
   right to remedy, 19, 23
   vicarious liability, 114

Daimler AG v. Bauman, 27, 53, 55
deferral of subsidiaries' income, 12

Democratic Republic of Congo, 7
Developing and transition economies, 12
direct parent company liability, 47
discovery
  Hague Convention on Taking Evidence Abroad, 134–35
  Letters of Request, 135
diversity jurisdiction, 35, 98, 125–26
Doctrine of limited liability
  Transparence doctrine, 51
Dodd-Frank Act, 90
due diligence, 14, 66, 128, 136, 154
  automatic liability, 81, 87–89
  corporate liability, 65
  devoir de vigilance, 48, 72, 74
  Guiding Principles for Business and Human Rights, 70
  legislation, 86
  overcoming limited liability, 44, 71–72, 74
  sexual harassment in the US, 66
  Switzerland, 51, 72
duty of care, 49–50, 74, 76–83, 85–86
  Chandler v. Cape plc, 49
duty to foreseeable victims, 81

early warning system. *See* Due diligence
Emmerich de Vattel, 17
enterprise liability, 46, 65–67, 69–70, 72, 74
Enterprise liability
  Employee Retirement Income Security Act, xxvii, 68
environmental damages, 14, 73
EU Commission, 69, 143
European Court of Justice, 117
European Union Agency for Fundamental Rights, 130
extraction industries, 15, 82
extraterritorial human rights claims, 36, 58
extraterritorial jurisdiction, 2, 159

Fed. R. Civ. P., 103
federal common law, 114, 118
federal preemption, 102–3
Fédération Internationale des Ligues des Droits de l'Homme, 153
fees and costs, 139, 141
Filártiga v. Peña-Irala. *See* Alien Tort Statute
First Judiciary Act, 25
foreign affairs doctrine, 3, 102
foreign affiliates, 1, 11–12
Foreign Corrupt Practices Act, xvii, 90
Foreign Direct Investment, xvii
foreign-owned subsidiaries, 29
forum necessitatis. *See* Jurisdiction by necessity

forum non conveniens, 3, 41, 57, 84, 90, 93, 104, 109, 159
  Aguinda v. Texaco, Inc., 119
  Aldana v. Del Monte Fresh Produce N.A., Inc., 121
  Bhopal v. Union Carbide Corporation, 119
  Bil'in (Vill. Council) v. Green Park Int'l, 123
  blocking statutes, 120, 125
  Choc v. Hudbay Minerals, 123
  Recherches Internationales Quebéc v. Cambior, Inc., 123
  Van Breda Club Resorts Ltd. v. Van Breda, 122

general personal jurisdiction, 107
Ginsburg, 105
Ginsburg, Justice, 105
global foreign direct investment, 11
Goodyear Dunlop Tires Operations, S.A. v. Brown, 27, 53, 55
Guidelines on Multinational Enterprises. *See* Organization for Economic Cooperation and Development
Guiding Principles for Business and Human Rights, 70, 127, 148

holding company, 10, 69
Human Rights Council, 20

in personam jurisdiction. *See* Personal jurisdiction
in rem jurisdiction, 58
Institute of International Law, 95
International Commission of Jurists, 32
International Court of Justice, 44
International Covenant on Civil and Political Rights, 17–18
International Covenant on Economic, Social and Cultural Rights, 16
International Criminal Court, xvii, 111
International Military Tribunal of Nuremberg, xvii, 111
International Tribunal for Rwanda, 112

Jesner v. Arab Bank. *See* Alien Tort Statute
John Ruggie, 142
judicial remedy, 2, 4, 15–16, 21–22, 45, 48, 109, 121, 138, 144, 158–60
jurisdiction by necessity, 41, 93–94, 96
  exceptional jurisdiction, 94

Kiobel v. Royal Dutch Shell. *See* Alien Tort Statute

labor and regulatory costs, 14
Lafarge, 112
law of nations, 23–25, 36, 111, 127
lead company. *See* Parent company

legal persons, 90, 109, 116, 154
Ligue des Droits de l'Homme, 153
limited liability of shareholders, 2, 26–27, 43–44
loser pays, 2–3, 59, 137, 158

Marbois affair, 24
Monterrico. *See* parent company liability

National Contact Points, xvii
Nicastro, 58, 98
Nigeria, 8, 31
no-costs ruling, 140
non-judicial grievance mechanisms, 4

Organisation for Economic Co-operation and Development, 4, 15, 21–22, 26, 159
Organization for International Investment, 13

parent company liability
  Guerrero v. Monterrico, 49
personal jurisdiction, 3, 27, 34–37, 52–61, 89–90, 93–98, 101–6, 130
  continuous and systematic business, 37
  general personal jurisdiction, 53, 55, 61, 95–96, 98, 105–6
  International Shoe Co. v. Washington, 53
  specific personal jurisdiction, 53, 55, 58, 61, 98
Phillip Blumberg, 46
pierce the corporate veil, 44, 46–48, 52, 80
Pierce the corporate veil
  Choc v. Hudbay Minerals, 47, 76
Pillar Three. *See* Third Pillar
political question doctrine, 3
potentially responsible parties, 87
presumption against extraterritoriality, 39
  touches and concerns, 39
presumption of extraterritoriality. *See* Presumption against extraterritoriality
Public international law, 112
pyramid approach, 10

Radu Mares, 81
red tape, 15
redress. *See* Right to remedy

responsibility of the sovereign, 16
Restatement (Third) of The Foreign Relations Law of the United States, 105
right to remedy, 16–17, 41

security forces, 1, 15, 78–79, 88, 110
self-regulatory initiatives, 48
sexual harassment, 66
Sosa v. Alvarez-Machain, 38
Special Tribunal for Lebanon, 112
Strategic Lawsuits Against Public Participation, 138, 150
  retaliatory lawsuit, 30, 148, 150
subject matter jurisdiction, 2–3, 26, 34–35, 89, 93–94, 124, 159

tag jurisdiction, 37, 56, 59
Third Pillar, 20
Torture Victim Protection Act, 36
Trafficking Victims Protection Act, 36, 117
transfer pricing manipulation, 12
Treaty on Business and Human Rights. *See* United Nations Treaty on Business and Human Rights

UN Committee on Economic, Cultural, and Social Rights, 16
UN Committee on Economic, Social and Cultural Rights. *See* UN Committee on Economic, Cultural, and Social Rights
UN Guiding Principles on Business and Human Rights, 20–22, 107, 128
United Nations Conference on Trade and Development, 10
United Nations Treaty on Business and Human Rights, 16
universal civil jurisdiction, 95
Universal Declaration of Human Rights, 17

vicarious liability. *See* Corporate vicarious liability

William Blackstone, 17
William Bradford, 25
William Paterson, 25
World Investment Report, 12

For EU product safety concerns, contact us at Calle de José Abascal, 56–1º, 28003 Madrid, Spain or eugpsr@cambridge.org.

www.ingramcontent.com/pod-product-compliance
Ingram Content Group UK Ltd.
Pitfield, Milton Keynes, MK11 3LW, UK
UKHW020209060825
461487UK00018B/1645